PLAYS BY SCOTS

1660-1800

The Gentle Shepherd (1729) by Allan Ramsay. Act III Scene 3.

Terence Tobin

PLAYS BY SCOTS
1660-1800

University of Iowa Press Iowa City

Library of Congress Cataloging in Publication Data

Tobin, Terence, 1938–
    Plays by Scots, 1660–1800.

    "List of plays and entertainments by Scottish
dramatists, 1660–1800": p.
    Includes bibliographical references.
    1. Scottish drama—18th century—History and
criticism. 2. English drama—Scottish authors—
History and criticism. 3. Scottish drama—18th
century—Bibliography. 4. English drama—Scottish
authors—Bibliography. I. Title.
PR8585.T6   822'.009   73–82159
ISBN 0-87745-047-1

University of Iowa Press, Iowa City 52242
© 1974 by The University of Iowa. All rights reserved
Printed in the United States of America

FOR LLOYD AND MILLIE TAIT

Contents

Illustrations

Foreword

Professor Tobin has shown a river for what seemed to many but a trickle in the quantity and variety of Scots' plays conceived, written, produced and criticized from 1660 to 1800. The theatres in the North over that span of years came only gradually to possess sufficient magnetism to call forth full efforts for a national drama. One can count the exceptions on the fingers of one hand. But the list of nearly a hundred playwrights who contributed from one to many plays each, directs attention to the great desire of Scotsmen to become dramatists both in the closet and on the boards. The overwhelming majority, as the author points out, sought for performance on the London stage, and wrote in rather traditional forms of comedy, farce, tragedy, interlude, and dramatic entertainment. He concentrates on telling—now briefly, now in more expanded fashion—the essential plots of many long-forgotten works. But the weathervanes are there, for he spots trends—religious, political, classical, pastoral—which attached the imaginations of the dramatists. Enough of the theatrical setting at Edinburgh and London is provided for the reader to see the plays in proper context.

Those familiar with the literature, politics, art, and music of eighteenth-century England are generally aware of the cosmopolitan nature of the culture, of the tremendous contributions made by the Irish, by the Scots, and by foreigners. For every Johnson, Fielding, Richardson, and Garrick, Arne, Hogarth, Gainsborough, and Wilkes two or three masters of their same fields came up, over, or down to London from outside— and the contingent of excellence flowing from Scotland was surprisingly large. One thinks of the Thomsons, Mallets, Smolletts, Boswells, Homes, Ramsays, Arbuthnots, Dows, and Butes of the age.

Professor Tobin has set forth for critical examination and ready comparison, the plays and their authors. In the pages on the Scots at home, the modern reader will be most amused by Christian Carstaires' *The Hubble-Shue* (ca. 1786)—as screwball a piece of tumult as ever came from the imagination of the "absurd." Of substance and impact on their contemporaries, however, are the works of Thomson, Mallet, Home, Mackenzie, MacLaren—their interests in the Scots language and accent, customs, manners, history, legends, myths, and melancholy. Their rhythms and experimentations count. But also in them, and in the others, humor, mockery, and nationalism peek through in play after play.

New York University
February 1974   GEORGE WINCHESTER STONE, JR.

Preface

Sarah Siddons once remarked that John Home was the only Scot who ever wrote "a decent play." Histories of British drama, which have neglected the works of Scottish playwrights, would seem to agree with the actress. Because this corpus of writing has been overlooked, and because a number of works discussed in this study are unfamiliar to specialists of Restoration and eighteenth-century drama, it seems expedient to concentrate upon the works themselves and to provide basic information on the subject. Plots, performances, selected contemporary criticism of the plays, some account of the theatre in Scotland, and the problems Northerners faced when writing for the London stage are the chief concerns of this consideration. Many of the plays discussed in this book have never been treated in other references. Hopefully this initial research will lead scholars to more extensive assessments of the Scottish contribution to drama.

As James Thomson addressed Frederick, Prince of Wales, in his Dedication to *Tancred and Sigismunda,* with "a warm and grateful sense," so do I wish to express appreciation for "goodness." Writing is often described as a lonely task. Without the assistance and encouragement of others, it is an impossible one.

The Penrose Fund of the American Philosophical Society and the Purdue Research Foundation awarded grants-in-aid which subsidized research at home and abroad. Librarians and scholars in America, England, and Scotland proved most helpful. Barbara Sherman typed various drafts of the manuscript with rare cheerfulness and patience.

Norma Armstrong's "The Edinburgh Stage 1715–1820: A Bibliography," Library Association of Great Britain, an unpublished F.R.C.S. thesis (1968), provided a number of the anonymous entries. Professor Fredson Bowers made valuable suggestions for the checklist of plays which appeared in *Studies in Bibliography* for 1970. The altered form of this catalogue is included, courtesy of the Bibliographical Society of the University of Virginia.

Professor Arthur Scouten and Dean George Winchester Stone read the manuscript and contributed much to the final form of the study.

The aid of the late Professor Curt A. Zimansky is also gratefully acknowledged.

Prologue

The earliest extant Scottish play, Sir David Lyndsay's *Ane Satyre of the Thrie Estaitis* (ca. 1540), indicates that the development of drama in pre-Reformation Scotland paralleled that of other European nations.[1] Notices of now lost plays, such as "Haliblude," a Corpus Christi passion play, probably performed in Aberdeen in 1440, and later programmatic dramas inspired by the incipient religious revolution, such as James Wedderburn's tirade against Roman Catholic corruption, "Beheading of Johne the Baptist," presented at Dundee in 1540, show that Lyndsay's outspoken morality was not unique.

Legislation against Robin Hood, Boy Bishops, and May Pole festivities began in 1555. Proclamations and statutes prohibiting these theatrically oriented recreations continued into the seventeenth century.[2] The vehemence and duration of the enactments against these drolls point to the popularity of the entertainments. There is much evidence to substantiate the early flourishing of a dramatic tradition in the North during the Mediaeval period.

The records of early drama in Scotland show that conditions there were similar to those in England, except that the Puritans gained control in North Britain at an earlier date. As the Kirk grew in strength, the toleration of plays diminished. The ministers no doubt feared that drama, which had proven a powerful weapon in their behalf, could also be used against them, even as Lyndsay had inveighed against the old Church. In 1575 the General Assembly abolished holy days except the Sabbath; they outlawed festivals, plays, and other entertainments

---

1 Anna Jean Mill, *Mediaeval Plays in Scotland*, St. Andrews Publications No. 24 (Edinburgh, 1927), gives an excellent, thoroughly documented account of the early development of drama in North Britain.
2 Thomas Thomson and Cosmos Innes, eds., *The Acts of the Parliaments of Scotland* (Edinburgh, 1844), II, 1555, c. 40, 500. The *Edinburgh Burgh Records*; Robert Pitcairn's *Ancient Criminal Trials in Scotland, etc.: A Diurnal of Remarkable Occurents, etc.;* David Calderwood's *History of the Kirk of Scotland: Calendar of State Papers relating to Scotland, etc.,* and like sources provide the information available about theatrical events in sixteenth-century Scotland.

which had been performed on saints' days.[3] This article of the Assembly was reinforced by the 1581 decision of the Scottish Parliament to prohibit observations of saints' days with festivals.[4]

In addition to ecclesiastical and civil curtailment of saints' feasts, writers had to submit plays to religious censors who drastically limited subject matter. The drama, which had existed traditionally as Sunday and holiday entertainment, was thus removed from a popular audience. With such constraint, which local presbyteries zealously enforced, the drama was in its death throes. What the Reformation with its censure of ceremony and festival had failed to do, the removal of the Scottish court to London in 1603 accomplished. Popular drama died in Scotland during the post-Reformation era, and theatrical presentations which are recorded indicate that by the seventeenth century drama was at best a court appendage.

By the beginning of the seventeenth century, plays of any kind were looked upon with disfavor by the Kirk. The Scots' innate love of spectacles and amusements found some satisfaction in the efforts of occasional strolling players, tumblers, tightrope walkers, and charlatans who found presentations in the streets an effective means of attracting crowds to the sale of their wares.[5]

Population, financial resources, climate, and the comparatively late development of civic institutions are factors which may explain the stunted growth of drama in Scotland.[6] The Northern reformation, a bourgeois movement, deprived the drama of its main source of talent and audience. Religious revolt also steered Scotland away from the humanism which was to produce Renaissance English drama.

Renaissance drama in North Britain is represented by one anonymous comedy, and four Senecan tragedies by Sir William Alexander. George Buchanan's school plays can be considered as part of this slim corpus.

Buchanan's Latin plays were written in exile. The Protestant poet fled Scotland to escape religious persecution and became a professor at the *College de Guienne*. The school, founded as a center for the new learning, required each staff member to compose a Latin play annu-

3 *The Booke of the Universall Kirk of Scotland. Acts and Proceedings of the General Assemblies of the Kirk of Scotland from the year MDLX*. Maitland Club Publications No. 45 (Glasgow, 1839), 1:332; see also p. 339.
4 *The Acts of the Parliament of Scotland*, III, 1581, c. 6. 212.
5 Terence Tobin, "Popular Entertainment in Seventeenth Century Scotland," *Theatre Notebook* 23 (1968):46–54.
6 Mill, *Mediaeval Plays in Scotland*, p. 101.

ally, which was to be performed by the students.[7] During the 1540s Buchanan translated Euripides' *Medea* and *Alcestis* from Greek to Latin, and wrote two original plays, *Jepthes sive Votum* and *Baptistes sive Calumnia*, both of which are closely modeled on classical dramas. Strident moralizing and elevated expression are the author's prime concerns. *Baptistes* is the more interesting because of its fiery political and religious commentary, which includes ridicule of David Cardinal Beaton at whose instigation Buchanan had been forced to flee his homeland. In the Prologue, Buchanan states his intention that the audience should make application between his ancient tale of the Baptist and the drama that was being played in his stormy era. John the Baptist's martyrdom by Herod is pointed as the moral of all religious and political tyranny. Liberty, fear of God and man, and the horror of oppression are themes in *Jepthes* and in *Baptistes*.

The next example of Renaissance drama appeared in 1603, when "ane verie excellent and delectabill Treatise intitulit Philotus" was published in Edinburgh. This comedy is probably a product of the 1590s. Like Buchanan's tragedies, *Philotus* is declamatory and overlong, yet it more nearly approaches drama in a modern sense than anything which had been written in Scotland until this time. The lengthy speeches tenuously unravel a complicated plot involving Philotus, a wealthy ancient, who loves Emily, a beautiful young girl; the old man unsuccessfully employs a *macrell*, or bawd, "to allure the madyn." The anonymous author of *Philotus* used *Riche his Farewell to Militarie Profession* as a source. Unlike Shakespeare, whose *Twelfth Night* was also inspired by the same work, the Scot adhered exactly to the earlier story.[8] The observance of Renaissance dramatic convention for romantic comedy, with its accompanying stock improbabilities, foreshadows the method of construction Northern playwrights followed throughout the period of consideration. In *Philotus* the introduction of the *macrell* is new; the language of the first edition[9] is Scottish in phrasing and vocabulary, but the imitative skeleton is British.

In the same year *Philotus* appeared, Sir William Alexander, the Earl of Stirling, published his first dramatic effort, *Darius*, which was

7 Donald M. Frame, trans., *The Complete Works of Montaigne: Essays; Travel Journal; Letters* (Stanford, 1957), 1:131. In "Of the education of children" Michel de Montaigne mentions his acting in George Buchanan's tragedies.
8 C. More Smith, "Of Phylotus and Emilia," *Modern Language Review* 5 (1910): 242–46.
9 Anna Jean Mill, ed., *Philotus* in *Miscellany Volume*. Scottish Text Society (Edinburgh, 1933), pp. 81–158. Miss Mill describes the changes in the various editions of the play.

printed in the Scottish capital in 1603. This tragedy was originally written in a hodgepodge of Scots and English dialects. Later Alexander
polished the language and reworked the plot, a practice he followed
with all of his literary works. *Croesus* and *Julius Caesar* in 1604, and
The Alexandrian Tragedy the following year, comprise his dramatic
output. Alexander later published these plays under the title of *The
Monarchicke Tragedies* (1607). The four works in the French Senecan tradition of Robert Garnier[10] share literary features. These closet
plays deal with falls of ancient princes: the downfall of Darius, the
overthrow of Croesus, the assassination of Caesar, and the death of
Alexander. The heroes of these epical narratives are flawed by ambition. The dramas open with lengthy expository prologues spoken
by Darius, Solon, Alexander's Ghost, and Juno, respectively. The dialogues are long and tedious, broken by occasional stichomythia, and a
chorus which permits the author to display his lyrical ability. The plays
are written in alternately rhyming verse characterized by alliteration,
antithesis, and affected conceits. The unities are dispensed with in
favor of prolix political incursions. The tragedies end with the death of
the main character. With the exception of the suicide of Croesus, these
deaths occur off stage. Other characters narrate endlessly the fate of
the hero, a final indication of the author's total unfamiliarity with
play making.

Thomas Dempster, whose pathological lies fill his autobiography,
was a professor who held many posts. From the safety of Douay, he
published an attack on Queen Elizabeth. In Paris, he published *Tra-
goedia decemuiratus abrogatus* (1613), a five-act drama. This classically
inspired piece, as well as his *Antiquitatum Romanarum Corpus abso-
lutissimum*, exhibits sound scholarship.[11] Dempster wrote Latin which
is prolific if not polished. The squabbling decemvirs speak in a plebian
fashion that would have provoked Claudius Appius.

Both Buchanan and Alexander were preoccupied with language
rather than action in their lengthy dramas. Both authors used ancient
settings and stories, which they intended to have contemporary significance. Buchanan's plays are more actable, no doubt because they were
written to be performed by his students. Although they exhibit similar

10   A. M. Witherspoon, *The Influence of Robert Garnier on Elizabethan Drama*
(New Haven, 1924), pp. 41–57; L. E. Kastner and H. B. Charlton, *Sir William
Alexander, Earl of Stirling* (Edinburgh, 1940), pp. iii–xiv.
11   Dempster's *Roman Antiquities* was placed in the *Index of Forbidden Books*
(1623). Later the same year, the new vicar of Rome, Pope Urban VIII, knighted
the author.

dramatic faults, not the least of which is a siccative classicism, the superiority of the Scot abroad, whose plays were written for theatrical representation, prefigures the situation which was to exist during the eighteenth century. The programmatic strains sounded in these plays may be considered a prelude to the political motifs of later Scots dramatists. While parallels can be drawn between these early playwrights and later writers, it is not possible to establish a dramatic continuum. The plays written by Scots during the era of the Reformation and the Renaissance certainly were unknown to the majority of dramatists of the Restoration and eighteenth century.[12] There is no extant play written by a Scot from the time of Alexander's political commentaries in dramatic form until after Charles II ascended the throne.

12   Allan Ramsay prepared a transcription of David Lyndsay's works for publication, but it was not published.

SCOTS AT HOME

1660-1800

SCOTS AT HOME   1660-1725

During the last forty years of the seventeenth century two plays by Scots were produced in Edinburgh.[1] Considering the tumultuous times Scotland was experiencing, the slim output by Northern dramatists is understandable. In the politically tense atmosphere fraught with religious radicalism, not only the drama but all secular literature faltered. Alexander Campbell in his *History of Poetry in Scotland*, waggishly observes that in the late 1600s "scarcely anything was relished in Scotland unless it was larded plentifully with the 'marrow of divinity'; hence the meagreness of profane productions, in the long lent of innocent hilarity. The muses were suffered to roam at large, unless any one of them thrumbed the harp of King David for the spiritual comfort of pious covenanters."[2] Cultural extremism, fostered during the late years of the Reformation, increased during the turmoil of the late Stuart dynasty, and did not abate until many years after Scotland's union with England, as the Jacobite uprisings illustrate. Coupled with the conditions of political unrest and economic disasters, most dramatically exemplified by the Darien affair, was the attitude that drama was diabolical. The Kirk nurtured the concept that the playhouse was the domain of Beelzebub. In writing of the early eighteenth-century attitude toward the drama, Hugo Arnot states in his *History of Edinburgh* that the "most popular divines represented the playhouse as the actual temple of the Devil, where he frequently appeared clothed in the corporeal substance and possessed the spectators, whom he held as his worshippers."[3]

Of the various elements which explain the poverty of the Scottish stage, religious censure is paramount. While it may seem simplistic to attribute clerical condemnation as the major reason for the precarious position of the drama, the controversy which John Home's *Douglas*

1   Terence Tobin, "A Checklist of Plays Presented in Scotland, 1660–1705," *Restoration and Eighteenth Century Theatre Research* 12 (May 1973):51 ff.; a list for 1705–1750 is forthcoming in *RECTR*.
2   Alexander Campbell, *History of Poetry in Scotland* (Edinburgh, 1798), p. 139.
3   Hugo Arnot, *The History of Edinburgh* (Edinburgh, 1779), 1:182.

provoked in the mid-eighteenth century illustrates the prime importance of religious censorship. And it was not until the late eighteenth
century, when the Enlightenment had become sufficiently widespread
to shake theocratic power, that the Kirk ceased to be the "devil's advocate" of the theatre.

To flirt with the satanic one must be potent. In the seventeenth
century such power belonged solely to the nobility, under whose aegis
plays were produced. After the Union of the Crowns, those who were
entertained by theatrical productions would have been familiar with
English playhouses. Since no immediate dramatic tradition existed, it is
not surprising that *Marciano, or the Discovery* is a facsimile of the
comedies which entertained Charles's court in the South.

Three years after the Restoration of Charles II, *Marciano* was published. The title page claims that this tragi-comedy was "acted with
great applause, before His Majesty's High Commissioner, and others of
the Nobility, at the Abbey of Holyrudhouse, on St. John's night, By a
Company of Gentlemen." There is no internal evidence to support the
conjecture that the play was written for this occasion. This piece is
mentioned in *Mercurius Publicus*, 15 January 1663, but no date of performance is given. In 1663, St. John's feast, 27 December, fell on a
Sunday, an extremely unlikely evening for the presentation of a drama.
The suggestion on the title page that *Marciano* was performed before
the Commissioner to the Parliament further complicates establishment
of the performance date, because the Earl of Rothes, the Commissioner, came to Scotland in May 1663.

Marciano is attributed to William Clerke, an Edinburgh lawyer,
who may have taken one of the parts himself in the amateur production.[4] The author's preface gives a picture of the condition of the
drama in the North:

> Although then it is not ordinar to apologize for Playes in general, at the
> publishing of any particular one; Yet, because this now appears as a
> City-swaggerer in a Country-church, where seldom such have been
> extant; and that the peevish prejudice of some persons, who know noth-
> ing beyond the principles of base, greazy, arrogant, illiterate Pedants,
> who, like the grasshoppers of *Egypt*, swarm in every corner of this
> Nation, and plague all the youth accordingly, is such, that they can-
> not have patience to hear of a Comedy, because they never see one
> acted: . . . .

4 William H. Logan, "Introduction," *Marciano, or the Discovery* (Edinburgh,
1871), p. v, says that Clerke acted in his comedy, but there is no documentation
to support this statement.

The writer goes on to cite the merits of the theatre, giving examples of Greco-Roman veneration for the stage, which teaches virtue as well as the art of speaking. After crediting the Jesuit practice of training students in oratory by presentation of plays,[5] Clerke boldly assays his countrymen's declamatory deficiencies:

> Wheras to deliver a speech naturally, that the action may sute the words, and the words the action; although dissonant to the pedantry of this age, who vote down the use of Stageplayes (as they call them) for no other reason, but because in them, such pilfring stinkards as themselves, are often discovered in their own colours; so ridiculous in their imperious behaviour, that non save themselves (whose innate stupidity doth much excuse their impudence) cannot but see it and abhor it; . . . .

Marciano opens with the title character staggering wounded on stage proclaiming:

> Lost—By Heavens—all lost,
> All our hopes blasted
> By *Jove*, without hope of recovery.
> O gods, commiserate our despicable estate.
>
> (I. 1)

Barbaro has usurped power in Florence and Duke Cleon has retreated to Savoy. Marciano and the Siennese have been defeated by Borasco and the rebel Florentines. Arabella determines to find her lover Marciano when she hears of this crisis. Marciano is captured by Borasco's henchmen at an inn, after much swordplay; Arabella is later taken prisoner. The captured pair meet in prison, but love behind bars is not for Marciano, and he escapes.

After the escape scene which involves a drunken jailer, a series of scenes deal with Arabella's fate. The Florentine Senate reverses the decision to liberate the heroine, who is then sentenced to be decapitated. Borasco tries to seduce Arabella, promising her freedom, but she refuses. At this point Barbaro dies, his followers are scattered, and

5 Students did perform plays in Scotland at this time. The vehicles presented subordinated entertainment to instruction, and the masters were most careful in their selection of vehicles, for as the case of William Bouok illustrates, schoolmasters could be dismissed for staging plays considered improper. Bouok was suspended "for his scandal in acting a comoedie wherein he mad a mock of religious duties and ordinances." See Terence Tobin, "School Plays in Scotland, 1656–1693," *Seventeenth Century News* 23 (1969):49.

Cleon is restored to his rightful position. Arabella and Marciano are united.

The play is a combination of heroic drama and Restoration farce. The main plot in blank verse is lightened by the comic subplot in prose. Pantaloni and his rich friend Becabunga, are deceived by Chrysolina and Marionetta, two "ladies of honour." The comic dialogue is the most natural since Lyndsay, and characters' speeches fit their personalities. The foppish Pantaloni frequently cites his mother as a final authority, and in aureate terms professes his love for the ladies. Manduco, an arrogant pedant, badgers his associates with pompous Latin phrases. The language of Pantaloni and Manduco is sufficiently artificial to render both types distasteful:

> *Enter Boy.*
> Madam, the two Gentlemen who call, *Casio* and *Leonardo*, desire to see you.
> MAN. Go tell them we are not within.
> CHRYS. Tell them we are not at leasure, Sirrah.
>
> *Exit Boy.*
> MAN. What are they?
> PANT. Ranting, young blades, like the times I warrand you, two fellows, that have frequented all your Stage-playes in *Italy*, and I heard our Chaplain say; and my Sister too (which is more) that Playes were very unlawful and impious.
> MAN. Playes are indeed profane, scelerate, abominable, yea abominably abominable—which I will maintain *multis argumentis*.
> PANT. Besides they are great mockers of such Gentlemen as us, who are better then themselves.
>
> (II. 2)

The structure of *Marciano* is weak, for it attempts too much. To concoct a politically expedient main plot about a general who gets his lady and aids in the restoration of a ruler is difficult enough. The injection of comic business into such heroics would tax a playwright thoroughly familiar with stagecraft. Clerke, like many of his countrymen who later attempted dramas, had little opportunity to learn what would work on the boards.

The next play presented in Edinburgh had premiered in London. In 1668 *Tarugo's Wiles, or the Coffee-House* by Thomas St. Serfe (Sydserf) was staged at the Tennis Court of Holyrood House. The author, who founded the short-lived *Mercurius Caledonius*, was sufficiently sophisticated to realize that recognition in the dramatic field was to be gained abroad. The father of the Scottish newspaper set a precedent in theatre as well as in journalism. St. Serfe was the first Scot to obtain a London premiere, a goal fellow dramatists continued to seek ever after. From 1668 until his death the following year, St. Serfe managed a theatrical company in the Canongate.

Dramatic activity was as slight in the reign of William and Mary as it had been under the Stuarts. In 1692 Archibald Pitcairne composed *The Assembly*, the sole Restoration comedy treating Scottish material written by a North Briton. Pitcairne, the most famous physician in Britain during the seventeenth century, whose Jacobite sympathies were as well known as his purported irreligion was notorious, railed against the obstreperous General Assembly. His dramatic contributions circulated privately until they were published after his death.

The Assembly was first issued in 1722, and subsequently went through several editions. After the octavo and duodecimo printings of 1722, textual and typographical corruptions occurred in subsequent editions of 1752, 1766, and 1817. Numerous emendations were made by editors in attempts to alter considered textual barbarisms. This post-humously published satire on religious hypocrisy remained in manuscript thirty years before it was printed. The ridicule of prominent churchmen and religious excesses was enjoyed by Episcopalian Jacobites in the seclusion of clubs and taverns considered unsavory by those who would have ordered the incendiary play to be burnt by the hand of the common hangman, had they known of its existence.

Seven years after the Fifteen, *The Assembly* appeared in London. It was not until 1752 that a preface was included. This introduction attempts to justify the deprecatory treatment of some of the characters who had real counterparts.[6] Solomon Cherry-Trees (David William-

6 John Genest, *Some Account of the English Stage from the Restoration in 1660 to 1830* (New York, n. d.), 10:183, bases his hypothesis that *The Assembly* was written by more than one author upon the preface, which does suggest multiple authorship.

> This play was begun just after the King of France took Mons [9 April 1691], as is clearly intimated in the first scene; but by reason of some gentlemen's going to the country, who were concerned about it, it lay dormant four months; then it was set about again, and was very soon compleated. We confess it was hastily huddled together; for we were not a fortnight about the whole work, by reason of the multitude of business the authors were intangled in.

This preface first appears in the second edition, which is a corrupt text of the play. It is likely that Pitcairne wrote the play, but did not compose the preface. A key such as this introduction provides would not have been necessary for the doctor's contemporaries. Had he provided the key, it is strange that he should have neglected to identify all of the characters based upon actual persons. See Terence Tobin, "Introduction," *The Assembly* (Lafayette, Ind., 1972), pp. 10, 20–21.

Archibald Pitcairne (1652–1713).

son), Clerk (John Spalding), Salathiel Littlesense (Gilbert Rule), Covenant Plain-Dealer (James Kirkton), Lord Whigridden (William Lyndsay, Earl of Crawford), and Timothy Turbulent (James Fraser of Brae) are labeled whited sepulchres:

> Mr. Fraser of Brae deserveth the name of Turbulent very well; for he's a huffing, insolent, cross-grain'd a fellow as ever lived. His whole trade, when he was young, was to debauch ladies waiting-women; but now, when he's graver, he talks obscenely, and shows a thing not to be named to the maid, as he did to a great many women lately at the cross of Dumfermline. Now, for women he takes wine, and drinks as great a quantity of hard sack, as curates do of ale. His party calls the fumes of the liquor the operations of the Spirit of God, and his fury and madness they term true zeal. The most part of the articles of the *Libella universalis* was made use of by him, to thrust out the Episcopal clergy of Fife.

Internal evidence suggests that Pitcairne drew inspiration from the General Assemblies of 1690 and 1692. For the first time since the interregnum the General Assembly met on 10 October 1690. In his message to the group, William III cautioned against extremism: "Moderation is what religion enjoins, neighboring churches expect from you and we recommend to you." Moderation meant little to the core of "antedeluvians" who had survived the Caroline ejection of 1661. Covenanters were in a retaliatory mood. *The Act of Assembly, anent a Solemn National Fast and Humiliation* reflects the spirit of the 1690 meeting: "there hath been in some a dreadful Athiestical Boldness against God, and his Providence the Divine Authority of the Scriptures, the Life to come, and Immortality of the Soul, yea and scoffed at these things." When King William's letters ordering the Assembly to desist were ignored, he sent Lord John Carmichael to adjourn the unruly gathering. In 1692 the King granted all who had taken the Oath of Allegiance permission to attend. The ministers disregarded this admonition, which they considered Caesarian interference. The commissioner again dissolved the Assembly. This long repression of Presbyterianism produced many martyrs. Most of the ministers identified in the preface to the play had been imprisoned for their faith. It must also be said that there were paranoid presbyters bent on reprisal. Pitcairne's bias was such that he depicted all presbyters as rogues considerably more heinous than "old priests writ large."

Pitcairne begins his extermination of fanatics with a conversation between two rakes. Will greets Frank, who has returned to Edinburgh.

Will, who has remained, gives his impression of Scotland after the revolution settlement:

> . . . for my own Part, I find no Reason to complain; for I find them as good Whoring and Drinking Times as ever: Only with this Difference; whereas, before we were *most Christian Drunkards,* we're now turn'd *most Catholick;* and the Compliments we took before out of *Cassandra* and *Cleopatra*[7] for our Mistresses, we're, now, beholden to the *Song of Solomon* for them. The Money we were wont to give to Bawds, we now give to Phanatick Ministers Wives: And whereas before Honest Fellows coin'd new Oaths at a Glass of Wine, we now send our Representative to Parliament to do it for us.
>
> (I. 1)

As the two friends sit in the tavern discussing topical events, Novel, a Jacobite newsmonger, and Abednego Vissioner, a Whig newsmonger, pester the traveler for information. Novel and Vissioner appear at intervals throughout the play to indulge in political ranting. Their incursions do not develop into a subplot. The newsmongers' heated exchanges are *scenas.* Their dialogue does not further the action, but functions like the Italian operatic device which provides for recitatives of impassioned character.

The second scene transpires at Lady Bigot's house. Mr. Wordie, a Presbyterian chaplain, reveals his desire for Lady Bigot's daughter, Mrs. Rachel, while discussing scripture with the two women. In the course of the conversation spiced with *double entendres* in a religious frame, Rachel reveals that she is pregnant with Wordie's child.

Weakness may flaw the kirk-ridden laity, but malice is the sin of the presbyters. The last scene in the first act consists of a session of the General Assembly. The splenetic religionists are bent on persecuting other sects and caviling about theological minutiae.

In the second act, tradesmen besiege Assembly member Lord Huffy, demanding reimbursement for items the ill-tempered knight has ruined with his lash. The scene shifts quickly to church, where Mr. Solomon absolves a fornicatrix. While the minister performs this ironic act from the pulpit, Will propositions Violetta by quoting the Song of Solomon. Lady Bigot adds to the merriment occurring in the pews. The old woman is captivated by Will's citations. Her niece, Violetta, is a match for the devil in quoting scripture. The third scene shows the committee in action again. Mr. Shittle, a complying Episcopal divine, tries unsuc-

---

7 *Cassandra* and *Cleopatra* are romances by G. de Costes, Seigneur de la Calprenède.

cessfully to buy his comfort from the Assembly. The committee refuses the cloying self-seeker, because they are even more hungry for power than for money. This quest for control is underscored by the presbyters' considerations about overriding Parliament.

The third act opens with Will and Violetta indulging in persiflage of an anti-Presbyterian hue. Will promises that Frank will court Laura, Violetta's younger sister. The lovers arrange a meeting at Lady Bigot's home. The rakes will don high hats and double-necked cloaks of kirkmen.

Will encourages Frank in his quest of Laura by outlining the caper. Mention of the clerical garb provides another opportunity to excoriate the ministry. To underscore the criticism of presbyters by the romantic principals, an entertaining scene transpires at Lady Bigot's house. Mr. Solomon makes advances to Laura. The minister fondles her bosom, while speaking of matters ecclesiastical. The final scene of the third act shows the committee in church again. They call on Mr. Turncoat, who rejects the Episcopacy and swears that he is a loyal Presbyterian.

The fourth act begins with the meeting of Laura and Frank. After the girl's initial aloofness, she, like her sister, warms to her suitor when she discovers that he shares her views on Presbyterianism. The second scene shows the committee wrangling over plantations and presbyteries, synods and sacraments. Characteristically they come to no conclusion. The third scene consists of commentaries by Frank and Will on the parade of deceivers, pedants, and opportunists. This long scene recapitulates the previous ridicule of the Williamite establishment.[8]

The fifth act begins with the newsmongers' discussion of the relative merits of filthy Romish Latin as opposed to good Presbyterian Latin. The second scene opens as Will and Frank, disguised as ministers, call on their ladies. They are greeted warmly by the girls' aunt. Their pietistic exchange with the old lady exhibits Pitcairne's comic power.

OLD L.   . . . O 'tis a sad World Mr. *Sam.*
WILL.   An abominable, accursed, unjust, malicious, ill-natured World.
OLD L.   A prying, Censorious, a Soul seducing, Gospel renouncing World.
WILL.   A Malignant, backsliding, Covenant breaking, Minister mocking World.
OLD L.   A filthy Idolatrous, Sabbath-breaking Parent dishonouring

8   In the 1766 edition Act IV, scene 3, is a brief violent skirmish between Lord Huffy and a soldier. The scene does nothing to further the plot and tells nothing new about the noble with the whip. This scene may have been inserted by the editor who emended the text extensively.

World; murdering, whoring, lying, coveting World—in a Word, it is
an uncharitable worldly World.
[*Enter Maid.*] There's a poor Man lost his Means by the West Country
Rable.
OLD L. Come you to tell me that, you baggage? beat him down
Stairs—. O Mr *Sam*, 'tis a troublesome beggarly World, a vain, gaudy,
Prayer slighting and Reformation overturning World.
WILL. [*Aside.*] Now I can say no more; she has run me out of Breath,
she is longer practised in the Trade than I.
OLD L. But how comes your Friend says nothing?
FRA. Then, Madam, 'tis an abominable, whoring, drinking, Reforma-
tion overturning World.
OLD L. That's said already.

(V. 2)

After drollery about which one of the imposters will give a sermon,
Solomon and Covenant enter. These two Assembly members are the
Lady Bigot's choices for her nieces. Frank and Will flee with their
ladies, meet Huffy as they are leaving, and Frank gives the brutish
noble his comeuppance. Solomon and Covenant tell the elderly lady of
her daughter Rachel's condition, and promise to cover up the dalliance
with a marriage ceremony. The couples return to chide Rachel and her
"bulky maidenhead."

In the last scene of the play, the convention summons Mr. Orthodox,
a noncomplying Episcopal minister, and seizes his church. After a reading of the outrageous charges against Orthodox, a Captain of the
Guard brings a letter from King William commanding the Assembly
to dissolve.

Pitcairne is probably the author of *Tollerators and Contollerators; a
Comedy Acted in My Lord Advocats Lodgeing, June 10, 1703.* The
epilogue of this playlet gives the gist of the conversations of the ten
characters.

> When church is in Comedians' dress,
> You may see how statesmen themselves express:
> What cursed, what foolish schism creators
> Are these sect of men whom they name Tollerators.

Some of the men Pitcairne had satirized in previous works appear once
more in this play. The opinions, allusions, and dialogue of *Tollerators*
and *The Assembly* correspond. After David Williamson exits angrily,
Viscount Tarbat and the Lord Advocate quarrel in the salty and direct
style of his five-act comedy:

TAR. God curse you for ane old whiggish divill; where Mr. Williamson's sermon befor the Assembly? wher Mr. Webster's Essay? and ther
whole preachings and writings are so bitter that I doubt not but they
have been insinuated by the devill in hell.
AD. O cursed wreatch, the quintisence of venom against God and his
cause. God curse you, and I am sure he will curse you, if you do not
repent: But not more of it.

Tolerators was not published until 1830, when George Kinloch included
the piece in his edition of Pitcairne's *Babell,* a hudibrastic satire on the
General Assembly, which contains the same prejudices the author
manifests in his comedies. It is possible that other Scots also tried dramatic writing, but there is no record of any play by a Northerner
published or produced in Scotland until the eighteenth century.

The only published drama of the generation that appeared in
Scotland was Alexander Fyffe's *The Royal Martyr, King Charles I* in
1705, the year the Union Parliament convened. This event may have
been the occasion for publication. John Genest was not hyperbolic
when he described this drama as one of the worst ever written.[9] *The
Royal Martyr* is a portrait of a paragon in jingling heroic couplets. As
the play opens Charles is concerned about treason. Queen Henrietta
and courtiers are reassuring the monarch, when the Duke of Richmond
enters to warn his sovereign of war. After the admonition, the opposition states its position. Essex lets the audience know that his quarrel is
with the senate rather than with the King. This soliloquy is the first in
a series which give the views of various factions. Covenanter Alexander
Henderson questions the imposition of "gaudie Rites." Dr. Hammond
states the Roman Catholic case. The scene then shifts to a chamber in
which Oliver Cromwell envisions victory.

Charles is imprisoned, and his family goes into hiding. The third act
opens with the song "Now the Lords, and the Levites, and the Lawyers go down." This is the only lyric in the piece labeled an opera in
the first edition. Cromwell crows about his conquest, then Thomas
Harrison reports on how the Roundheads took Charles prisoner:

> Whilst Drums and Trumpets did the noise resound,
> I with my Squadrons did his Coach surround;
> So whilst the Idol King himself would shew,
> They'd in that Glorious Servitude him view,
> Nor Grandeur from Captivity they knew.

9   Genest, *Some Account of the English Stage,* 10:152.

> At full Career we marcht along the Plain,
> And in this Pomp he drag'd about his chain.
>
> (III. 1)

In disguise the Queen and the Prince visit the King in prison; this melodramatic confrontation proves too much for Henrietta. The Prince supports his mother: "Madam you'r in a Swoon, / And whilst I'd bear you up, ye still fall down."

In the fifth act Charles is beheaded on stage, and participants in the Civil War exchange ideas which demonstrate that exciting history can be transformed into dull fiction.

A second edition of Fyffe's drama came out in 1709; it was more correctly identified as a tragedy. The play was revised if not improved in the 1712 edition. An insertion entitled "To her Majesty's Principal Secretaries of State, etc." was printed after the fulsome dedication to Queen Anne in an effort to curry favor, which is the *raison d'être* for *The Royal Martyr*.

The Interlocutor was written during the early years of the eighteenth century, but it remained unpublished until 1803. This playlet is credited to Alexander Pennecuik, M.D.[10] Dr. Pennecuik owned Newhall, the estate after which Allan Ramsay drew the setting of *The Gentle Shepherd*.[11] In his Tweeddale manor, Pennecuik entertained Ramsay and other friends with ribald dialogues, such as "The Webster's Wife's Tears over her Husband's Testicles, who Castrate Himself: In a Dialogue 'twixt her and the Matrons of Middleton." Pennecuik's "The Mermaid: A Dialogue betwixt two Country Clowns, staring on the Sign of the Mermaid, at a Tobacconist's Shop" exhibits a high degree of dramatic potential. The speculations of Georgie and Jamie on the Mermaid, whose parents fed her fish in Lent, thus producing the tail responsible for sexual complications, are highly entertaining. The dialogues are much superior to *The Interlocutor*, which causes one to question the attribution to Pennecuik.

If *The Interlocutor* is the work of Pennecuik it antedates 1722, the year the doctor died. The one-act comedy in verse is early eighteenth century in feeling and diction. The play deals with the bawdy preoccupations of Sir John, the Just-Ass of the Peace, who tries to seduce July, a serving wench. To foil the knight lurking in the shadows below stairs,

---

10   William Brown, "Writings of Alexander Pennecuik, M.D., and Alexander Pennecuik, Merchant," *Publications of the Edinburgh Bibliographical Society 1901–1904* 6 (1906):117–31.
11   *The Works of Alexander Pennecuik* (Leith, 1815), p. 28.

July warns Sir John of the arrival of Mr. Grue, the procurator. Grue intimates to the girl that Sir John is impotent, and as the interlocutor scorns the noble as "the shaughland legged wight / With his poker, in the yard alight," July determines to serve both swains the anaphrodisiac of toasted cheese.

Dr. Pennecuik's works have been confused with those of Alexander Pennecuik, the merchant, who produced *curiosa* as raffish as those of his medical uncle. The nephew, noted for his dissipation, could also write biting satire. *The Flight of Religious Piety from Scotland, upon the account of Ramsay's lewd books, &c., and the Hellbent Play-house Comedians, who debauch all the Faculties of the soul of our rising generation* exhibits Alexander Pennecuik's penchant for the Juvenalian. This pamphlet is not a defense of Kirk principles, but rather an effort to infuriate his competitor Allan Ramsay. Pennecuik was more adept at satire than frolics of pseudo-classic shepherds. His pastoral, *Corydon and Cochrania*, is lifeless. This playlet was written to entertain guests at the wedding reception of the Duke of Hamilton in 1723.

For the same event, Allan Ramsay wrote *The Nuptials: a Masque On the Marriage of his Grace James Duke of Hamilton and Lady Anne Cochran.* This masque is not polished professional entertainment, but it contains a happy combination of neoclassical convention and rustic diction, which Ramsay would later employ to greater advantage in *The Gentle Shepherd. The Nuptials* commences with Calliope accompanying herself on a violin-cello to four quatrains of praise for the bride and groom. The Genius of the family attired in scarlet announces that he will lead the guests. Venus and three Graces, together with Minerva and Hymen, next enter to wish the couple well in Scotticisms touched by the classics. The goddess of love promises the newlyweds happiness:

> And bear frae ilka Glance, on douny Wings,
> Into his ravish'd Heart the softest Things:
> And soon as *Hymen* has perform'd his Rites,
> I'll show'r on them my hale Idalian Sweets.

Ganymed enters, flagon in hand, and the cup bearer and Bacchus toast the company. After the healths, the participants dance. Then the ladies lead the Duchess away to be undressed, while the muse of heroic epic sings an epithalamium.

Ramsay composed *An Ode, With a Pastoral Recitative on the Marriage of the Right Honourable, James Earl of Wemyss and Mrs. Janet Charteris* in which shepherds Rosalind and Armyas discuss in dialect

how the beautiful Charterissa will go far away to become the wife of
the Thane of Fyfe. There is no record substantiating that this pastoral
was presented at the nobleman's wedding.

Allan Ramsay reputedly wrote a libretto of twenty-four lines for
Bocci's *A Scots Cantata.*[12] The poet who managed the first resident
company of players in Scotland also produced creditable prologues and
epilogues, but his stature as a dramatic writer rests upon *The Gentle
Shepherd,* the most popular pastoral in eighteenth-century British
theatre.

The Gentle Shepherd was not written for a London audience, but
rather grew into a theatrical from ecologues which Ramsay had published previously. "Patie and Roger" (1720) became the core of Act I,
scene 1. "Jenny and Meggy" (1723) forms the basis for Act I, scene 2.
"By the Delicious Warmness of the Mouth," a song of 1721, Ramsay
incorporated into Act II, scene 4. The pastoral became a ballad opera
at the request of Haddington Grammar School boys, who wished to
present the story of Peggy and Patie for their annual school play. The
boys had seen the pastoral comedy performed by strolling players in
Edinburgh in 1728. Ramsay obliged, and the elementary school children performed the piece at Taylor's Hall on 22 January 1729. The pastoral became a favorite with audiences everywhere. It was performed
for more than a century, and was mounted in more than 160 different
productions in Scotland, England, and America.[13] Tyrone Guthrie's
candlelight production for the Edinburgh Festival in 1949 demon-
strated that this pastoral still charms theatregoers.

Unquestionably, *The Gentle Shepherd* is the major Scottish contribution to the drama in the early eighteenth century. Ramsay depicted
Scots shepherds in their natural habitat in a more genuine fashion than
most writers of pastorals. He brought a freshness to the highly artificial
form, chiefly by his dialectical approach considered novel at the time.
Written in Scots, *The Gentle Shepherd* actually did not require a glos-
sary, but contemporary Englishmen thought the language unintelligi-
ble. George Chalmers states that John Gay visited Ramsay in Scotland
to assist Alexander Pope in reading the play, for Pope wanted certain
Scotticisms explicated.[14] This story, which has been called apocryphal,
does help to explain why burr is a rarity in Northern dramatic writings
for much of the century.

12 Burns Martin, *Allan Ramsay, a Study of His Life and Works* (Cambridge,
Mass., 1931), p. 115.
13 Martin lists recorded performances of *The Gentle Shepherd* in Appendix C.
14 George Chalmers, *The Life of Allan Ramsay* (London, 1800), p. 104.

Translations and imitations of *The Gentle Shepherd* abounded, but they suffer by comparison with the original. In translation the paste-board characters' idealism and Christmas panto fatuousness become apparent. The imitations make the languor of the action patent. These common faults of pastorals, which had made the genre obsolescent by Ramsay's time, are less noticeable in *The Gentle Shepherd*, because the dialect disguises the artifice, and makes the play seem vital and honest.

Original in his poetic approach, Ramsay was conventional in plot. Patie, the gentle shepherd, loves Peggy; Roger, a well-to-do shepherd, loves Jenny. Symon and Glaud are two old tenants of Sir William Worthy, the *deus ex machina*. Bauldy, a deer, replaces the satyr who is always outwitted in pastorals. Patie and Peggy are about to announce their love when Worthy arrives in disguise. He tells them that he is Patie's father, and obliges his long lost son to go on a journey, for he does not approve of Patie's love. The fifth act provides a happy ending, however. Mause, an old woman, supposedly a witch, reveals that Peggy is the daughter of Sir William Worthy's sister, and the lovers are united.

The story of a shepherd ignorant of his gentle birth, falling in love with a shepherdess, who learns that she is a descendant of aristocracy, has antecedents. The plot is reminiscent of Giovanni Guarini's *Il Pastor fido*. Mirtillo, who has a divine heritage, marries Amarilis. Damoetas and Mause function in about the same capacity. Guarini is refined: Ramsay is rustic. It is this difference which made the romantic *Gentle Shepherd* popular theatre later in the century. Ramsay splashed the pastoral with local color; he added a realistic wash to the stilted delineations of aristocratic shepherds. The result, like the portraits his son painted, was a smooth, flattering yet recognizable product.

Facile talents such as Allan Ramsay's invite criticism from contemporaries. William Forbes of Disblair was one of the many who felt constrained to carp at Ramsay's easily turned phrases. Forbes, who wrote *Allan Ramsay Metamorphosed into a Heather Bloter Poet in a Pastoral between Oegan and Milibiae*, also published a drama entitled *Xantippe, or the Scolding Wife* in 1724. This poem in banal iambic pentameter is an enervating treatment of the *Conjugium* by Erasmus. Xantippe, a jealous and imperious termagant, berates Socrates mercilessly. Phoebe, her even-tempered adviser, counsels that reason and suavity are more advantageous ploys. After protracted exchanges the scolding wife is convinced. The point of view expressed in *Xantippe* is similar to that of the author's better known doggerel, *An Essay upon Marriage* (ca. 1704), which he wrote after he had gone through a scandalous divorce. This dramatic poem, which shows Forbes's disenchantment with women, was almost certainly not intended to be performed. The distinction between stage and closet plays, however, is of slight importance until at least the second quarter of the eighteenth century,[15] when a resident theatrical company was established in Edinburgh. The existence of any works which are dramatic in nature is noteworthy in a country where abrogation of the theatre had become a tradition.

1725-1750

Before Allan Ramsay founded the Edinburgh Players in 1733, visiting companies and strolling performers had presented entertainments sporadically in the Scottish capital. Since troupers of the ilk who would go to the *Thule Ultima* of the English speaking theatrical world have rarely presented new dramatic works, these groups offered slight hope to local playwrights desirous of having their efforts staged. Thomas St. Serfe, Stephen Grege, and James Underwood probably managed theatre companies, but record of their activities is slight. Like most fledgling theatrical companies, the Edinburgh Players did not make it a practice to venture into world premieres. No official record of their performance of a new drama exists. The only known plays which appeared in Scotland during the brief tenure of this troupe would have been unlikely choices for any group. Two plays were published in 1733: John Hunter, a minister, had a religious drama entitled *The Wanderer and Traveller* privately printed in Glasgow; Gabriel Nesbit published *Caledon's Tears, or Wallace, a tragedy, containing the Calamities of Scotland, from the death of King Alexander III to the betraying and butchering of the faithful Father of his Country, Sir William Wallace of Ellerslie.* The latter play, which covers a twenty-year span of events, is perhaps the earliest effort by a Scot to mine the rich ore of national history and legend for dramatic subject matter. Ralston Inglis records in *Dramatic Writers of Scotland* that this play (which makes use of Thomas the Rhymer, who predicted the death of Alexander III),

15 Allardyce Nicoll, *A History of English Drama 1660–1900* (Cambridge, 1959), 3:217–28, argues cogently for the conscious separation of plays for the theatre and for the study after 1790.

includes illustrative notes.[1] James Grahame also employed annotation nearly seventy years later in his treatment of Mary Queen of Scots. Grahame was conscious of the distinction between plays for stage and study. He was also aware of working with a genre which had become established—the epical representation of national heroes in dramatic frame. Nesbit, who published *Caledon's Tears* before James Macpherson was born, may be considered a harbinger of the romantics in the thrall of ancient legends of the barren hills.

Rather than fostering a national drama, the mundane consideration of box office receipts was paramount for the Edinburgh Players, who like most provincial companies were often in financial straits. In 1736 the troupe was sufficiently affluent to move into a remodeled building in Carrubber's Close; this was the first regular theatrical establishment set up in Scotland. The playhouse opened 8 November, with productions of *The Recruiting Officer* and *The Virgin Unmasked*, the sort of British fare which became staple. The puff in the *Caledonian Mercury* praised the theatre "which is thought by all judges to be as complete and finished with good taste as any one of its size in the three kingdoms." The newspaper also published the prologue spoken at the opening. The verse, as well as numerous anti-theatrical tracts by Scottish divines, shows that the stage had to cope with forces which had thwarted the theatre since the days of John Knox.

> Long has it been the business of the stage
> To mend our manners, and reform the age.
> This task the muse by nature was assign'd,
> Ere Christian light shone in upon the mind;
> Ev'n since these glorious truths to men appear'd,
> Her moral precepts still have been rever'd,
> And when the sacred monitors have fail'd,
> Just satyre from the stage has oft prevailed.
> Tho' some sour criticks full of phlegm and spleen
> Condemn her use as hellish and obscene;
> And from their gloomy thoughts and want of sense,
> Think what diverts the mind gives Heav'n offence.[2]

Edinburgh did not get much chance to determine whether this theatre was reformatory or "hellish and obscene," because the playhouse was closed immediately after the passing in 1737 of the Licens-

---

1   Ralston Inglis, *Dramatic Writers of Scotland* (Glasgow, 1868), p. 90.
2   *Caledonian Mercury* 15 November 1736. See also *Caledonian Mercury* 16 September 1736.

ing Act, and the building in Carrubber's Close became a qualified Anglican chapel.[3]

The year after the passage of the New Act (10 Geo. II, cap. 28), which forced the theatre to cease operation, Adam Thomson's ballad opera, *The Disappointed Gallant, or Buckram in Armour,* was published in Edinburgh. From the author's remarks in the preface it would seem that the comedy was written around 1733. Although there is no definite record of performance, *The Disappointed Gallant* may have been presented during the final season of the Carrubber's Close theatre. There are several advertisements in newspapers during this time which mention that comedies were presented, but the plays are not named. Thomson says in his preface that he was fifteen when the play was staged. The prodigy's claim as well as his name may be invention. Nothing else is known of the teen-age dramatist, and in a town the size of eighteenth-century Edinburgh, during a period much concerned with genius, this is as unusual as the appearance of the author's name on the title page. In Scotland profane works were almost always published anonymously. This practice, which arose from necessity and became customary, persisted through the Waverley era.

In *The Disappointed Gallant* the author makes use of local color, and the action of the three-act farce takes place in Edinburgh. The business which bustles at the expense of credibility, slows for songs set to Scots airs. The tale of Sandy Buckram, a "brave little tailor," is replete with comic conventions of the day. Devices used to snarl situations are predictable, but the play has entertaining moments. Buckram is being cuckolded by Sir Robert Careless, with whom Sandy's shrewish wife, Jean, is infatuated. Lady Careless permits Mr. Rover to pay her court. Belinda loves this gentleman of fashion as well, which further complicates the amorous machinations. Sir Andrew Trimmer and an heiress have an affair, aided by scheming servants, Tom and Molly. The adventures of this host of *enamoratti* include locking Sir Robert in a chest, a comic duel between Rover and Trimmer not unlike the sword-play in *Twelfth Night,* and disguising Buckram as a maid. The resolution of the intrigues is abrupt. After Buckram dons armor to fight a duel, Jean is miraculously transformed into a submissive wife. If this comedy is the juvenile effort its author purports it to be, it is proficient, for it is comparable to numerous comedies of the period.

3   See Allan Ramsay's poem which protests the closing of the Edinburgh play-house: "To the Hon. Duncan Forbes of Culloden," *Gentleman's Magazine* 7 (1737): 507. Also see Frederick A. Pottle, *James Boswell: The Earlier Years 1740–1769* (New York, 1966), p. 461.

Dramatic production ceased from 1737 until 1741, when Edinburgh once more enjoyed theatrical entertainment. Under Thomas Este's management, plays were given in conjunction with concerts. The following advertisement in the 12 March 1742 issue of the *Caledonian Mercury* indicates how Britons skirted the 1737 law:

> By desire of his Grace the Duke of Hamilton, for the benefit of the Master Hamiltons, at the Taylors' Hall in the Cowgate. To-morrow being the 13th instant, will be perform'd a Concert of Vocal and Instrumental Musick, after which *gratis* that celebrated comedy, called She wou'd and she wou'd not, or the Kind Imposter. To which by desire, will be added, the Honest Yorkshire-man, performed by Liliputians.

Admission was charged for the concert, after which plays were presented free of charge, a practice generally followed in unlicensed London and provincial theatres. This evasion of the Licensing Act seemed to satisfy Scots legalists, since there was not a season for the rest of the century when some professional theatrical was not offered in the Northern capital.

In 1742 a notice appeared describing Patrick Coldstream's production of his "Turnus and Aeneas." The manuscript by the master of Crail Grammar School in Fyfe indicates that the play was intended to instruct rather than to delight the pupils. Children declaimed the drama for their parents, who listened to neoclassic oratory about Roman bravery. The play is insignificant as dramatic literature. The highly complimentary notice of "Turnus and Aeneas" is important, however, as an indication of how firmly entrenched theatricals had become in the education of Scottish gentlemen since the Restoration.

> *Crail, Aug. 24.* This day the students of our grammar-school made their publick appearance, (as has been long usual here,) before the vacation. They acted the tragedy of Turnus and Aeneas, composed in blank verse by the master, before a numerous audience, among whom were several persons of distinction, and all were satisfactorily entertained with their elegant behaviour and good address. This method of acting publickly the masters' compositions, from Terentius Christianus, &c. has been thought most conducive to give the boys an easy pronunciation and a modest assurance; and all they do in this manner, being timeously given them for their employment at spare hours, does not retard their other exercises. There are also yearly orations delivered at Candelmas, at which time there is a visitation and examination of the school by the magistrates and minister, for whom are produced themes, versions, specimens of writing, arithmetick, &c. and this school being

situate remote from any avocations which might intercept attention to
learning and study, the boys under so good a master, make an uncommon proficiency.[4]

In 1745 William Lyon, one of the actors in Este's company, published
an adaptation of Sir John Vanbrugh's comedy, *The Mistake*, entitled
The Wrangling Lovers, or Like Master Like Man.[5] The title was later
altered to *Lovers' Quarrels* and played many seasons in the Northern
theatre. This play has a long history of transformations. Molière borrowed from Italian plays *Interresse di Nicolo Secchi* and *Sdegni amo-
rosi* and incorporated *lazzi* of the *commedia dell'arte* for his *Le Depit
amoreux*. Vanbrugh translated Molière, and followed the French playwright scene by scene, but changed the locale from France to Spain,
and did not retain Molière's mildly pessimistic tone in his early comedy
of intrigue. The English version is a different play from its French
model. William Lyon's farcical afterpiece takes Vanbrugh's dialogue
verbatim. Lyon rearranges the sequence of events, beginning with
Vanbrugh's third act scene in which Don Felix confronts his son with
the youth's clandestine engagement to Leonora. Shortly after the confrontation, Lyon backtracks to Vanbrugh's second act to introduce the
pedantic tutor, Metaphrastus, who expounds in both plays: "The Title,
Master, comes from *magis* and *ter*, which is as much to say, Thrice
worthy."

When a five-act comedy involving twelve characters is condensed to
an *entr'acte* requiring seven players, motivation and characterization
must suffer. Lyon omits the initial mistake, the delivering of Leonora's
letter to the wrong suitor; this error sets the original comedy in motion.
Lines which Vanbrugh assigns to Don Lorenzo and his servant, Lyon
gives to Don Carlos and his clever man Sancho. The amalgamation of
two suitors and their servants into one of each is not apparent, because
Vanbrugh does not provide notable distinctions in the characters of his
beaux and their servants. Lyon concentrates on the *commedia* ele-

4   William H. Logan, ed., *Fragmenta Scoto-Dramatica* (Edinburgh, 1835), p. 16.
5   James Dibdin, *Annals of the Edinburgh Stage* (Edinburgh, 1888), p. 56, notes
the title change. Bonamy Dobrée, ed., *The Complete Works of Sir John Vanbrugh*
(London, 1927), 3:83, mentions that *Lovers' Quarrels* has been attributed to William King. This may be another adaptation, but it is likely that Dobrée is referring
to Thomas King's interlude, "Lovers' Quarrels or, Like Masters Like Man." George
Stayley, the Edinburgh actor, did *Metaphrastus, or the Wrangling Lovers*, for his
benefit on 3 April 1765. This five-act comedy is still another version which was
revived several seasons in London in the late 1700s. See *The London Stage 1660–
1800, Part 5: 1776–1800*, ed. with a critical introduction by Charles B. Hogan (Carbondale, Ill., 1968), 1:240; 2:904.

William Lyon (?–ca. 1748).

ments, thus making up in brisk pace what the piece lacks in plot and subtlety.

An anecdote published in the *Dublin University Magazine* a century after Lyon played the Irish capital purports that the dramatist once won a crown bowl of punch for repeating verbatim an entire issue of the *Daily Advertiser* the day after the bet was made. In addition to a good memory, Lyon possessed a knowledge of contemporary theatre-goers. The most arresting departure is the new importance given the servants in *The Wrangling Lovers*. All of their lines appear in Van-brugh, but Lyon features Sancho and Jacinta, Leonora's maid, in his adaptation. The Scot's play ends not with the Restoration couple as Vanbrugh's does, but with madcap servants, who, after slapstick imi-tation of their superiors' bickering, make up. The featuring of the menials places *The Wrangling Lovers* in the tradition of farces such as *The Lying Valet* and *High Life Below Stairs*, the bourgeois entertain-ments which point to the expansion of audience that took place during the rise of modern commercial theatre.

William Hamilton of Bangour is best known for his ballad, "The Braes of Yarrow." His poem, "To the Countess of Eglinton with the *Gentle Shepherd*," accompanied some early editions of his friend Ram-say's play. Hamilton, an ardent Jacobite, had to leave Scotland during the rebellion of 1745. While in France (ca. 1745–49), the poet translated into verse Racine's *Mithridate*. The first scene of the first act is the only part of this effort which was published. The lines are facile, romantic, and after the manner of the dramatic rhyme of the French dramatist, rather than an imitation. Xiphares tells Arbates of Phar-naces' pursuit of Monimia.[6] Xiphares declaims in diction characteristic of the rest of the fragment:

> Nor duty further binds my tongue, since here
> I now no rival but a brother fear;
> Nor is this flame the passion of a day,
> A sudden blaze that hastens to decay;
> Long in my breast I pent the rising groan,
> Told it in secret to my heart alone.
>
> (I. 1)

The playhouse in Scotland was dependent upon the middle class for its audience. A wide spectrum of this group, however, still thought the

6   Nelson S. Bushnell, *William Hamilton of Bangour: Poet and Jacobite* (Aberdeen, 1957), pp. 52 and 94, cites Monimia as a recurring favorite of Hamilton's. Bushnell observes that the defeat of Mithridates parallels the Pretender's condition.

William Hamilton of Bangour (1704–1754).

theatre invidious. From 1741 until 1767, when a license was granted for legitimate theatrical operation, the pitched battle between church and stage evolved into a cold war, but the financial struggles seldom abated. The Edinburgh playhouse, like its counterparts outside London, was continually in dire financial need.[7] In 1746 the actors, most of whom were miserably underpaid, split into factions. Maintenance of two companies compounded the difficulties of getting through theatrical seasons. The better thespians joined Sarah Ward, Edinburgh's leading actress, to present productions in a new theatre in the Canongate. The other scion remained at Taylor's Hall, where until 1757 they gave programs considered inferior to those of Mrs. Ward's troupe.[8]

At mid-century the theatre in Scotland was still a precarious operation in one town. Its unstable position factors in the exodus of dramatically inclined Scots to London. James Thomson, David Mallet, and Tobias Smollett succeeded in having their works produced in the English capital. John Home tried desperately to interest David Garrick in his plays, but the minister had to be content with an Edinburgh premiere. Home's *Douglas* brought the Scottish theatre to the attention of all Britain. More important, the success of this tragedy inspired other Northerners to attempt playwriting.

1750-1775

Two years before John Home created a sensation with *Douglas*, the company at the Canongate Concert Hall staged Samuel Hart's *Herminius and Espasia* on 25 February 1754. The tragedy, which ran three performances, was uninteresting, according to David Erskine Baker, who cited a bit of dialogue to substantiate his unfavorable opinion of the play: "In the third line of it, however, we are informed, 'friendship is the wine of life.' Espasia, speaking to her confidante Ardelia, says:

7   Allan Ramsay, *Some Hints in defense of Entertainments* (Edinburgh, 1727); John Lee, *A narrative of a remarkable breach of trust, committed by a nobleman five Judges, and several advocates of the Court of Session in Scotland* (London, 1772); and John Jackson, *The History of the Scottish Stage* (London, 1793), 2, all discuss the lack of funds in the Edinburgh theatres.
8   Dibdin, *Annals of the Edinburgh Stage*, pp. 59–62, 83.

Douglas (1756) by John Home. Act IV Scene 1.

'Friendship, Ardelia is the *wine* of life,
That, mingled with the fall of harsh affliction,
Sweetens the nauseous drought, and wins the wretched
To bear his lot of suff'rance here below.' "[1]

When the new theatre manager of the Canongate, West Digges,
produced his first premiere, it was better received than Hart's play.
Digges placed an advertisement of the forthcoming production in the
local press:

A *New Tragedy* called DOUGLAS, written by an ingenious gentleman
of this country, is now in rehearsal at the Theatre, and will be performed as speedily as possible. The expectations of the public from the
performance are in proportion to the known talent and ability of the
Author, whose modest merit would have suppressed a Dramatic work,
which we think by the concurrent testimony of many gentlemen of
taste and literature will be an honour to this country.[2]

When the tragedy of frustrated mother-love and youthful idealism
opened, 14 December 1756, with West Digges as Douglas and Sarah
Ward as Lady Randolph, it became a *cause célèbre*. Theatrophiles
were as entranced by a national drama as presbyters were incensed
that one of their number had contributed to the infernal institution.
There is a frequently quoted anecdote about the first nighter who
stood up in the pit and enthusiastically roared, "Whaur's yer Wully
Shakespeare noo?" Many clergymen would have been ecstatic had
Home joined the Bard the night after the premiere.

The bibliography of the writings occasioned by *Douglas* is ponderous.[3] None of the copy expended on the tragedy was more advantageous from the standpoint of publicizing the play than the "Admonition
and Exhortation" issued by the Edinburgh Presbytery on 5 January
1757. This statement, which labels entertainments pernicious and
harmful to morality, titillated readers of British newspapers to see the

1   David Erskine Baker, Stephen Jones, and Isaac Reed, eds., *Biographia Dramatica, or a Companion to the Playhouse* (London, 1813), 1:98, lists *Herminius and
Espasia* as the work of Charles Hart. *Edinburgh Courant* 12 February 1754, identifies the author in typical manner as a "Scots gentleman." *Scots Magazine* 25 (1754):
212, says the author is S_____l. Hart. Ralston Inglis in *Dramatic Writers of Scotland*, p. 52, concurs with this identification; he hypothicates that the dramatist is
"the Rev. Samuel Hart (1720–1783) who died in South Carolina."
2   *Caledonian Mercury* and *Edinburgh Courant* 4 December 1756.
3   See Alice Edna Gipson, *John Home: a study, his Life and Works with special
reference to his tragedy of* Douglas *and the controversies which followed its first
representation* (Caldwell, Idaho, 1917).

play that had provoked such an outcry. The opening paragraph gives the flavor of the harangue made by the Kirk a month after one of her own ministers had so far forgotten his calling as to make an offering for the temple of Beelzebub.

The Presbytery taking into serious consideration the declining state of religion, the open profanation of the Lord's Day, the contempt of public worship, the growing luxury and levity of the present age—in which so many seem lovers of pleasure more than lovers of God—and being particularly affected with the unprecedented countenance given of late to the Playhouse in this place, when the state of the nation and the circumstances of the poor, make such hurtful entertainments still more pernicious, judged it their indispensable duty to express in the most open and solemn manner, the deep concern they feel on this occasion. The opinion which the Christian Church has always entertained of stage plays and players as prejudicial to the interest of religion and morality is well known, and the fatal influence which they commonly have on the far greater part of mankind, particularly the younger sort, is too obvious to be called in question. To enumerate how many servants, apprentices, and students in different branches of literature in this city and suburbs, have been seduced from their proper business by attending the stage would be a painful, disagreeable task.[4]

The clergy's animus against Home was born of the fear that the theatre might prosper, that crowds at secular pastimes in the Canongate might set trends which would weaken Kirk power. Ministers who had attended the opening of *Douglas* were called before presbyteries to answer for their behavior. Home was summoned before the Presbytery of Haddington, and subsequently resigned his post as minister of Athelstaneford on 7 June 1757.

Writings occasioned by the play filled bookstalls, where the public could choose from a host of lampoons, ballads, religious tracts, and defenses. Among the more entertaining specimens is Adam Ferguson's *The Morality of Stage-Plays Seriously Considered.* Dr. Ferguson cites Joseph and his brothers as biblical proof for defending the theatre. Dr. Alexander Carlyle of Invernesk, who attended the rehearsals of *Douglas,* as did a number of other literati,[5] wrote a pamphlet worth mention. Carlyle had defended his sympathetic position on the theatrical ques-

4 "Admonition and Exhortation by the Reverend Presbytery of Edinburgh, to all within their Bounds, January 5, 1757," *Edinburgh Courant* 7 January 1757; *London Chronicle* 8–10 March 1757.
5 Robb Lawson, *The Story of the Scots Stage* (New York, [1913]), pp. 117–18, describes a rehearsal of *Douglas* at which William Robertson, Adam Ferguson, Hugh Blair and other notables read parts for a select group of friends.

tion successfully before his presbytery. He then proceeded to use Swift's tactics in *Reasons Why the Tragedy of Douglas should be burned by the Hands of the Common Hangman*. This satire on the behalf of his friend, like those of the Irish Dean's, went over the heads of those who were the objects of its ridicule. At least one author selected the dramatic form to berate Home. *The Deposition, or Fatal Miscarriage* and *The Philosopher's Opera*, both published in 1757, have been ascribed to John MacLaurin, Lord Dreghorn.[6]

The Deposition, according to the preface, was presented as a puppet show in Allan's Close on 31 January 1757. Rather than a record of presentation, this information seems to be a satirical fillip, a common practice in dating "performances" of dramatic squibs. *The Deposition* opens with Poetaster and Lady Tearsheet exchanging professions of affection and sentiments of anticipation for the happy outcome of his dramatic production. Their rhetoric is identical to that of Home's characters.

In the second act Poetaster has a vision of Shakespeare. Atheos, a lady of his bedchamber, has also been disturbed by shades. The ghosts have condemned *Douglas* to Lethe's stream. In the last act the moderator of the General Assembly charges Poetaster with frittering away time in London. Robula pleads the poet's cause on the grounds that there is no shame attached to writing a perfect tragedy. Lucius condemns the minister for seeking the bubble of reputation. After the balloting Poetaster reenters and determines to earn his living from the theatre, whereupon he is informed that Lady Tearsheet can no longer share the bed of an impecunious lover. Poetaster then decides to go to the West Indies.

The Philosopher's Opera begins with a situation similar to that of *The Deposition*. Mr. Genius expresses his love for old Mrs. Sarah Presbytery. Mrs. Presbytery objects to Genius's hand on her breast, but opines that this suitor is an even better reformer for the present age than her first husband, John Calvin, because her sons now "have acquired a jaunty air, a military swagger, and a G—d-d—n—me look." The scene changes from the drawing room to Arthur's Seat, where Satan is late for an appointment, because he has been so busy in the town below. In the second act Satan (Digges) and Genius (Home) meet; Genius, the philosopher who manifests his hellish pride in his anti-Christian writing is Satan's own. In the last act of this loosely constructed ballad opera, Mrs. Presbytery is entertaining lachrymose ladies, who praise *Douglas* because of the tears it provokes. Genius,

6   Ralston Inglis, *Dramatic Writers of Scotland* (Glasgow, 1868), p. 143.

Satan, and his band enter and dance with the company to celebrate the playwright's engagement to the elderly Sarah.

Douglas provided material for satirists well into the nineteenth century, as is evidenced by George Smith's *Douglas Travestie*. Like most spoofs published long after a subject is topical, Smith's threadbare poem of 1826 is wearing:

> My name is *Norval*, brook it weel or ill;
> My father herds his sheep ayont the hill;
> A cautious carle, fond o' gatherin' gear,
> An' guides the thing he has wi' unco care;
> Yet guid's he wis, he had a thrawart scheme
> Wi' me; he held me hollin' on at hame—[7]

(II. 1)

The spate of writings which *Douglas* occasioned in Edinburgh and later in London, coupled with the censorship of the clergy, gave Home's first produced tragedy more widespread publicity than any other play previously done in Scotland. This controversy kept the Canongate packed for an unprecedented six-night run. London capitalized on the Scottish furor over *Douglas*. John Rich brought the drama to Covent Garden on 14 March 1757. Later David Garrick, who had rejected *Agis* and *Douglas*, did nearly everything Home could produce. This acclaim has led Harold William Thompson to call Home's best remembered work the "Scottish Declaration of Literary Independence," because the tragedy, based on a Scottish ballad, first produced in the North, won all Britain on its merit.[8]

John Home came from an old and respected line, and his background caused additional consternation among his detractors. Like Home, Eleonora Cathcart (Lady Houston) was well connected, which figured in the staging of her play, *The Coquettes, or the Gallant in the Closet*. This comedy was performed on 10 February 1759.[9] *The Coquettes*, a reworking of one of Thomas Corneille's comedies, probably *Les Engagements du hasard*, was staged through the efforts of Lady Houston's fourth cousin, James Boswell. The student at Edin-

---

7 George Smith, *Douglas Travestie: to which are added Poems and Songs chiefly in the Broad Scottish Dialect* (Aberdeen, 1826), p. 21.
8 Harold William Thompson, *A Scottish Man of Feeling; Some Account of Henry Mackenzie, Esq.* (London, 1931), p. 46.
9 *Caledonian Mercury* 10 February 1759. James Boswell, *London Journal 1762–1763*, ed. Frederick A. Pottle (New York, 1951), p. 5, says that "The Coquettes" ran three performances. There is no indication in the press that the play ran more than one night.

burgh College wrote a prologue for his relative's work, saw it through
rehearsal, and when the translation failed, Boswell took the blame as
well, for his cousin refused to claim it.[10]

Boswell's first known publication, *A View of the Edinburgh Theatre
during the Summer Season of 1759, containing an Exact List of the
Several Pieces represented, and Impartial Observations on Each Performance,* a collection of *Edinburgh Chronicle* reviews, appeared when
he was nineteen. Boswell had an abiding interest in the theatre, but
his contributions were peripheral. He wrote dramatic criticism, prologues, epilogues, and drafted a comedy, but abandoned the project.
James Boswell, Robert Burns, and other proficient Scots writers who
possessed a sense of the dramatic devoted their skills to other genres.
Among those Northern lights who wrote in other literary forms, James
Macpherson exerted the greatest influence on late eighteenth century
British drama. The Ossianic poems provided source material for melodramas until the Waverley vogue.[11] By 1760, when the first of Macpherson's "translations" appeared, the plays synonymous with Northern
drama in the popular estimation had been written. In a 1762 issue of
the *North Briton,* works of Home and Ramsay, the two plays by Scots
most frequently performed in London, were used as an allusion to Lord
Bute's influence: "The managers of both theatres have received orders
to lay aside the custom of representing the tragedy of *Tamerlane* on
King William's birthday and instead thereof to entertain the public on
that occasion with Home's *Douglas* and the *Gentle Shepherd.*"[12]

Bute was considered less than sterling in a number of English circles,
but his reputation was untarnished at home, as Baillie's *Patriotism!*
(1763) illustrates. This supportive farce, which casts the prime minister's opposition as rogues, was quickly snapped up by those who came
to the capital for the session.[13]

10   Pottle, *James Boswell, The Earlier Years,* p. 40, 465. In addition to dramatic
criticism, prologues, epilogues, and an attempt at a comedy which he abandoned,
Boswell probably provided the inspiration for *Songs in the Justiciary Opera.*
11   James Macpherson's dramatic poem *Comala* (1762), the story of the Princess
Comala who so loves Fingal that she dies from a surfeit of emotions as she observes
the hero victorious in battle against Caracul, is as close as the poet came to writing a
play. This work was the basis for David Erskine Baker's *The Muse of Ossian* (1763).
12   *North Briton* 7 (1762):11–12. See also p. 48.
13   Baillie was probably a member of the Edinburgh Faculty of Advocates. His
Christian name eludes scholars. The following manuscript notation in a copy of
Patriotism! owned by George Chalmers, attests to the popularity of the play: "This
farce is a ridicule of Wilkes, Churchill, etc., and the faction who opposed and
calumniated Lord Bute. It was published at Edinburgh, at the sitting down of the
session, 1763; all the copies were soon bought up, and there was a great demand
for more." This copy contains a manuscript key. (National Library of Scotland.
Hereafter cited NLS.)

As *Patriotism!* opens, Creole (Bedford) thinks that Slyboots (Pitt the Elder) has resigned too quickly. Slyboots assures Creole that this is a matter of policy, and that Lord Norland (Bute) is in power only because Slyboots could not have made peace which would be acceptable to the war profiteers. In a long speech typical of the piece, Slyboots explains his position on the Caribbean and other New World colonies:

> By your leave, good Sir! It is very natural for you to be fond of the sugar-islands. The engrossing of the whole sugar-trade by a few rich planters, was a scheme too lucrative not to excite their warmest zeal. But others have their particular views and interests as well as you or I, and will prosecute them with the like attention. The interest of you sugar-merchants, however great in the metropolis, would have signified little opposition to the bulk of the nation: and how could we have held up our faces to our other American islands, and those concern'd in them, had we left them expos'd to the same dangers and injuries which occasion'd such a bloody and expensive war? No, no Mr Creole; whatever partiality I may have for you, and however much might be inclined to gratify you in all your views in return for your important services, I durst not run so great a hazard as that of incurring the indignation of the far greater part of Britain by giving up North America.
>
> (I. 1)

The second act is more play-like than the first, which resembles a political tract. Act II consists of a dinner party given by Lord Ortolan (Newcastle). Among the Whigs attending are Scrivner (Chesterfield), and Lord Bruin (Cumberland). The company indulges in name-calling, and draws up ten resolutions satirizing Whig tactics; and when gouty Slyboots excuses himself, his fellow politicos denounce him as a turncoat, whom they will manipulate because of his popularity. They really wish to make Bruin the party head.

The last act takes place in John Wilkes's rooms. The author of Number 45 of the *North Briton* is reading *Paradise Lost:*

> "So farewell Hope, and with Hope farewell
>   Fear;
> Farewell Remorse, all goods to me is lost
>   Evil be thou my good."—
> My own case to a tittle!

Wilkes bemoans his Canadian loss and rails against Bute:

> To be revenged on thee, I would commit—
> even sodomy of soul.—Brave Churchill!

> whose brain, but thine or mine, could have
> conceiv'd, or whose pen, but ours could have
> express'd such a noble delicate idea?
>
> (III. 1)

Wilkes shows his visitor Mercurio (Temple), Charles Churchill's compilation of a Political Vocabulary, for which Wilkes paid five pounds to
Churchill, who wrote it in a brothel. The method of composition for
the word list is a model for extreme propagandists:

> With these we do just as musicians with a few notes.—We compound,
> diversify, or transpose them, at a pleasure, and so chime them weekly
> in the ears of the people as a new political tune . . . Here is the word
> Scot, which in the grammarian style, I may term a *radical word.* Under
> this you have, *The Scot; The Scots Favourite; Scottish prime minister*
> . . . *Scots Jacobite; Scots harpies, Ec.*
>
> (III. 1)

Churchill enters, and Wilkes, who is going into exile in France, directs
his friend to continue the hue and cry about the Peace of Paris, the
Cider Tax, and hungry Scots.

Baillie's caricatures drawn in broad strokes result in delineations
which, like Hogarth's thumbnail sketches, are recognizable at a glance,
yet require study because of attention to detail. The author relies
chiefly upon exaggeration in his political cartoons. The difficulty with
Patriotism! is that the political climate it ridicules was such that it
almost defies such satirization. Baillie escaped falling into the pit of
the obvious by crowding his play with allusions that require his readers
to be abreast of political events.

The overly evident which crept into much comic writing of the
period is apparent in Andrew Erskine's *She's Not Him, and He's Not
Her,* which opened at the Canongate on 6 February 1764. This farce is
of the variety which gives an audience a sense of superiority in that
they are able to anticipate the outcome. The title reveals the plot. As
She's Not Him opens, Sophia has her confidante Harriet don men's
clothes to test her fiancé Frankly. Sophia tells Frankly of her "husband"
whom the beau threatens to cuckold. When he encounters Harriet in
disguise he is attracted to the "man's" face. In the second act Frankly
turns the tables by disguising his man Belmont as a woman. Neither
of the masqueraders is suited to imitating persons of the opposite
sex. Frankly observes that Belmont-turned-female to seduce Harriet-
turned-male possesses the *"je ne sçai quoi* of one of those engaging
females that follow a camp for the sake of plunder."

Sophia, convinced that Frankly does love her, is shocked to hear that her intended has sired three sets of twins in as many years. In the midst of Belmont's absurd account of trials as a curate's daughter who has children out of wedlock, the servant falls instantly in love with Harriet. The maid in men's costume demurs from the advances of the bogus curate's daughter: "I have a religious scruple or two; allow me a couple of days to get rid of them, and I'll fly with you to Japan." Frankly and Sophia unmask their gulls and the couples unite.

The epilogue to *She's Not Him* contains four lines of asterisks, which a note explains are "irrecoverably lost," in the tradition of *Tristram Shandy*. It is unfortunate that Erskine was not more proficient in his conception, because a number of his comic rejoinders are highly respectable, but these, even as the strings of asterisks, are lost in the farce. Erskine in a 7 July 1762 letter to Boswell wrote, "I confess, indeed my bashfulness does not appear in my works, for them I print in the most impudent manner." It is difficult to determine whether impudence or inertia caused Erskine to permit performance of *She's Not Him* in the state it was printed, since he had received adverse criticism of the play in 1761 in *The Cloaciniad*, which damned the comedy in *Dunciad* fashion:

> A Grubstreet ballad-maker was your fire;
> But to be born in *Scotia* was your doom,
> As once I made a friendly trip to H——.
> Go prosper then, may each succeeding lay
> Be still more stupid than your first-born play.[14]

In 1764, the same year *She's Not Him* appeared, John Wilson brought out his tragedy *Earl Douglas; or Generosity Betray'd*. In 1760 Wilson had published anonymously a dramatic essay of the same title. The tragedy, based on the murder of the Earl of Douglas and his younger brother David, is similar to the account of the fate of this claimant to the Scottish throne as told by Patrick Abercromby in *Martial Atchievements of the Scots Nation*. Wilson followed this history, adding sentimental and moralizing incursions in his hagiographical treatment of a national hero. As the blank-verse tragedy begins, Sir William Douglas and Lord Fleming discuss current civil strife. Fleming provides necessary background on the Earl's bravery and personal history:

> Your noble uncle took you from the nurse:
> His countess often set you on her knee

14 *The Clociniad* (Edinburgh, 1761), pp. 23–24.

> Beside her daughter, kissing both by turns,
> And bade her daughter kiss her future husband.
>
> (I. 1)

After Douglas's love within the third degree of kindred has been introduced to foreshadow romantic complications, the dowager Countess arrives. The widow, who has been gloomy, rejoices truly at her son's homecoming. This contrasts to the false jubilation Crichton expresses because Douglas is once more in their midst. In the final scene of the expository act, Douglas muses on his nation's independence in a manner unmistakably Jacobite:

> When Scotia's state was govern'd by her peers,
> She rose from ruin to renown and power:
> Shut from her councils, peaceful they retir'd,
> And to their country sacrific'd revenge,
> While o'er their heads their base inferiors rose.
>
> (I. 6)

The Chancellor and the Regent want cohesion and fear that Douglas's following of peers will create factions. Fleming cautions Douglas not to trust the wily Chancellor Crichton's pleas for peace and unity. When his Lady Beatrice's confessor pronounces that her love for her relative is incestuous, Douglas's domestic scene becomes as taut as the political tightrope he must walk. Crichton the younger desires Beatrice also, a further complication in the lovers' relationship.

At a banquet a bloody, raw bull's head, which functions as a Judas kiss, is set before Douglas. He is taken prisoner, then decapitated. Livingston enters, after the heads of the martyrs have been displayed on the castle walls, with the report of the suicide of Crichton's son, who was guilt-ridden because of his part in the assassination to gain his own amorous ends.

Earl Douglas is prolonged by the author's obeissance to the five-act structure. Melodramatic turns impede the tragedy. The philosophical preoccupations are stitched rather than woven into the pattern of the synthetic Mediaeval fabric. The poetry in which Wilson tells his historic tale is facile. When the blank verse is not overshadowed by Shakespeare or Home, it is accomplished. The author concentrates upon poetic expression rather than on creating a producible drama; but, in spite of its panoramic sweep and other characteristics of closet drama, *Earl Douglas* could be acted. At the risk of venturing into the perils of psychoanalyzing the dead, it seems unfair to suppose that some Northern playwrights, particularly if they possessed Wilson's education and background, wanted their plays staged.

Amyas Bushe's *Socrates* is an example of a gentleman's use of the drama for extra-theatrical purposes. An excerpt from the second scene of the play was published in the *Universal Magazine* in 1758. Four years later Bushe printed the complete work, which deals with the philosopher's noble triumph over Athenian castigation. In Socratic fashion the protagonist questions students about causality, and investigates the nature of man and his relationship to God. Socrates' approach to divine mysteries is more Calvinist than classic, and in later acts, which cover the sage's trial, imprisonment and death, he is the epitome of Christian resignation. In his sermon in competent blank verse, Bushe makes effective use of choruses, but the piece is homiletic rather than dramatic.

John Drummond, who stated in his *Collection of Poems for Reading and Repetition, etc.* (1762) that his purpose was to provide "an exercise to promote the improvement of youth," included dramatic readings, which like Bushe's *Socrates*, were intended to inculcate Christian morals. For students of rhetoric, Drummond extracted *The Death of Hector* and *The Redemption of his Body* from Alexander Pope's translation of the *Illiad*. These companion pieces focus upon what the author termed the "affecting transactions in that poem." Drummond included *The Death of Teribazus and Ariana* in his text *The Art of Reading and Speaking in Public, etc.* (1780). His method of construction is typical of the adaptations schoolmasters prepared for their students. *The Death of Teribazus and Ariana* is taken from Richard Glover's poem *Leonidas*. The dramatist took Act I from Book I, Act II from Book II, and Act III from Book VI. The almost verbatim transcription in dramatic form lacks continuity, but as the marginal glosses which give the desired expression indicate, this text was designed to give students of elocution a means to improve public speaking, while they absorbed the gallantry that transpired at Thermopylae.

The Devil to Pay: or, The Play-House Metamorphos'd. A Farce in Two Acts. As it was acted at the Canongate Theatre, January 24th, 1768 [sic], was published in 1767 but was never performed. Patrons purchased the pamphlet for tuppence at the door of the theatre that had been torn by squabbles, which arose when James Dawson and David Beatt, the theatre managers, decided not to rehire George Stayley, a popular actor.[15] The playlet in verse contains a series of short

15 The following manuscript notation by Alexander Gardyne is written in *The Devil to Pay* (NLS): "This is probably unique—it was sold at the Door of the Theatre for 2d and refers to some Managerial rows in which Stayley was Concerned."

slapstick scenes enacted by local thespians. Shuffle (James Aickin), a good man but a poor actor, endures a raging Captain Sneer (Thomas Young); Poop (Simeon Quin) then propels Stayley off the stage. In the second scene Sopscull (Thomas Lancashire) recounts the Canongate riot that occurred on 24 January 1767. This version of the fracas coincides with Stayley's account of the epic battle he described in *The Theatrical Hurricane* as "all to ruin and confusion hurl'd."[16]

John MacLaurin, to whom playlets occasioned by *Douglas* have been ascribed, concocted a theatrical squib in 1769 on the fight for the theatrical patent. His "tragedy" in one scene, *The Public*, consists of a monologue by John Lee, the theatre manager, who has held a meeting at the Cross Keys Tavern to enlist supporters against David Ross, the other contender for the license. Lee returns to the public house to assure the innkeeper that fame of his tavern will spread, because it has housed the auspicious meeting, despite the actor's certainty he has lost the fight.

The efforts of Lee, Stayley, and the "public party," as their supporters called themselves, were in vain. Ross received the patent, and on 9 December 1767, David Ross starred in *The Earl of Essex*, the first play legally performed in Scotland. The Canongate Theatre in Skinner's Close became the Theatre Royal, for as Boswell noted in his prologue for the first licensed production "lov'd George's free enlighten'd age / Bids Royal favour shield the Scottish stage."[17] With the prestige of the patent came a new theatre. On 16 March 1768, the cornerstone was laid, and despite its inscription, part of which exhorted: "May this theatre tend to promote every moral and every virtuous principle,"[18] at least one clergyman threatened to raze the sinful structure before the roof was on. The Theatre Royal despite difficulties did open 9 January 1769, two years to the night after the first legal performance in North Britain.[19] It was not until 1773 that a Scot's drama, Henry Mackenzie's *Prince of Tunis*, premiered in the playhouse located on the site of the present General Post Office in Shakespeare Square.

Of the works published in the North during the years when the the-

16 [George Stayley], *The Theatrical Hurricane, or All's Well that End's Well* (Edinburgh, 1767).
17 James Boswell, "Prologue at the Opening of the Theatre Royal in Edinburgh, December 9th 1769," in Dibdin, *Annals of the Edinburgh Stage*. See Appendix [p. 493]. This prologue was frequently reprinted during the eighteenth century.
18 *Sketch of the History of the Edinburgh Theatre-Royal Prepared for this Evening of its Final Closing*, May 25, 1859 (Edinburgh, 1859), p. 4.
19 Donald Mackenzie, *Scotland's First National Theatre* (Edinburgh, 1963), presents the ninety-year history of the Edinburgh Theatre Royal.

John Finlayson (fl. 1770s).

atre in Shakespeare Square was new, John Finlayson's *The Marches Day* (1771), is among the more entertaining. The play is based upon the old custom of riding the marshes, which consisted of burgesses cantering the limits of their royalty. *Marches Day* draws from the ceremonies which took place at Linlithgow. The first act treats of preparations for the parade; it opens with a pair of cobblers, Cockwell and Little Watty, anticipating their enjoyment of the event. The shoemakers speak in broad Scots, which the author felt obliged to footnote. In the second scene Avarus, a magistrate, bickers with a tradesman about the pennies charged for refurbishing the wig he will wear to the festivities. In the third scene, the hammerman and his son discuss their poverty, and Quotewell, a spoof of the romantic paragon, assures his offspring that their financial predicament is noble by quoting platitudes. In the last scene of the first act, Jawbone, a pompous individual, disparages Jackie for his provincialism and inelegant language. The comic device of scorning accent gained favor with Scottish dramatists in the last years of the century.

JAWBONE

All I know about it is this, if thou hadst been garrison'd at Minorca, that Billingsgate tongue you possess, would have cost you your life.

JACKIE

I wou'd na ha' been sic a scaticraw† as you wou'd ha ta' en't.—You may get a shilling i' the day for sitting on a cherry-tree and fearing awa the burds. I'll speak to ° ° ° °, and see if he'll gi' ye bread:—what think ye o' that?—

† scaticraw — scarecrow

(I. 4)

In the fifth scene Mrs. Humwell, a woman of common sense, is courted by Avarus, who tries to impress her with his importance. Her other admirer, Thomas Lecture, attempts to win her esteem by displaying his pedantry.

In the second act, the proclamation of the annual festival is read, Quotewell spouts a bit of misapplied scripture, and a group of tradesmen march forth singing ballad opera airs about their callings. The light lyrics are too lengthy, as often happens in fledgling musicals, and the parade of the professions palls. The third act consists of a banquet at which several guests indulge in verbal horseplay at Quotewell's expense by pretending to misinterpret the deacon of hammermen's biblical references. The convivial dinner with its hearty burlesque of table talk on religion, war, and foreign politics makes the final scene anticlimactic. Mrs. Humwell becomes engaged to Jawbone, a fate which she has done nothing to deserve. The betrothal is a ruse to permit the characters' return for the finale.

Marches Day, with its local color, gossipy intimations about characters who, perhaps, had actual counterparts, and humorous incidents has the verve of comic folklore. This vitality is such that a key is unnecessary, because the types who speed through the action possess the humanity which makes them recognizable, interesting, and funny.

The Planters of the Vineyard; or a Kirk Session Confounded is flawed by the obscurantism which circumscribes works when the allusions are too local. The comedy by a customhouse clerk who used the pseudonym "Mr. Lothian" was inspired by the clamor which arose when the newly ordained the Reverend John Logan first preached in South Leith. The key to this 1771 play does little to illuminate the proceedings.[20] Parishioners discuss the Reverend Mr. Flighty (Logan), who has established his "infallibility" despite a sensual personal life. Pamphlet (Robert Oliphant, Postmaster General of Scotland) tries to settle by reason the judgmental assertions church members let fly in the tavern. Ironsides ("The whole Calton Elders and Captain George Steil") cautions detractors for different reasons:

> Take care, Sir—dinna speak that way of Mr Flighty—gude sooth! the clergy are black craws to shoot it—As the Apostle says, It's not a canny thing to speak against pastors. Ye ken weel enough what Paul says that drunken cappersmith, the Lord reward him, *Corunce*, chap. iii.
>
> (III. 1)

As the parishioners continue to imbibe, it becomes increasingly apparent how unfit the sodden are to select a minister. *The Planters of the Vineyard* ridicules religious hypocrisy in such a narrow frame of reference that the play is largely of local antiquarian interest.

Among the writers who published comedies during the last decades of the eighteenth century, Jane Marshall is conspicuous for her incorporation of neoclassic and romantic paraphernalia in *Sir Harry Gaylove, or Comedy in Embryo*. Her 1772 publication favors the sentimental; it serves as an example of what occurred when the world of sensibility, with its innate goodness, relieved drama of its tension.

Miss Marshall had written *Clarinda Cathcart* and *Alicia Montague*. These epistolary imitations of Samuel Richardson emboldened the writer of omniscient romances to construct a play, a highly unusual

20   *The Planters of the Vineyard* (NLS) contains a manuscript key.

endeavor for a Scots woman. In the preface to her comedy, which she describes as a history of disappointments, the author tells of her efforts to have the vehicle accepted for London then Edinburgh production. She enlisted the aid of several influential men, among them the Earl of Chesterfield. This statesman, who hesitated to champion anything, replied to her request in his peculiar diplomatic way: "Whatever fate may attend your comedy, you may justly have the satisfaction of knowing, that the dialogue, the sentiment, and the moral of it, do honour to a young and virgin muse."[21]

The product of the virgin muse, like other novelistic British dramas of the day, manifests the influence of the incompatible form upon a theatrical work. The abrupt scene shifts, introduction of characters who are dispensed with summarily, and the cant preached continually show the impress of the novel of sensibility. The moral discourse, which praises values of a narrow domestic world, impedes the action. Several incidents which exhibit dramatic potential are told rather than acted. The talk, as well as the predictability, which arises, in part, from the sentimental sense of poetic justice, is more bearable in a novel than on the stage.

In *Sir Harry Gaylove*, Belmour's revelation of his plight to Sir Harry sets the play in motion. Their exchange exhibits the writer's fondness for the trite:

> SIR H. Come, come, Charles, I'm a wild young fellow, that's certain;
> yet, when occasion requires, I can be serious: Give me to understand
> the nature of your grievances, and my name is not Harry Gaylove, if I
> do not fall on a way to remove this mountain of difficulties.
> BEL. Reduced from an affluent fortune to these five pieces, (*emptying
> his purse*) obliged to ask favours from those I despise, with scarce any
> hopes of success. Oh Sir Harry! time past cannot be recalled. I have
> bought at an exorbitant price, and am now bankrupt in everything but
> experience.
> SIR H. And, like a spiritless dog, you repine at the purchase. Let me
> tell you Charles, a grain of experience is worth a mint of money.
>
> (I. 1)

Belmour has been cut off without a farthing by a penurious uncle, who is Ophelia's father. Ophelia Godfrey discusses Belmour's predicament with her servant, Maria, as sententious a confidante as ever a senti-

---

21 *Biographia Dramatica*, 2:275, prints the entire letter. Bonamy Dobrée, ed., *The Letters of Philip Dormer Stanhope 4th Earl of Chesterfield* (London, 1932), 6: nos. 2613, and 2936, reprints the portion Jane Marshall quoted in her preface to *Sir Harry Gaylove*.

mental heroine had. Mr. and Mrs. Godfrey converse about their daughter's matrimonial possibilities, and Mr. Godfrey decides in favor of Mr. Leeson, in a scene such as Jane Austen would later ridicule when writing of the Dashwoods and the Bennets. The last scene of the first act takes place at Whyte's Coffee-House, where Belmour confides to Sir Harry his love for cousin Ophelia.

The second act opens with Mr. Leeson pressing his suit with Ophelia, who expresses her lack of interest in this ancestor of Mr. Collins with a maximum of gentility. Ophelia's disdain causes Leeson to utter a line borrowed from a Ramsay song, which incorporates the excesses of sentimental diction: "By the delicious moister of your lips, fair creature, I swear you talk very strangely." Leeson, a man of mundane duplicity, admits that he is hypocritical and believes that the entire world is like himself: "since the fall of our first parents, 'tis the figleaf which covers our infirmities." His attitude toward life provides Ophelia with an opportunity for homiletic aphorisms.

The scene shifts abruptly to Lord Evergreen's house, where the aging rogue and his housekeeper, Mrs. Coaxer, rehearse for his conquest of Ophelia in a manner reminiscent of Lady Wishfort's prinking preparations for Sir Rowland. There are hints of Congreve throughout the work, but sympathy for the absurd condition of those who will be bested is understandably absent.

The third act provides contrast to the civilized bourgeois love rituals in its depiction of aristocratic depravity. After a coach accident, Ophelia has been abducted in a fashion similar to one of Alicia Montague's near escapes from the virtuous path. In the manner of Miss Marshall's other heroines, Ophelia enters the Lord's lair, the aged noble tries to seduce her, and she exclaims: "Help me, heaven; Oh! Oh!" Lord Evergreen's plans for wickedness are foiled by his daughter Harriet. She sends for her beau, Sir Harry. He spoils her father's plans and manages to rescue the "famously trepann'd young lady," who is united with Belmour unscathed.

Ophelia during her incarceration in the Evergreen household remains pure, because of the elderly seducer's bout with gout. Sir Harry persuades Evergreen to give up his hostage by reason rather than by heroics. The hero suggests that the abducted girl's relatives have gone to the Lord Chief Justice for a warrant. Since this will mean confiscation of Evergreen's estates, the old man sees the light. If the older and more wicked members of this society are ruled by money, the younger, higher types are governed by right sentiments. Sir Harry justifies his threat which frees Ophelia, as the "way of the world." His beaten

uncle counters with a peculiar paraphrase of Matthew 6:1, ". . . that
you look thro' the magnifying end of the prospect of your uncle's follies,
then whip it about when you venture to look on your own." This
accusation is without justification, for Sir Harry Gaylove, like Harley,
displays tender and virtuous sensibility to every worthy sufferer.

In *Sir Harry Gaylove* virtuous characters, personifications of the
inherent nobility in mankind, display the way of the upright world by
fighting passionate fire with moral fibre. The triumph of youth over age
is accompanied by reason and justice, if not absolute truth. This sense
of values blends ideal and real in the Mackenzian manner. The reward
for these principles is romantic and material. In the final pairing of the
couples, Belmour, who has been in prison for his attempts to rescue his
love, is united with Ophelia. Sir Harry, the reasonable man of feeling,
is united with Harriet Evergreen. The victory of this generation of
paragons seems to provide a brave new way of the world, in which
perfection of the human condition is not only possible but imminent.
This new rational and sensible order does not admit further conflict.
Moral victories bring about utopian conditions; this *Weltanschauung*
tends to diminish if not demolish the conditions requisite for drama.

Henry Mackenzie subscribed to *Sir Harry Gaylove*. He was interested in Miss Marshall's comedy, because he was trying to persuade
Garrick to produce a tragedy of his own. When he read the script
sent by William Robertson, the Drury Lane manager was no more
impressed with Mackenzie's *The Prince of Tunis* than Mackenzie was
with *Sir Harry Gaylove*. Mackenzie wrote to Elizabeth Rose that the
comedy was not "destitute of merit," but he was not enthusiastic about
the product of a fellow purveyor of sensibility.[22]

On 14 February 1771, the Reverend Hugh Blair wrote an acquaintance of his favorable reaction to *The Prince of Tunis*. The minister
noted for his own rhetoric was particularly fond of the line at the
beginning of the third act, "Scaring the dimply cupids from their
Seats," and liked the "good poetry" in "animated and high style." The

22 "You are good-natured to Miss Marshall's Play; yet I do not think it destitute
of merit, tho I cannot go as far as you, or the noble Lords whose opinions are pre-
fixed. But I make great Allowance for the Difficulty of the Attempt, a Comedy
being, I imagine a Performance, which it is no less difficult to execute in the whole,
than it is easy to discover Faults in it's Parts; because taking it as a whole, it must
be the Production of a Fancy, chaste as well as vigorous; while it's Parts are composed of Materials drawn from real life." Henry Mackenzie, *Letters to Elizabeth
Rose of Kilranock on Literature Events and People 1768–1815*, ed. Horst W.
Drescher (Edinburgh, 1967), 7 October 1772, pp. 119–20. Mackenzie mentions
that Miss Marshall's play is to be performed at Covent Garden in a letter of 15 September 1769 (p. 21).

qualities Blair admired flawed the play. Mackenzie based his drama in the rich style on a section from William Robertson's *History of Charles V*. In his concentration upon poetry the playwright neglected dramatic action. Until the fifth act the historical source moves more rapidly than *The Prince of Tunis*. The characters speak at rather than to each other in dialogue strewn with archaisms, similes, and figures of speech that masquerade as aphoristic wisdom. Using the Home formula in an endeavor to provide trenchant commentary upon the human condition, Mackenzie inserted so many elegant pronouncements that the tragedy resembles Shakespearean burlesque.

The story features the trials of Zulima. This lady is in love with Arassid, whom she believes dead. The heroine encounters Barbarossa, the usurper whom she eventually marries, in a scene which shows the result of the dominance of language over action.

> BAR. My Zulima! my bride! That name demands
> A warmer look, Why turns thy moistened eye
> From Barbarossa? he's a suitor still.
> The sterner customs of an eastern husband
> His love foregoes; but Zulima requites him
> With unrelenting coldness.
> ZUL. No; she feels
> The gratitude that Barbarossa's love,
> And Barbarossa's friendship, well demand.
> She can no more; perhaps her nature wants
> The warmth, that glows in more exalted minds.
> BAR. For me alone she wants it. What condition
> Of love assiduous, of unwearied service,
> Can win her smile for me?
> ZUL. Alas! her cheek,
> In sorrow steeped, has lost the power to smile.
> Ah! too unworthy of assiduous love,
> And much too humble for unwearied service,
> She only asks the privilege of mourning.
> BAR. Inhuman to herself! Can ceaseless tears
> Re-animate the dust of fallen virtue?
> Can the loud wailings of affliction break
> The fettered sleep of death?
> ZUL. I know they cannot;
> But reason may not measure what we should be,
> When thus we are. There is some hidden power
> More forcible than are a thousand reasons,
> That will not be outpleaded.
> BAR. Such power there is,
> That weans us from our woe. Unheeded Time
> Creeps, like some thrifty pilferer, on our thoughts,

Henry Mackenzie (1745–1831).

Till by unvalued atoms he has stolen
Accumulated sorrows. But for thee
He rolls his suns in vain; thy cherished grief
Mocks every common cure.

(I. 1)

Zulima discovers through Heli, one of Barbarossa's officers, that Arassid is alive. She then hears that Arassid is dead at Barbarossa's hand and vows vengeance—a poisoned cup is sent to Barbarossa. As Zulima is finally reunited with her true love, she is told that Heli, her long lost father, has drunk the cup which was intended for Barbarossa. In despair Zulima takes her life. Barbarossa comes upon his dying wife and raves in madness.

When the play by the novelist, who had created the popular *Man of Feeling*, opened at the Edinburgh Theatre Royal on 8 March 1773, it ran five nights. In his *Anecdotes*, Mackenzie says that *The Prince of Tunis* ran "7 consecutive nights (equal to 70 in London) to full houses." This egotism gave the play a better run than *Douglas* enjoyed when it premiered.

Mackenzie's tragedy was reviewed enthusiastically in the *Edinburgh Courant:*

The play was received with very great applause. It is many years since a new play has been ushered into the world at our Theatre. It has been generally allowed that dramatic genius has been on the decline for several years in Great Britain, and we must give our assent to this opinion. We may affirm that if the testimony of a genteel and crowded audience may be credited, *The Prince of Tunis* will hold a distinguished rank among modern Tragedies. The fable is interesting, and language poetical, the sentiment just, and the catastrophe affecting. The play upon the whole was extremely well acted. Mrs Yates' powers were called forth and shone conspicuously in the unfortunate Zorlima [*sic*], and the unhappy fate of the virtuous Heli was fairly represented by Mr Digges. When the curtain draws up the audience are surprised with a most picturesque scene, when Mrs Yates appears as the Genius of Scotland, and speaks an excellent prologue.[23]

Mackenzie was well pleased with his first venture in the theatre. The letter to Elizabeth Rose, which he wrote the night of the opening, glows with satisfaction:

The Prince of Tunis was received with utmost Applause; more, much more I fear that he merited[.]Mrs Yates however could not receive too

23 *Edinburgh Courant* 9 March 1773.

much. Tho a little flurried with an unlucky Accident which happened
when she came to the Prologue, to wit the falling down of The End of
the Lamps, yet She acted with that Power which ever seizes the Heart
& wrings it. I must be partial; but I speak the Language of many less
so, when I say, that her Zulima stands amongst the foremost of the
Characters with which [s]he has delighted us. Digges was the same
excellent old man he alwise is as Heli. The Rest of the Players wonder-
fully well tho not a little heightened from being engaged in a thing
unusual to them.[24]

The Prince of Tunis was a local success. The author continued to try
to recapture the thrill of a theatrical victory, but never again would he
hear the utmost applause for one of his plays.

In 1773 Mackenzie went to London to attend to the prepublication
details of *The Man of the World*. Armed with a letter of introduction
from William Robertson, the novelist met Garrick, and it is probable
that he showed the theatre manager *The Spanish Father* at this
encounter.[25] The arbiter of the English theatrical world thought the
catastrophe, a filicide, "too horrid for the stage," and rejected the
tragedy.

The next new full-length production staged in Edinburgh was as
packed with action as *The Prince of Tunis* had been devoid of it. On
19 February 1774, John Jackson's *Eldred, or the British Freeholder*
was presented at the Theatre Royal. The Scottish actor's play had
opened in Dublin, where it had met with the same cool response it
received in the Scottish capital. *Eldred,* a bourgeois tragedy set in the
time of Hengist, is a war-time love story peopled by characters who are
more wildly romantic than most of the Ossianic offspring. Against a
backdrop of untamed nature, Edwena, who sings of woe, explains her
melancholy to her confidante Eliza:

> HAIL, god of war! to thee I sing;
>   Assuage my piercing woe:
> My ELIDURE from dangers bring;
>   O save him from the foe!

(I. 1)

In gratitude, the heroine has secretly married Elidure, who saved
her from a raging stream. The Saxon girl then fell in love with the
Northern warrior.

24   Henry Mackenzie, *Letters to Elizabeth Rose,* pp. 128–29.
25   In the preface to *The Spanish Father,* Mackenzie states that Garrick examined
the manuscript in 1775. Thompson in *A Scottish Man of Feeling* (p. 165), believes
that the date should be 1773.

Edwena's father, Lochrine, enters with Brennus, whom he has chosen to be his son-in-law. Brennus, a heroic leader, is enamored of Edwena, but must attend to public concerns before his personal life. Brennus becomes involved in truce negotiations with the enemy. His quandary about entering into a league of amity in order to effect an eventual truce is particularly poignant as he contemplates private peace in Edwena's arms. Jackson's theatrical experience is evident in his skill in ending this and other acts on an anticipatory note as well as his piecemeal revelation of character. Brennus appears to be a sympathetic character early in the play.

In the second act Lochrine and Brennus discuss the older man's lands. Brennus is happy at the prospect of owning extensive properties, but is puzzled that a small piece of land surrounded by Lochrine's estates does not belong to his prospective father-in-law. Lochrine explains that the elderly and obstinate Eldred holds this farm and will not sell his property at any price. Brennus's suggestion of ousting the freeholder vitiates sympathy for the man whom Edwena may not marry. During his consideration of taking Eldred's land by force, Brennus is interrupted by a servant, who announces that Vortimer is waiting to discuss negotiations. Elidure, Vortimer's spokesman, and Brennus meet, but the two men manifest antipathy for each other, and Brennus defers action on the proposed league which would curtail strife.

As the third act opens, it is apparent that Brennus is more fortune hunter than lover. He determines to win Lochrine's favor by obtaining the freehold. While the ambitious villain urges Lochrine to set the date of the nuptials, Eldred enters to tell of an omen he has encountered in the forest. The freeholder has heard a whistling sound, which led him to save a drowning hare, and he now wishes to present it to Edwena.

In a woodland tryst scene, Elidure tells his wife of Brennus's command to arrest his father Eldred for treason. Elidure had approached his father's cottage as the old man was attacked, and in an attempt to save his parent killed one of the officers. Subsequently, Brennus has charged Elidure with murder. Eldred is taken before Brennus in shackles, and shows fortitude in the presence of his enemies, where a witness swears falsely that the old man has committed treason. Christlike, Eldred refuses to defend himself, and Brennus sentences him to death. Edwena pleads for the prisoner's release, hears that Elidure is dead, and swoons. Eldred cries out, "O save that sinking excellance," a line representative of the diction.

In the resolution Elidure wrests his wife from the clutches of Brennus, Lochrine kills himself, and Eldred is released. *Eldred* is encapsulated in the last line: "And righteous wrath and impious over take."

Henry Mackenzie attended one of the initial performances of *Eldred* He detested Jackson's performance in the title role, and in a 21 February 1774 letter to Elizabeth Rose criticizes the play itself: "As to the Merit of the Piece, there are some Situations happily enough contrived for acting, & some poetical Sentences & Sentiments above what I should have been apt to expect; but there is a want of *Taste* to regulate the *Invention*, the familiar becomes frequently *ludicrous* & the attempted *Sublime* almost always fustian."[26]

Mackenzie was a better critic than playwright. He as well as other dramatists produced imitations rather than original conceptions. Shades of Home and Macpherson haunted Northerners. These spirits required an exorcist if drama were to take a new direction in language and subject matter, but no talent strong enough to expel these forces appeared until the end of the century, when the Wizard of the North began his literary career.

1775-1800

In the last quarter of the eighteenth century more Scots wrote plays than ever before. As Robert Burns observed, the market was glutted with Northerners' subscription publications. These works were often the kind which were consigned to the top library shelves of the author's friends, who purchased the volume but never slit the uncut pages. Most of the plays were poetic exercises included in a book of miscellanies. Some of the now forgotten works were published and staged in towns other than Edinburgh. For the first time since the Reformation, plays were originating in the smaller towns of North Britain. There were a greater number of efforts which dealt with national subject matter, and although these endeavors did not develop into a distinctly Scottish corpus, there was a "tartan" trend in drama.

Like the melodramas of most Scots writers, Henry Mackenzie's *The Spanish Father* remained in manuscript, unperformed from the 1770s until he published it in his *Works* (1808). Although *The Spanish*

26   Henry Mackenzie, *Letters to Elizabeth Rose*, p. 84.

Father is better theatre than *The Prince of Tunis*, it contains a number of defects peculiar to melodrama, some of which Mackenzie acknowledged in the preface to his second mature tragedy. The author states his fondness for the tragic figure Alphonzo, gives his moral intention, and mentions the difficulties he had in fitting dialogue to situation.

> In the enthusiasm natural to youth, I had conceived it standing on the high ground of heroic virtue and honour, fierce and implacable in vindication of those principles, yet open to that humanity and tender feeling, which I had perceived frequently to belong to minds of that description. Such a character, in unskilful hands, is sometimes apt to develope itself in bombastic expression. There is a good deal of such expression in the first copy of this play, which, even at that time, I had taste enough to be sensible of. I find several passages of that sort, in the scroll now before me, which, though they possessed some poetical beauty, I had struck out, as going beyond the simplicity of nature, and the style appropriate to the situation. Some perhaps still remain open to censure on this score.

Mackenzie prints one of Ruzalla's original romantic outbursts as a footnote, although this speech was not relevant to the dramatic situation. The dramatist's retention of poetry he could not bear to delete points to his prime concern in playwriting.

The Spanish Father begins with poetic descriptions of the principals, Alphonzo and his compassionate daughter, Ruzalla. In the usual over-long Mackenzian exposition, it becomes apparent that the Toledans are models of landed gentry. Alphonzo advising Ruzalla sounds like a country squire:

> ALPH. . . . Methinks my cautions wrong thee;
> But thou'rt the treasure of thy father's age,
> And, like the miser trembling o'er his hoard,
> He fears, he knows not why.
> RUZ. Oh! speak not thus,
> Nor add to all those debts of past indulgence,
> That make a wretched bankrupt of Ruzalla.
> ALPH. My two brave boys have fallen for their country—
> Peace to their souls! for I have heard their fame.
> Thou, my Ruzalla, art the single ray,
> That gilds the evening of thy father's age.
> Could'st thou but know how dear this bosom holds thee—
> Thou canst not, till thy heart has felt the throb
> A parent's feels! —Wipe off that falling tear.

Amidst the gentleness that suits her sex,
Even soft-eyed woman has a proper pride.
Revere thyself—the daughter of Alphonzo.

(I. 1)

The fatherly counsel is ironic, for the second act opens with Ruzalla's confession to her sympathetic confidante that she is dishonored, because of her affair with King Rodriguez. Later the lovers meet in a pastoral setting, and as the act ends, Alvarez, the crafty minister, poisons the king against his enamorata and her father, a deed far more evil than the physical poisoning that occurs in *The Prince of Tunis*.

The third act contains a climactic confrontation between the outraged Alphonzo and Rodriguez, which exhibits Mackenzie's dramatic power:

ALPH. Dost thou threaten me? —Urge thee no further!
Must I then stoop, and bear indignity?
By Heaven, I will not so betray the rights
Of freedom, or of manhood! Thou shalt hear me.
ROD.   Shalt hear thee? Dost thou know me?
    On thy life—
But I forgive thee for Ruzalla's sake.
I found her—much less haughty than her sire.
ALPH. Found her!—less haughty—found her!—
Speak it again, that I may tell thee, king!—
Thou darest not.—
ROD.   Darest not, traitor! —Hear it all then,
And let that honour thou presumest to lift
In proud defiance 'gainst thy sovereign, know
Rodriguez for its lord. —Montverdo's groves
Witnessed the joys thy beauteous daughter gave me.

(III. 1)

In the fourth act the imprisoned Alphonzo gives a verbal flashback describing his daughter as a child. This scene contrasts strangely to Alphonzo's castigation of Ruzalla, whom he calls vile, and disowns at the end of the act.

In the catastrophe Alphonzo and his child agree that she must die to expiate her sins. The curtain falls on this tragedy of blood, after father has killed daughter, and lover and father slay each other. The character of Alphonzo, an humanitarian sensitive to all except his own daughter, presents a behavioral deviation memorable in melodrama.

When Mackenzie was sixteen he wrote *Virginia, or the Roman Father*, which he published nearly sixty years later. In 1820 he had this

drama printed for distribution to select friends. Mackenzie acknowledged in a perceptive note that the play was defective because of his
concentration upon declamation at the expense of incident. As a juvenile work, one might consider *Virginia* as a beginning step on the
writer's sentimental literary journey; the poetry has a polish which
indicates that the author took pains in revising the play before it was
printed.

The familiar story with its elements of virtue and seduction, lends
itself to Mackenzian sensibility. Appius admits his love for Virginia to
Appulinius, who formulates a plan to gain custody of the girl. Virginia
has escaped the influences of a thoroughly corrupt Rome, and is good
and artless by her own admission. The heroine, who "loves to cry for
pity oft," is as brave as she is pure, and courageously prefers death to
the forced marriage arranged through political chicanery. Some of the
actions and particularly the philosophical excursions on freedom and
virtue resemble those expressed in *The Spanish Father*.

Mackenzie wrote dramatic criticism for *The Mirror* and *The
Lounger*, the Scottish imitations of *The Spectator* he edited. Of the
observations on theatre written by the Northern Addison for his short-
lived magazines, his essay on Hamlet is the most notable. In general,
his comments are worth mention as examples of the implementation of
sensibility as a critical tenet.

In addition to his plays and criticism, Mackenzie contributed to the
theatre by acquainting his countrymen with European drama. He
delivered a paper on the German theatre before the Royal Society of
Edinburgh on 21 April 1788 which was a secondhand account of contemporary Continental plays.[1] Since at that time Mackenzie did not
know German, he gleaned his information from French translations.
The *Schicksals-tragödie* school, which was influenced by George Lillo,
appealed to Scottish belletrists. Mackenzie's paper aroused so much
interest, according to John Gibson Lockhart, that Walter Scott considered it the beginning of Scotland's fascination with German literature.
Shortly after his influential address Henry Mackenzie collaborated on
Dramatic Pieces from the German (1792), a volume of translations of
plays by Johann Wolfgang von Goethe, Johann Gesner, and Cornelius
von Ayrenhoff.

Alexander Fraser Tytler, Lord Woodhouslee, who had published the
popular *Essay on the Principles of Translation* (1790), rendered Fried-
rich Schiller's *The Robbers* into English in 1792. Tytler advocated

1   *Transactions of the Royal Society of Edinburgh* (1792), 2:154–92.

Mackenzie's approach to translation. In the critical preface to *The Robbers*, he quotes "the man of feeling" and follows his method of softening the original with sensibility. Tytler's translation of the Act I line of Francis to his father, Count de Moor, illustrates the process: "*Wir wurden noch heute die hoare aufrasen uber everm sarge*" [We will not tear our hair over your coffin today], becomes "Heaven forbid that I should e'er abridge your days!" Alexander Thomson adhered to Tytler's principles in compiling his *German Miscellany* (1796). Thomson's English versions of plays by Alfred Meissner and August von Kotzebue stress the sentimental.

In 1776 Christian Edwards published her *Miscellanies* and included a drama with novelesque insertions. Her romantic musings are quite similar to Mackenzie's. *Otho and Rutha* opens with the hero's disconsolate confession to Rutha that he deserted Sabina when their home was attacked and his wife was forced to flee with her children. Rutha preaches patience in coping with life's difficulties:

> Honours, like shadows, pass ere well perceived; or, like a midnight-meteor, quickly die. It is virtue only that can make us smile, in spite of Fortune's frown. Rich in itself, it needs no borrowed ornament; but looks most bright seen through the glass of sharp Calamity.
>
> (Part I)

The hero is comforted by Rutha's reassurance. The friends then visit a Hermit, who reinforces Rutha's consolation by extolling acceptance of one's lot. Sabina and Otho are reunited at the hermitage.

The second part of the work begins with Otho's prayer, then shades into a narrative of the hero's history, which is not in dramatic form. Otho's account of his life, although unfinished, bears no more resemblance to the biography of the tenth-century German emperor than does John Keats's *Otho the Great,* despite the repeated protestations of Miss Edwards that the story is true.

David Robertson included *The Dying Indians, A Dramatic Ode* in his *Poems* (1784). This poem is not cast in dramatic form. The wounded Yangzu and Oobeea contemplate going to heaven in this graveyard treatment of noble savages. Oobeea speaks throughout the piece. His final prayer to the Great Spirit Yohewah is characteristic:

> Shroud us in the whitest deer-skin,
> Lay us deep in yonder gloom:
> Here, that savage Mohawk torture:
> Let his scalp wave o'er our tomb.

One might call quasi-dramatic works such as *The Dying Indians* conversation pieces, for like the paintings of Johann Zoffany they combine portraits, nature imagery, and some theatrical elements.

John Wood, who published *The Duke of Rothsay* (1780), created a play based upon Albany's seizure of Rothsay to obtain power. *The Duke of Rothsay* rises above the melodramatic morass of closet dramas. It is a sophisticated dramatic achievement. The characters' motivation is psychologically oriented and remarkably complex. James I is depicted as a sniveling old monarch who makes Rothsay a surrogate to replace the son Albany has sent abroad, ostensibly to be educated. Albany, a misogynist with homoerotic tendencies, is ruthless in his quest for political as well as personal dominance. Rothsay is a near stoical man, romantic yet practical. The hero speaks plainly, but with sufficient diplomacy to make his foil Ramorgny seem all the more vapid in his florid superfluities.

As in many serious plays, particularly those under the influence of melodrama, the villain is more fascinating than the hero. Albany's unnatural proclivities constitute a counterpoint which retrogrades his quest for power:

> ALBANY: Though perverse Nature lock'd me in the womb,
> And brought into the world a puling changeling:
> And oft my mother said so; for I was
> Her only darling, tho' but second son,
> And she the only woman ever was
> I cou'd abide: the sex to me is wormwood;
> A bane, that poison ev'ry manly virtue.
>
> (II. 1)

The King gives Rothsay to the charge of Albany. The minister professes affection for the young Duke, who has been betrothed several times. To Albany's knowledge, Rothsay is still single.

> I ever lov'd you, Rothsay, and still more
> Thou art endearing for thy prudent conduct,
> In declining proffer'd matrimony,
> 'Tis weak in princes in their youth to wed.
>
> (II. 2)

Albany asserts that concubines are preferable to dull marriage, but Rothsay recoils from such overtures. The minister dismisses his intimations as cajolery to test his charge's sense of humor.

Shortly after this exchange Rothsay is warned that his life is in danger. In the third act Dorothea Borthwick slips past the guards to bring Rothsay, her imprisoned brother-in-law, a cake. Wood makes good use of the historical legend that Rothsay starved, to underscore Albany's treachery. The incarcerator intercepts Dorothea and reassures her, as he gives Rothsay the food, that she will not come to harm because of her prison visit. He then stabs the girl saying: "Thus perish all womankind who'd seek / To cross me in my golden line of hope." This action emphasizes Albany's sexual as well as political motive for starving Rothsay into submission.

Dorothea and Euphamia Borthwick have prevailed upon their father and Crichton, Dorothea's suitor, to rescue Rothsay whom Euphamia has wed secretly. Crichton kills Albany, but they arrive too late to save the young Duke who dies in his wife's arms.

Scottish legend inspired comedy as well as tragedy. Paton's *William and Lucy* (1780), is based upon the ballad "Auld Robin Gray." The story told in the ballad is superior to the ballad opera. In the original work Jenny loves Jemmy, who is away at sea, but she marries Robin Gray, because he has helped her parents, shortly before her sailor returns.

In the bourgeois adaptation Lucy awaits William, but her cousin Lydia reminds Lucy that her father is indebted to Robert. To the tune of "Bessy Bell and Mary Gray" Lydia sings in Act I an admonition of practicality:

> Though Cupid may not wound your heart,
>   Yet Robert's wealth should charm you;
> No raptures though his love impart;
>   His opulence might warm you.

The selfish Lydia, who wants William for herself, convinces Robert that making her cousin's father solvent will win the girl of his dreams. The second act lists to the melodramatic. The songs are sprightly then melancholy by turns. The heroine's mother, a materialistic sort, who was the instrument of William's leaving, laments her daughter's loveless wedding to Robert. Money matters gain precedence over romantic concerns, for Lucy requires little persuasion to grub for the pound in the manner of her forebears. In the contrived resolution William returns to Lucy, and understanding Robert takes Lydia on the rebound.

William and Lucy was rejected by the Edinburgh Theatre Royal, but managers in the capital and in Glasgow accepted entertainments of

the same rank during the 1780 season, when John Riddel's masque
"George's Natal Day," played Scotland's two largest towns. The tribute
to the monarch commences with a reclining Britannia, who frightens
the Goddess of Peace by describing the horrors of civil war. (A pacifist
theme recurs frequently in Riddel's poetry.) In the second scene Britannia enters a pavilion in the clouds where the Olympian chorus
salutes Jove. Britannia with drawn sword begs the father of the gods
to sheathe her weapon, and Jupiter assures her that rebellion will be
quelled. In the third and final scene Britannia commands the foe:

> Hew down the bands that dare our rights oppose!
> And now wide o'er th' Atlantic's roaring tide,
> Conducted safe by Ocean's watery God,
> In dread array our warlike vessels ride,
> With sudden death and awful thunders load.

Guardian angels sing a grand chorus honoring George III, and various
gods hymn tributes to the sovereign.

Six years after the politique masque was presented, Riddel published
Malvina (1786), a blank-verse Ossianic tragedy. The plot of *Malvina*
contains a number of familiar turns frequently used during the period.
Malvina loves Rinval, but must wed Prince Uther to prevent civil war.
The Prince hears of his love's marriage plans and battle ensues. The
victorious Uther carries the Virginian heroine to England. Malvina
escapes her captor in the same forest she discovers the dying Rinval.
When he expires Malvina faints. She recovers to castigate Uther, who
promises to exchange her imprisoned father for Malvina's passion. The
girl chooses suicide at the end of this literary exercise which attempts
to combine the tender melancholy of a Macpherson love story with a
political strain derived from the revolutionary events of the late century.

Riddel, a surgeon and librarian, wrote occasional pieces, as did many
gentlemen. Like most of his fellow dramatic practitioners, Riddel was
unfamiliar with the playhouse. Archibald MacLaren had theatrical
experience which he obtained as a member of touring companies. He
wrote more dramas than any other playwright born north of the Cheviot
Hills, but the scores of pieces brought him little fame and less fortune.
MacLaren's career belies Byron's observation that "the most prolific
are the most popular authors." This playwright's dramatic bibliography
consists of more than eighty titles. The list is misleading, however,
because the dramatist frequently reissued the same works under different titles. From his first publication in 1781 until his death in 1826,
MacLaren wrote at least sixty original plays.

MacLaren's range is such that examination of a few of his entertainments acquaints the reader with the scope of his output. His first known play, *The Conjurer; or, the Scotsman in London* (1781) was printed in Dundee. The comedy was performed in Edinburgh in 1783. It had no doubt been staged in provincial towns before this, since MacLaren had joined Mrs. Ward's company in Montrose, after soldiering in America. The redcoat, who became an actor, found that his forte was dialectical humor. In *The Conjurer* he included the character of Torrence O'Fagan, a role tailored to his talents. The obtuse stage Irishman fancies Delia, a coquette who is dangling two other suitors: Ramble, a Scot, and Suckpot, a fop. To inform the girl that he seeks her favors, O'Fagan sends a letter that exemplifies MacLaren's broad, provincial comic approach:

> *To Miss* Delia.
> Madam, Please to ask this letter from Miss Sucky, for she has it in her pocket; but if she does not mention it herself, I believe you had as well let it alone, as I intend to try her contegrety; for between you and me, she is a very great slut, and always keeps back my letters sometimes when she does not deliver them.
>
> (I. 1)

To win Delia the Irishman enlists a confederate to impersonate a Frenchman from whom he protects Delia; this ruse provides another opportunity for dialectical humor. The wise Ramble uses trickery to better advantage than O'Fagan. He beats the Janis at her own game. The Scot plants goods on Delia and the fop, each of whom believes the other is a thief. A Northerner outsmarting Southern circles must have won favor with Scottish audiences, since the trend in British comedy was to cast the Scot as a rustic dupe.

In 1784 MacLaren's *The Coup de Main, or, The American Adventures* was printed in Perth. The plot of the musical, that had opened in Dundee the previous season, is as complicated as a Mozart opera. The tangled incidents are peopled with characters who execute violent antics to provoke laughter. Two captains vie for the hand of the same girl. Before Captain Lovewell gets Phoebe, the dramatist employs the dialect comics, disguises, a letter, and other devices he used continually.

In 1790 MacLaren published *Humours of Greenock Fair; or Taylor made a man* in Paisley. This comedy had premiered two years previously in the town mentioned in the title. The musical is constructed on a single premise: the comeuppance of a domineering wife who scorns her husband's drinking. Before Joe Pimple gets the upper hand he meets a Highland boatman who speaks Erse. This first known use of Gaelic in a North British theatrical is scripted in such a way that the audience receives a translation, testimony to the moribund state of the old language. "How do you, Mr Pimmal, mo chulain goalich"; the boatman then adds the English near equivalent, "you're fine whelp."

The same year that MacLaren put out *Humours of Greenock Fair*, he also published *The Highland Drover; or, Domhnul Dubh M'Na-Beinn* [Black Donald Son of the Mountain] at Carlisle. In this comedy he greatly expanded the use of Erse dialogue. MacLaren played the Drover, a role which contemporaries considered his *pièce de résistance*. As the play opens Hartly plans to spirit Lydia away from her guardian, Mr. Hog. Hartly outlines his scheme to Ramble, but is interrupted by a pair of Highlanders, Domhnul [Donald] and Donacha [Duncan], who enter complaining about their inability to make themselves understood.

> *Domh.* Droch co'd hail air a bhaille mhosach so, a Dhonachi, cho n'eil ach Bearla, Bearla, aig gach baist a tha tachairt orm; ach coma leatsa a laochain bithidh sinneaig an tighe fhas't, far an tuig aid sin, ach bi falbh agus thoir an airre air a chrobh; agus theid mis agus feuchaidh mi am faigh mi Callum mac Peather mo sheann—mhaithir; chuala mi Gu bheil e ann so bhaille sa, bi falbh a laochain.
>
> (I. 1)

MacLaren provided the following translation in the printed script:

> A bad meeting to this ugly town Duncan, there is nothing but English, English with every trifling fellow I meet with; but, never mind my good fellow, we'll be at home yet, where they'll understand every word we speak; but go you lad and take care of the cattle, and I'll go and try if I can find out Malcolm, and son of my grandmother's sister, I have heard that he lives in this town, go my good lad.

Duncan and Ramble meet; each understands the language of the other, but both stubbornly adhere to chosen tongues. Their mutual distrust inspires Duncan to let loose a string of Celtic imprecations. Ramble asks Betty Campbell to intercede. Duncan is delighted with the girl from Inverary, when he discovers they are related. His account of her genealogy, a corollary to the saying that all Scots are Jock Thompson's bairns, exemplifies MacLaren's capabilities in exaggeration of ethnic characteristics:

> A bheil sios agad Ban-charraid dhomhsa thu? tha odha brathair mo shean-athair, posda air bean chindh dhuit, Ian mor mac Ian, 'ic Dhug-

hail, 'ic Dhomnul, 'ic Dhonachi, 'ic Alastoir, 'ic Shemuis, 'ic Eoin bhig
mhic Ian duin Agus a nis mo tha padhagh no acras ort a fhad, agus a
bhis peign ann an sporran Dhonuil Dhubh's a do bheatha a ghællad.

(I. 1)

Translated as:

. . . do you know that you're a relation of mine, the grandson of my
great grandfather's brother, was married to a namesake of yours, big
John the son of John, the son of Dugald, the son of Donald, the son of
Duncan, the son of Alexander, the son of James, the son of little Hugh,
whose father was brown John; and now my girl, if you are either hungry or thirsty as long as there is a penny in black Donald's purse you
shall be welcome.

Betty's protector is Mac na muic [Son of a sow]. This relationship
parallels Lydia's predicament. When Duncan realizes the similarity of
the situation to his own, he is sympathetic and abets the elopement
plans. Duncan distracts Hog, who does not understand Erse, by engaging him in conversation. This equivoque enables Lydia to join her
fiancé.

In the altered version of *The Highland Drover* MacLaren brought
out in London in 1805, Lydia has additional suitors. The Gaelic is transformed into dialect. After the elopement there is an anticlimactic chase
and other unnecessary elongations which diminish the freshness and
originality of the comedy meant to entertain a Northern audience.

MacLaren once more used an arranged betrothal in 1795 to produce
dramatic tension in *The Scottish Volunteers*. The play, which opened
in Greenock and was published in Paisley, is a variation of the Mac-
Laren formula. Flourish, the man chosen for Sophia, has no use for the
army. The captain she loves is the embodiment of a recruiting poster.
After disguising and slapstick involving drunks, a favorite MacLaren
ploy, the girl and the patriot are united.

Four years later MacLaren turned *Scottish Volunteers* into a ballad
opera, which he entitled *Old England for Ever! or A Fig for the Invasion*. The author expanded the role for the supporting actress, made
the hero more chauvinistic, and inserted jingoistic lyrics and speeches
that interrupt the flow of the comedy. The abrupt changes, which do
not improve the original, were made to make the play more politically
expedient and hence salable, for MacLaren admits in the preface that
poverty motivated him to have this revision published in Bristol.

In 1799 MacLaren used the Irish insurrection in an attempt to sell
copies of *The Humours of the Times; or What News Now* which he

had published originally as *What News from Bantry Bay? or, The Faithful Irishman*. The same year MacLaren also published *The Negro Slaves*. It was presented in Edinburgh and was published by subscription, in another effort to capitalize on the topical. This plea for humanitarianism in ballad opera form treats of the plight of Quako, an educated slave, who is more lucid than his boorish master, Racoon, under whose tyranny he suffers. The most unusual aspect of this afterpiece is the use of dialect to express serious sentiments. McSympathy, the spokesman for humanity, utters his objections to the cruelty of slavery in Highland Scots.

What News from Bantry Bay, which treats the plight of those who were hanged for wearin' o' the green, as well as a number of other works MacLaren rushed into print in the early decades of the nineteenth century lack the comic power of his theatricals written for provincial presentation. MacLaren never again manifested the proficiency he evinced in *The Highland Drover*. During the last years of the eighteenth century he moved to London. Although details of his biography are sparse, the many Soho addresses the author gives at the ends of his prefaces indicate that he had more landlords seeking back rent than subscribers to his plays. In England MacLaren catered to what he considered London tastes. His better comedies have a Celtic élan which is missing from farces such as *London Out of Town, or The Family Genius's* (1809). This musical farce opens with the usual banter between Hopewell and Friendly on the battle of the sexes. The Scottish element is reduced to the cavorting servants Cuddie and Jenny. MacLaren concentrates upon comic devices, such as pedantry involving misused Latin, rather than the matter at which he excelled.

In the preface to *The Elopement; or, A Caution to Young Ladies* (1811), the actor-dramatist explains the circumstances which forced him to support his large family[2] by writing for the theatre. After nearly eleven years in the army MacLaren was mustered out of the service, but was unable to obtain a pension because his landlady had used his discharge papers to light her pipe. The preface to his 1815 piece, *The Ways of London; or Honesty is the Best Policy*, is also a play for sympathy. MacLaren's account of door to door peddling of his extra copies of subscription publications etches, with the precision of a mezzotint,

2 In the preface to *The Second Sight: or, A Tale of Other Days* (London, 1817), Archibald MacLaren mentions his family: "To those who wonder that all my children are not grown up during the eighteen years I have been in London, I must say, that some of them are growing up, and that some of them have grown down, even to the grave, for I have buried five, and yet I have five still remaining."

the plight which befell the Scot who could please local audiences but could not capture the more sophisticated crowds of Drury Lane.

The Scottish dramatic output was as bankrupt as MacLaren during the last years of the century. The agglomerations of entertainment, that variety seeking patrons demanded, contributed to the impoverishment of Georgian theatre. An Edinburgh advertisement for a 1787 performance of John O'Keeffe's *Young Quaker*, which included James Brown's 1783 farce, *The Frolic*, and other local inconsequences, displays the pile of fluff which was presented and then retired:

> 'The Maid that tends the Goats', a song by a gentleman of this city, to be sung by Mrs Kemble—a hint at the secret, by Mrs Kemble, as a Freemason's wife, to be followed by *The Frolic*, after which a farce called *The Fool*, the whole to conclude with *Away to Leith Links, or a Golfing we will go*.[3]

New serious plays were still being presented, but none won public acclaim. John Jackson's "Sir William Wallace, of Ellerslie; or, The Siege of Dumbarton Castle" opened 26 July 1780. The *Edinburgh Courant* criticized Jackson's tragedy on the Scottish hero as a ghost of the historical prototype.[4] At the opening of "Sir William Wallace," another Jackson piece, "Tony Lumpkin's Rambles through Edinburgh" was included in the program. In addition to this localizing of O'Keeffe, the Edinburgh theatre manager probably did other afterpieces to stuff playbills for audiences desirous of varied theatrical fare, but there is no record of which ephemerae he wrote.

Three years after John Jackson took over the management of the Theatre Royal in Edinburgh, he accepted John Logan's *Runnemede*, which was first presented on 5 May 1784. Logan had tried to interest London producers in his tragedy, but his drama was vetoed by the Lord Chamberlain. Mackenzie in his *Anecdotes* observes that the censor "thought it had too much liberty."

Runnemede treats of the granting of the Magna Charta; the main plot is a thinly veiled plea for the Whigs. The subplot, adapted from Voltaire's *Tancrède*, is the more entertaining element in the play. Elvina who loves Elvine, is ordered by her father Albermarle, to marry Arden, a Norman, for the good of her country. The catastrophe is dissipated by Elvine's return to his love. (Supposing the heroine to be guilty of infidelity, Elvine rushes into battle, where he learns otherwise,

---

3   Cited in Dibdin, *Annals of the Edinburgh Stage*, p. 200.
4   Donald Mackenzie, *Scotland's First National Theatre*, p. 10.

and returns to wed the chaste Elvina.) The political plot, which presumably is the main concern, concludes with the granting of the Great Charter. The dramatic preparation for the attainment of the fundamental constitution of English liberties is deficient. There is much pageantry but little doubt that the political goal will be achieved. As a result, the play lacks suspense.

Logan, a writer of the tender and pathetic school, was author of other plays which are mentioned by the editor of his *Works,* but "Electra," "The Wedding Day," one act of "The Carthegenian Heroine," and three acts of a tragedy on the death of Mary Queen of Scots were never published.

Logan had long been interested in theatre. He used the drama as metaphor in a love letter to Mrs A on 26 November 1767:

> A free and a Married life seems to me to resemble Comedy and Tragedy. In the first we are continually diverted with humorous fancies and storys, we see the parties cast out or be reconciled; we see them part with one another in one act and join hands in another: the whole concludes with Merriment and Matrimony. In the last we are disposed to be more serious, we feel the higher passions and view the higher virtues exercised; we are deeply concerned in the plot and interested in the fate of the persons; The conclusion of all is Death. . . .

Logan's amorous activities had agitated "the planters of the vineyard" who were dissatisfied with him when newly ordained, as "Mr. Lothian's" squib mentions. Logan had talent, and early in his career he won the patronage of the creative establishment. His drinking, piracy of Michael Bruce's poems, and other dubious activities disposed his second parish in South Leith in 1781 to pay the wandering shepherd forty pounds a year to stay away from his flock. Logan's staged endeavor (*Runnemede*) was the *coup de grâce.* In 1786 the minister was forced to give up his clerical post. After laicization Logan went to London, where he pursued a literary life, which included contributing to *The English Review* and translating Louis Mercier's drama *Le Deserteur.* Although giving up the ministry was no sacrifice for Logan, the consequence of writing *Runnemede* demonstrates that prejudice against the theatre still flourished in North Britain.[5]

In the land that produced Lord Monboddo, who prefigured Darwin with his flute-playing orangoutang, and Lord Kames, who sentenced a chess-playing cronie to death with a cheery "Checkmate, Matthew,"

5   See J. S. Marshall, ed., *Letters of the Rev. John Logan* (Edinburgh, 1961), Introduction and pp. 46–48.

as well as a generous supply of other eccentrics, it is fitting that Scotland should be the home of a likely candidate for the most *outré* dramatist of the century. Little is known about Christian Carstaires. The Fyfeshire governess dedicated her playlet, *The Hubble-Shue* (ca. 1786), to the "Honorable Antiquarian Society." A key might solve conundrums such as the sword brandishing Gustard, whose only function seems to be to frighten the cat. In the light of theatre of the absurd, there is a temptation to formulate multiple hypotheses to explicate the topsy-turvy uproar of *The Hubble-Shue*. This rare play is an interesting analogue to William Blake's *The Island in the Moon*, which Geoffrey Keynes dates 1784–85. These satires of psuedo-intellectual circles share more than compulsive Italian song.

   The Hubble-Shue is reprinted line-for-line, beginning on the opposite page, from the first edition in the National Library of Scotland to intrigue present-day readers.

THE

HUBBLE-SHUE.

N.

'TIS false—'tis a mistake—there's not one word of truth in it.

M.

Never was a man so astonished—if he had been shot out of the mouth of a cannon he could not have been more confounded.

Enter Lady Gundie.

Good God—there is not one great name in the whole town that is not in her list.

No wonder than he was in a passion.

She flew at him like a tiger.

N.

No—no—he was in no passion.

For God's sake let us hear some of her poems.

M.

Her poems!—some of them are pretty—
enough to be sure—and feeling—as one
might say, (takes a great snuff).

But, for the dramatic piece, certainly never was any thing so ridiculous.

N.

Her dramatic!—the thing she calls the
Scundum is ten times better than the dramatic.

M.

Dare you, Sir—that's altogether an imposition—that verse was written by her sister.

*Enter Gustard with a drawn sword
and the cat runs in beneath the bed.*

Scene II.

*A door opens—and discovers a long table
with twenty covers—a fine sideboard,
with a display of silver plate—chi-
na—glasses, &c. &c. The company
usher'd in by fine powder'd footman—
The* Scrivener *and his* Wife—*their
three* Daughters—*a* Fat Minister *and
his daughter—other two young Ladies—Mrs* Umphry, *a widow—a*

West Indian Student—*three* Lieutenants—*an* Irishman—*an old* Ensign
and a Colonel.

The Lady of the House.

Do you chuse a little soup, Ma'am?

Mrs ———

I am terribly fatigued—I would rather
have a pâte.

Fat Minister.

Hobbernob Miss—Colonel, I fancy our
bonny lasses at home are little short of the
three *tits*—you took at the battle of *Mal-
plackuy.*

Colonel.

I can remember yet how they blush'd,
when they were set up amongst us young-
sters.

Fat Minister.

They would be educate in a nunnery.

Colonel.

She had the most enchanting voice—the
one with the dark hair.

Ensign.

It was the sweetest evening.

Mrs Umphry.

Give me the pepper.

Irishman.

Zoms—Miss—take care of your fea-
thers—has the scoundrel spilt [*sic*] the gravey
down your back?

Ensign.

Colonel, do you remember the locket—
on her white arm?

Colonel.

And her mild blue eyes.

Fat Minister.

Ay—ay—He's wanting to introduce his
story again—And to tell us, how she lookt
when the soldiers crowded round the tent
to listen to her song.

Colonel.

Sweet was her song.
> And soft the enchanted Air,
> That Angels paused and hung
> Their golden harps.

Ensign.

She did not know at that time that her
lover was wounded.

Fat Minister.

Come, Nan—give us one of your songs.

—Yes, papa.

> Down in the vale
>> the dew hung on the rose.

Fat Minister.

None of your vales, nor your dews and your roses—and your flowery fields, and your mirtle groves.

Play, Up and ware them a' Willie.

Miss, are you for a gig?

Colonel.

Ladies—good night—I have seen the time when I would have passed up amongst the gayest—I am now an old fellow.

Fat Minister.

And has a tear for pity.

Colonel.

Yes, Sir, and a heart that can feel the happiness of others.

They all crowd round him—O, Sir, you must not leave us—you must not go away.

[*The company move to the withdrawn room.*]

Fat Minister.

Come, Miss, give us your Italian—.

Miss.

Yes, Papa.

Si   li   si   ti   o   to
Ki   li   qui   si   o   so
Fa   la   se   scud
Qui   a   vi   a   vi   a
Que   a   vi   a   ve   a
Qui   a   vi   a   bo.
&c. &c.

[*Enter Mrs Consul and her Grandchild.*]

Mrs Consul.

Madam, I beg you ten thousand pardons, it was not in my power to wait upon you at dinner; there is no separating my Grandchild and the little black girl.

Child.

O, Mamma, I'm frightened.

Mrs Consul.

Why are you frightened?

Child.

The little girl says a great fish (a crocodile) came out of the water (the Ganges) and devoured her father—and a fine gentleman came running with a sword and stab'd the monster—and her father was all bloody, and she would have been killed; but the fine gentleman took her away, and they were carried by black mans with muslin on their head (turbans)—and the fine gentleman gave her to a great lady—All the fine things could not make her forget her poor father —He was very hungry, and as she lay on his arm, beneath the tree where the ugly monster came, he was giving her a little rice—it is all—the last—mor-sel.

Fat Minister.

Hold your tongue, my bonny dear, and you and the black girl shall go to the dancing school.

Child.

No, Mamma. —*Crys.*

Mrs Consul.

No my love.   (*One of the gentlemen takes her on his knee—dries her eyes.*

A Footman enters.

The coach is come, Madam.

The Lady of the House.

Madam, we are going to the play; will you be so obliging as make one of the party? It will divert miss.

Child.

Take me home, Mamma, take me to Cloy.

T.

A name for a dog.

Mrs Consul.

Come my dear—excuse me, Madam— my child is really not well—feel her hand— I am afraid she's feverish.

[*The Apothecary steps aside and whispers.*] Madam, you had better give miss a little Senna and a puke, if it operates six times it will be sufficient.

They go to the Play-house.

Mr Woods comes on the stage and makes a genteel apology, that the play, from an accident, must be put off for half an hour.

In the mean time, Mrs Kennedy (though not expressed in the bills) obligingly appears and sings

How sweet's the love
That meets return.

Then a beautiful young girl, dressed in the character of Spring, sings, and scimming along the stage,

When you hear a mournful tale
Laugh and hide your tears.
When you hear a mournful tale
Laugh and hide your tears.
La-a-a-a- laugh, &c.

This is poor entertainment (*from one of the boxes.*)

An orange from the footmans gallery hits the Irishman such a blow on the nose. —He flies upon the stage, drawing his dagger—throws one of the players heels o'er head—wounds Mr Hallion—makes such a hubbub, the gentlemen from the pit are obliged to interfere.

The house in great confusion—the company crowding to the door with great difficulty get to their coaches—a dreadful storm —a dark night—a Nabob's carriage driving like Jehu—the coachman being drunk overturns one of the hackneys—they shriek frightfully, and the Minister roars like a bull.

The old Ensign, chancing to walk on foot, comes up and helps to lug them out.

In 1787 Andrew Shirrefs, a bookbinder, published *Jamie and Bess, or The Laird in Disguise.* This imitation of *The Gentle Shepherd* was staged at Aberdeen, Elgin, and Inverness. The play was reprinted in Shirrefs's *Poems* in 1790, which also contains an "Address in Scotch, on

the decay of the Language, etc." This lamentation on the demise of
"guid auld Scots" praises Aberdonians who alone, according to the
author, retain their native tongue.

Jamie and Bess transpires in the country northwest of Aberdeen,
where the characters speak intentionally quaint Buchan dialogue. Shirrefs's concern was the creation of stage dialect to entertain rather than
transcription of regional speech. Banky[6] informs Sir Archibald of Bess's
supposed intentions:

> Some cantrip-castin' cock, wha spells can read,
> I understand has turn'd auld Lucky's head.
> Her niece is bonny, and, gin she be spar'd.
> She hopes to see her wedded to a laird.
>
> (II. 2)

The knight observes that in former times people married for love rather
than position and money. The sentiments the characters express mirror
late eighteenth century bourgeois manners rather than the mores of
Scots peasants or even Ramsay's romantic concept.

David Morison included a ballad opera in his *Poems* (1790). This
tale of the laird and the lass, *Jack and Sue: or, The Fortunate Sailor*,
is analogous to Paton's *William and Lucy* as well as to Ramsay's *Gentle
Shepherd*. Jack has gone to sea to raise money in order to settle down
with Sue. The heroine's confidante, Ketty, expresses her distrust of
Jack's notions. Ketty has a stock pawky turn of mind, characteristic of
secondary characters in light plays.

> KET. Good troth ye gab like ony printed book,
> But trulins ou'd afore they leap shou'd look
> I dinna like the idle wild romances,
> That fill our lads heads wi' sic foolish fancies.
> When they come hame wi' broken arms or legs,
> They crack o' diamonds bigger than goose eggs;
> How Indian Queens forsooth, at ilka ear,
> Wear lumps o' gowd as big's a honey pear.
> And rattle aff sic tales, when round the fire,
> That doth our lads wi' wonder all inspire.
> Weel may they stretch their tales to ony size,
> An blind for want o' skill our ladies eyes;
> For nane can check the daft like tales they tell,
> But book lear'd folk, or wha's been there themsel'.
>
> (I. 2)

6 Banky was played by Archibald MacLaren in the Aberdeen production on 12
January 1788.

Thimble, a tailor, loves Sue; a young squire desires her as well. Despite their plans to win the girl, Sue remains faithful to Jack. When he returns, he paints an even more glamorous picture of life at sea than Ketty foretold:

> Why faith, we sailors live as sailors ought,
> We brave all dangers, that's ne'er done for nought;
> Like lords we live at sea, like kings on shore;
> When money fails, we go to sea for more.
> Thus happy lives we lead, content's our aim,
> A friend to friends, to enemies humane;
> Who wou'd not then join in our heartsome core,
> And live the life that princes now adore?
>
> (III. 2)

Andrew Greenfield's *Henrique, Prince of Sicily* was published posthumously in his *Poems* (1790). The unfinished tragedy is drawn from *Gil Blas*, the same source James Thompson used for *Tancred and Sigismunda*. Greenfield, an Episcopal minister, began the poetic drama several months before his death in 1788, but completed only three of the intended five acts.

Greenfield takes Alain Le Sage's consolatory position on the vicissitudes of life. The divine is also indebted to William Shakespeare for facets of characterization. The Hamletesque details end in perplexing *cul de sacs*. Blanche is to be Henrique's queen as the action begins. Leontio adopts Henrique as a son. Blanche has a premonition of disaster. In the second act Henrique is forced to accept his cousin Constantia as consort. Constantia resembles Ophelia as well as Gertrude. In the third act of the tragedy, courtiers discuss the ill-fated wedding of Blanche to Alvaro, the chancellor who plots against the King of Sicily. After the bride resists Alvaro's advances the groom encounters Henrique, but the hero does not kill his rival out of respect for Blanche. In the beginning of the fourth act, Henrique accuses the woman he loves and once respected of marrying Alvaro for spite because he has officially agreed to take Constantia for consort in order to obtain the throne. As Henrique yearns to encounter Alvaro once more, the play ends.

James Mylne, like Greenfield, was deprived of seeing his closet plays through the press. Mylne's son George brought out his father's *Poems* in 1790. This volume, which contains two melodramas, *The British Kings* and *Darthula*, occasioned Robert Burns's advice on Scottish subscription publications:

Andrew Shirrefs (fl. 1780s).

My success, perhaps as much accidental as merited, has brought an inundation of nonsense over the Land. Subscription-bills for Scots poems have so dunned, and daily do dun the Public, that the very term Scots Poetry totters on the brink of contempt. For these reasons, if publishing in magazines, etc. any of Mr. Mylne's Poems be at all prudent, in my opinion it certainly should not be a Scottish poem. The profits of the labours of a man of genius, are, I hope, as honourable as any profits whatever; and Mr Mylne's relations are most justly entitled to that honest harvest, which fate has denied himself to reap.[7]

Mackenzie considered the Laird of Lockhill possessed of "considerable Marks of unguided Genius."[8] This estimate of the gentleman farmer's verse is generous, for although Mylne's poetry is readable because of its directness, his style does little to alleviate the tedium of the long Ossianic dramas.

The British Kings is a one hundred seventy-three page study of tragic and fatal consequences arising from unknown identities. As the play opens, Lena, disguised as a boy, has escaped the clutches of Cadwallan. The King of the Britons attacked Lena because her husband, Osrick, King of Northumbria, is the rapist's foe. Cadwallan is unusually restive about his mode of revenge, which is intended to foreshadow the ultimate unraveling of identities in which the British King learns that his enemy, Osrick, is his supposedly dead son. Lena informs Kenwal, King of Wessex, that Cadwallan has killed her father, Edwin, in the foulest possible way. The King of the Britons, when he was a dinner guest, violated the *comitatus* by slaying the previously wounded Edwin in his own hall.

In the second act, Lena and her husband meet. Bathetically she tells Osrick of her "fate worse than death." The news motivates Osrick to headstrong action. In the third act the Druid reveals relationships of several of the principals. The seer is unsuccessful in his attempt to tell Osrick of his origin. This is necessary if the drama is to end tragically. Having been informed that the hero is curious about his lineage, it is difficult to countenance the King's reaction as the Druid tries to inform him of his identity.

DRUID
Twice ten times has that oak renew'd his shade,
Since thy fair mother with her infant son,

7 Rev. P. Carfrae had requested Robert Burns's advice with regard to publication of James Mylne's works. In his letter Carfrae mentions "two complete and regular tragedies" and a "farce in three acts." Mylne's comedy was not published. F. H. Allen, ed., *The Letters of Robert Burns* (Boston, 1927), pp. viii, 175.
8 Henry Mackenzie, *Letters to Elizabeth Rose*, p. 75.

Thyself, came hither. —"Wretched babe,"
     she cry'd,
"I have preserv'd thee from their cruel swords,
From flames, at midnight rais'd for horrid ends."—
                    OSRICK
No more! —I'll hear no more. —My ears are shut!
I find thou know'st the story of my birth.—
Seal yet awhile thy lips, thou holy man,
To that mysterious secret. —I have sworn
This day to rest in ignorance. —This day
Fills up the crisis of my fate. —I'll hear
At my return whate'er thou hast to tell.

                                              (III. 2)

In the fourth act Cadwallan learns from the Druid that Osrick is his
son, and realizes the heinousness of his attack upon his daughter-in-
law. Lena overhears this revelation and goes mad.

The fifth act catastrophe is a parricide. Cadwallan lets his son run
him through to atone for his having wronged Lena. Arthur and Kenwal
bicker over who is to rule Britain. The ruler of Camelot is portrayed as
a petty and petulant individual. The now insane Lena is disposed of by
an unexplained death, presumably the result of her madness. Arthur is
proclaimed king, and Kenwal, who is legal heir to the throne, voluntarily retreats to a cottage with Elfrida.

Lena shares the fate of a number of unfortunate heroines who go
mad and die in late-century melodramas. Although they succumb pri-
marily for purposes of pathos, death from insanity was as acceptable to
the eighteenth century as Juliet's drugged demise is to a late twentieth-
century audience. Death lists in *Scots Magazine* and other periodicals
of the time attributed the cause of death to madness in a number
of cases.

Lena's death is more justifiable than Mylne's cavalier appropriation
of history for dramatic purposes. The author brings in some authentic
paraphernalia of the seventh century, such as the *comitatus,* but the
correspondence of the characters in the drama to historical counterparts is nominal. Cadwallan is drawn from Caedwalla, the West Saxon
King who slew Osrick, the Northumbrian ruler. In the play, King
Arthur succeeds Cadwallan. Arthur antedates his predecessor by at
least a century. The Druid, whom Mylne introduces apologetically as
the last of his kind, is, by conservative estimate, half a millenium too
late.

Mylne's *Darthula* is a romance set mainly in third-century Ireland.
It is a tale of a Celtic king's daughter who evades a tyrant's lust, loses
her father and brothers, and gets her beloved Nathos. The struggle of

good and evil forces for the Irish throne provides the conflict of the main plot. Cairbar, a tyrannical King of Erin, has a noble brother, Cathmor, who until the last act disapproves of his brother but remains loyal. Darthula notes the disparity in the two: "Vile and contemptible mankind would be, / Were all like Cairbar! But the few like Cathmor / Still make us of our general nature proud."

The most unusual feature of *Darthula* is the use of the chorus. The choruses function in the same manner as their classical Greek predecessors, but Mylne's versions are *sui generis*, as is illustrated by the robust Kiplingesque soldiers' chorus, which provides an extraordinary change of pace in the antique proceedings:

> EIGHTH SOLDIER
> Away, silly fopling! How vainly ye rave!
>   To think that such dunces as you,
> Will e'er by the fair be esteem'd like the brave,
>   Such painted moth-flies
>   The ladies despise;
>   Though rolling your eyes,
>   Though heaving soft sighs,
> Ye think ye are wonderous charming!
> Though smiling most sweetly, though looking so wise,
> Though frisking and lisping out ignorant lies,
> The conduct of soldiers ye dare criticise,
>   And of battles and sieges determine!
> A soldier who wants both his limbs and his eyes,
> Is worth twenty tribes of such vermin.
>
>   (Chorus 4)

A number of Scots writers, James Mylne among them, tried to ape the rustic image of the Ayreshire ploughman, and attempted to pass themselves off as untutored. John Learmont, in the prefatory address to his *Poems* (1791), described himself as a gardener by profession and a poet by propensity. The proclivities he manifested are imitative of Ramsay, Ferguson, and Burns. The pastoral he included in his volume, *The Unequal Rivals*, is reminiscent of Ramsay.

Jamie loves Minia. His rival, Lord Patria's son, is infatuated with the girl as well, but Minia wishes to marry Jamie. Her love is strong enough to withstand the blandishments of Young Patria, who uses money to obtain the advantage over the impoverished hero. Jamie expresses the romantic ideal in Act I as he envisions life with his true love:

> The hamely cottage, an' the canny wife,
> Young healthfou bairns ga 'en reeling in it rife,
> Seem aye to me the sweetest joys o' life.

Lord and Lady Patria provide contrast to the rural folk. The urban couple have values as false as their overly elegant diction. Young Patria is instrumental in Jamie's imprisonment on a trumped-up charge. Learmont provides a *deus ex machina* in the persons of Mr. and Mrs. Moral, the long-lost parents of the hero. This couple functions as a foil to the immoral Patrias. The Morals bring about the happy ending for the clean-living country characters. Jamie and Minia have love and money at the conclusion.

In *The Unequal Rivals*, Learmont emphasized the superiority of simple rusticity, a motif also found in political playlets of the day. These closet dramas manifest a social consciousness too controversial for theatrical presentation. One of the more mature plays that opted for reform is *Elim and Maria*, a two-act pastoral "by a Friend of the oppressed," printed in Glasgow in 1792. The agricultural dilemma arising from rotten boroughs occasioned this piece. *Elim and Maria* suggests that exorbitant rents and abominable taxes make insolvent tenants whose only solution is emigration. The play follows the dialectic of a pro-agrarian organization, the Friends of the People. The movement's spokesman in the play is Wilmor, a wise old shepherd, who embarks for the land of promise where soil is cheap and there is little toil, as does the hero Elim, who leaves Maria behind. The heroine's parents will not permit her to go with Elim to America; the melancholy pastoral ends with the lovers' parting.

The author of this work, which was published the same year George III issued a proclamation against seditious writings, no doubt remained anonymous because of the inflammatory nature of his democratic tendencies. The dramatist has been identified as Thomas Muir, a man much concerned with parliamentary reform. Muir belonged to The Associated Friends of the Constitution and the People, a group accused of supporting the French Revolution and desiring the overthrow of the British government.[9]

The Philistines; or The Scotch Tocsin Sounders (1793), takes a light approach to show the ignorance of the supporters of the French Revolution. The scene at an Edinburgh Jacobin club opens with a song which leaves no doubt as to who are Philistines:

9 "Elim and Maria," *Notes and Queries*, f.s., 10 (1854):414, provides tenuous evidence that Thomas Muir wrote the pastoral. John Earnshaw, *Thomas Muir Scottish Martyr, etc., Studies in Australian and Pacific History*, vol. 1 (Cremorne, New South Wales, 1959), makes no mention of *Elim and Maria*.

> Since we are swine,
> On blood we'll dine,
> And rest on desolation;
> Like Sans Culottes
> We'll sharp our snouts,
> And dig up all the nation—

Joseph Bable, a schoolmaster, and Bob Riot, a carter, conduct an idealistic discussion in dialect on the gentility of the Friends of the People.
Other tradesmen argue about the value of the revolution with respect
to the political concerns of Britain. When confronted by the authorities,
the workers deny complicity in any *coup d'état*. The Constable believes
them, and, in diction which contrasts to the burr of the uninformed,
ends the play with a statement of the author's position: "Poor misled
men! your situations excite sympathy; but what kind of characters are
those *gentlemen*, who, revenge disappointment in unreasonable expectations, have not scrupled to pursue means, which if God had not prevented them, might have ended in the loss of thousands of lives, and in
the utter ruin and destruction of our native country."

Modern Politics, or the Cat Let out of the Pack (1793), takes a
position similar to that of *The Philistines*. John Dunt, a Presbyterian
blacksmith, and Gibby Grunt, a seceding weaver, are both Friends of
the People, but they oppose each other on national issues. Mr. Tacit
Neuter, a schoolmaster, is a friend of the country and speaks for
appeasement, whatever the cost. Their dialogue conjures up what a
French Revolution would do to Great Britain.

Brissot's Ghost! or, Intelligence from the Other World (1794), is
another warning of the perils of wearing the French cockade. The setting is a meeting of the Friends of the People. The proceedings are
interrupted by the spectre of Jean Pierre Brissot de Warville, the
Girondist leader, who had been guillotined by the Jacobins in 1793.
Brissot reveals that the real motives of the revolutionaries are not egal-
itarian. The ghost tells of the horrible conditions in his homeland,
which have come about through the irresponsibility of the power mad,
and warns against British imitation. After this apparition the Friends of
the People decide to disband.

William Brown, a Dundee editor, has been identified as the "Tam
Thrum," who wrote the political plays *Look before ye Loup; or, A
Healin' Sa' for the Crackit Crowns of Country Politicians* (1793), and
Look Before Ye Loup Part Second: or Anither Box of Healin' Sa' for

the Crackit Crowns of Country Politicians (1794).[10] The earlier of the
playlets is superior. Through ale house conversation of local types the
reader discovers the mean between the extremes of Charlie Clod,
the representative of the revolutionary left, and Harry Heeltap, the
representative of the unthinking establishment. As the play opens,
Sandy Snip, Simon Shuttle, and others argue about their constitution
in the light of Thomas Paine's *Rights of Man.* The conversation evolves
into a dialogue between Harry and Charlie. Harry explains to his friend
that a constitution for Scotland would not mean that one would be "as
free as the French," for the French do not possess the liberty of which
Paine speaks. They discuss taxation and religion. Charlie, imbued with
the French revolutionary spirit, is for banishment of religion. Harry,
ever loyal to the establishmentarian vagary, advocates "a religion of
natures." Harry wins every time with arguments as sophistical as Charlie's are radical. The discussion ends amicably with the two singing
"God Save the King," and giving three huzzas for George III.

The second *Box of Healin' Sa* is a less effective repetition of ideas.
The same characters convene in the pub, take sides about the French
Revolution and the British Convention. They finally decide after a discussion of the qualifications of Simon Shuttle, their convention dele-
gate, to leave politicking to the experts. "Tam Thrum" had expressed
this sentiment in the introduction to his 1793 play: "To be plain wi' ye
lads, you have ta 'en us aw fraw our ploughs, our shuttles, an' our
needles, to mak' constitutions, an' mend governments; you've deprived
us of our innocence, our happiness an' contentment."

Religious as well as political concerns were expressed in dramatic
form by writers seeking a livelier approach than tracts or catechisms.
The pseudo-dramas on religious topics are often as unorthodox in content as form. *Edinburgh Delivered; or, the World in Danger* appeared
in 1782. This dramatic poem opens with two weird sisters, Matha and
Drina, who have summoned Satan. Matha describes a hellish scene
which took place on Arthur's Seat:

> A Satan came, who told us, they
> From Ætna's flames had bent their way,
> Commission'd, by some pow'rful spell,

10   Inglis, *Dramatic Writers of Scotland,* p. 22, assigns the authorship to William
Brown. He may have confused the author with the Edinburgh bookseller by the
same name who printed *Look Before Ye Loup* in its Scottish editions. *Look Before
Ye Loup* (1793), was published in Philadelphia as well as Edinburgh. The Scots-
Irish settlements in Western Pennsylvania provided a market for a dialect play, as
the early writings of Hugh Henry Brackenridge attest.

> To sink all Edinburgh in hell,
> For it to them was rightly suited
> For follies and for crimes reputed.
>
>   (I. 1)

The second scene transpires inside the mountain, where Ardrakle pre-
siding over the furies tells the host of Scottish turpitude. Empeto is the
most dramatic sinner in the parade which proves the demon's assertion.
This rake has progressed from scarlet coat in dapper youth to rags in
debtor's prison, where he is held for gambling. In the second act the
coven awaits the devils. The evil ones meet in council, and as the fate
of the town is sealed, Oralyn materializes from Aetna's flame to avert
the diabolic decision. The spirit saves Edinburgh for the moment.

   *Poetical Dialogues on Religion, in the Scots Dialect, between Two
Gentlemen and Two Ploughmen* (1788) substantiates Benjamin Frank-
lin's observation that "Persons of good sense . . . seldom fall into dispu-
tation, except lawyers, university men, and men of all sorts that have
been bred at Edinburgh." In the first three dialogues Donald and
Dubbin uphold liberal and conservative views respectively. Donald is
ecumenical in his approach to religion:

> I've heard this news as weel as you,
> And I am glad to find it true;
> Because my very saul would sing,
> To see Religion form a ring,
> Embrace, in one harmonious Kirk,
> Pope, Prelate, Pagan, Jew, and Turk;
> To see your bletherin' bigot hand
> Whip'd forth from every peaceful land.

The rational liberal does not succeed in convincing his hypocritical
adversary that factional prejudice is wrong.

   The fourth dialogue between Theophilus and Hippolitus also ends in
an impasse. Theophilus, who "tends his bothy" and says his prayers,
stands for liberty. Hippolitus, who believes religion is superstition,
advocates license. These participants in the last of the *Poetical Dialogues* conclude, as does Ebenezer, who says "I have known few
converted from their opinions in controversy," at the terminus of *A
Conversation Between John, a Baptist, and Ebenezer, a Seceder, on the
Faith of the Gospel Occasioned by Mr M'Lean's Treatise on Christ's
Commission to his Apostles*, which was printed in Edinburgh in 1798.

   Plays which were staged dealt with nothing as crucial as political or

religious controversy. William Richardson included *The Indians* in his
Poems, chiefly Rural (1774). He recast this work as a tragedy which
played at the Caledonian Theatre in Glasgow and the Richmond Theatre near London (ca. 1790). The tale of love and vengeance among
the noble savages resembles the Pocahontas myth. *The Indians* contains a number of odd combinations. The names of the characters are
of the vowel-haunted Ossianic variety. Ononthio, Onaiyo, and others
speak diction more suited to Quakers than primitives. In Act III, the
scene following Mariano's plea to Chief Ononthio to save Sidney, the
patriotic British captive, is the high point of the piece, and Indians
brandishing tomahawks dance about the fettered Englishman chanting:

> 3rd Ind.   Come, my brethren, fierce and grim,
> Fill the cauldron to the brim.
> Fuel in the forest hew,
> Cypress, pine, and baleful yew,
> Fill the smoke and smould'ring fire
> Round the sooty sides aspire.

The fifth Indian threatens: "Bend th' elastic bow to fly / With his hairy
scalp on high," but Sidney is saved by the Indian heroine.

Gavin Turnbull, an actor-writer, published his *Poetical Essays*
(1788), which contain "Pastoral I." This poem has been given in check-
lists as a drama, but the rustic exchanges between Colin, Alexis, and
Corydon are not of the dramatic sort. Turnbull played at Dumfries in
his interlude, *The Recruit* (ca. 1792). His playlet treats of a nagging
wife who drives her husband to enlist in the army. John Burness's
adaptation of *The Recruit* was printed about 1819.

In addition to short pieces, original five-act plays were being staged
outside the Scottish capital. Matthew Nimmo's *The Fatal Secret: or
Truth Disguised* was performed and published in Dundee in 1792. This
prose tragedy is a story of love among the North African nobility. The
improbabilities are inaugurated with the news that Prince Mulyzeden
is going to wed Princess Belraiza. Court observers are surprised by the
betrothal, because the Prince and his best friend, Abdomor, had vowed
never to marry. The closeness of the men parallels the relationship of
Belraiza and her lady-in-waiting, Zatilda. The ladies are miserable at
the prospect of breaking their vows to remain single.

The narrative becomes more plausible when Belraiza admits that she
prefers Abdomor to her royal fiancé. Mulyzeden discovers that his
betrothed and his closest companion love each other. The Prince then
imprisons Abdomor, and Belraiza pleads that Abdomor be spared the
rack. The Prince releases his former friend and offers amnesty, if Bel-

raiza will be his bride. North Africa is on the verge of revolt, because of the complications which have arisen by the delay of the marital-martial alliance, but Belraiza refuses to wed a man she does not love. Zatilda desires Mulyzeden, and stabs herself because she cannot have him. The Prince also commits suicide out of frustration. As Abdomor prepares to go to war against Belraiza's uncle, the Moroccan king, his love promises to join him on the field of battle.

James Norval's tragedy, *The Generous Chief*, was performed in Montrose about 1792, and the following season another tartan tragedy, Thomas Scott's *Edwin and Catherine, or the Distressed Lovers* was published in Paisley. This 1793 romance employs as many melodramatic clichés as Nimmo's *Fatal Secret* to tell a story of the crises which beset those who wish to marry for love. Scott begins his tragedy with MacGregor's refusal to permit his daughter, Catherine, to wed Edwin, an orphan. Reynaldo, the heroine's brother, sympathizes with his sister:

> But well I know the dear, dear, tender thoughts,
> The soft sensations, that in crowds arise,
> Throb round her heart, and innocently play,
> With love, and longing to her absent Edwin.

The second act opens with Catherine weeping in a wood. The girl's musing in this romantic spot is cut short by Reynaldo, who informs her that MacDonald has been chosen for her husband, whereupon Catherine faints.

It becomes evident in the third act that MacDonald seeks only the MacGregor fortune. Euphrasia, Reynaldo's love, has dissuaded the lady of MacDonald's choice from marrying him. The impetuous MacDonald seeks vengeance, and his violence surfaces when he meets the heroine, who fights off his advances. Catherine utters: "Off-off! thou monster—assist me, heaven! / Else I'm undone—thy vows are binding on me." Reynaldo carries a spear to the rescue and saves Catherine's virtue.

In the fourth act Euphrasia and Catherine discuss their dreams, which seem to presage disaster for the heroine. The dreams are diversions as are too many other distresses of the tale. MacDonald intercepts a letter to Catherine from Edwin, and learns that the hero is staying with a hermit on the Isle of Pomona. MacGregor also finds out that Edwin is now Lord of Pomona; he then plans to rematch his daughter to Edwin in order to gain support in his plot to overthrow the king.

In the final act MacGregor wounds his son, who is disguised as MacDonald. Reynaldo kills his father. Young MacGregor's assassination is then reported. MacDonald is about to stab Catherine, whom he thinks is Euphrasia, but discovers her true identity in time. Edwin enters in chains under guard, as Catherine is about to commit suicide. Her lover throws off his chains and saves her. One of the bogus guards is Reynaldo in disguise and, after the battle in which MacDonald is killed, the two pairs of lovers unite. The innumerable twists of the serpentine plot militate against even perfunctory characterization. The surprises are inserted to provoke additional gasps of breath, but there is little motivation and no preparation for these contrivances. This piece is an example of the small-town dramatist imitating his more polished fellows by implementation of every fashionable ploy in one play.

In 1794 William Mickle published *The Siege of Marseilles* after exhaustive efforts to get his tragedy produced. Earlier Home helped Mickle with script revision to make it acceptable to Garrick, who told Boswell that *The Siege* was rejected (1770), "not from its deficiency in spirit but in form." Mickle then offered the drama to the local theatre. When his work fared no better in Edinburgh than it had in London, Mickle submitted the play to Sheridan. The Irish dramatist never sent it back from Dublin.[11] Boswell restrained his fiery friend from making Garrick the subject of a new *Dunciad*, and Mickle contented himself with a waspish preface to *The Siege of Marseilles*, in which he takes to task the Drury Lane manager and the plays chosen for presentation.

Mickle used a passage from William Robertson's *History of Charles V*, which deals with France during the reign of Francis I, as a point of departure for his drama. The dramatist follows the historian's account of the Bourbon collaboration with Charles V of Spain to regain estates seized by the French monarch. Erminia, the heroine based on Louisa of Savoy, Countess of Chateaubriand, is the center of attention throughout the five acts which adhere to the unities. This she-tragedy of jealousy and irresolution does possess a theme, which may be expressed as "frailty thy name is woman." Erminia is a conventionally delicate creature, apt to come unstrung upon slight provocation, as her four swoons prove. Erminia becomes unbalanced at her husband's death. Mickle prepares for the fate of his heroine with greater care than many of his fellow melodramatists. Raymond looks upon his wife and observes:

> A little while, for lift she but her eyes,
> And the first thistle flower that catches them

11   "An Account of the Life and Writings of William Julius Mickle," *Scots Magazine* 51 (1789):532–34; concluded (1789):581–83; George B. Hill, ed., *Letters of Samuel Johnson* (Oxford, 1892), 1:422.

Catches her fancy too, and thither speeds she,
Oh Heaven, what haggard imperfection blots
Thy fairest work!

(II. 4)

The noble repeats the frailty motif in the next act as he wonders about his wife Erminia:

Woman thou slave of gaudy vanity,
What trifles win thee! O had Heav'n
but made thee
Constant as lovely.

(III. 3)

Although Erminia never summons terror, she does manage to convey pity. Demented, the heroine imagines that her dead child is upbraiding her in a truly original mad scene.

In addition to *The Siege of Marseilles* Mickle wrote several other dramas which were not published and which are now lost.

Robert Heron, the first biographer of Robert Burns, suffered humiliation when his *St. Kilda in Edinburgh; or News from Camperdown* opened 21 February 1798. Before the final curtain it was doomed. Archibald Constable, the publisher, noted in his copy of the comedy why *St. Kilda* failed in Edinburgh:

This play was damned on the first night of its appearance. . . . This was brought about not only by the demerits of the play, but also by a joke of Henry Brougham, the late Lord Chancellor. In the 6th Scene of the 2nd Act, p. 30, the President, after proposing the health of Admiral Duncan, said 'What toast shall we next drink?' upon which Brougham (who was sitting next to me in the pit) called out 'We'll drink Good Afternoon.' After this no more of the play was heard without roars of laughter and the curtain was dropped.[12]

In his preface Heron accuses the audience of administering Jedburgh justice to the work he intended to be a comedy of "genuine Scottish manners, neither disguised nor absurdly caricatured." Heron explains that he chose English rather than Scots, because he believed Edinburgensians and Hebudians did not speak a pure dialect. He was also of the opinion that the actors were incapable of delivering pure Scots dialogue.

Heron was a respectable bookman and critic, but these faculties did

12 Archibald Constable's copy of *St Kilda in Edinburgh* (NLS).

not help him to construct the kind of situation comedy popular with
his audience. Brougham's remark was funnier than any one-liner in the
play. The pomposity Heron exhibits in the preface to his comedy and
in his *History of Scotland* is a fatal characteristic in a comic writer. *St.
Kilda* is notable only as a conscious effort to create a Scottish drama,
for Heron lacked the common touch necessary to produce a genuine
artifact of an essentially rural society.

The comedy is a combination of romance and patriotism. *St. Kilda*
deals with the difficulties which arise when Jeanie's Hebudian sweet-
heart William goes away to fight the Dutch. M'Coul, the caw-fisted
cawdie, offers to find the girl a new lad. Johnstone, a wealthy lecher,
wants Jeanie, and M'Coul panders for him by spreading false news of
Admiral Duncan's defeat at Camperdown. When the heroine hears the
lie about the outcome of the naval battle she faints. Johnstone, who is
about to spirit her away to his lair, is prevented from carrying out his
scheme by the returning heroes of the Camperdown victory who rescue
Jeanie.

The hint of rape caused "Timothy Plain" to label the play "replete
with the grossest indecency" in his *Scots Chronicle* review. Heron, the
former preaching assistant to the Reverend Hugh Blair, was furious
about the remark. As Heron asserts in his preface, this observation is
unwarranted. Plain's phrase was picked up by theatrical historians,
and this attempt at more realistic use of local color, which Heron
achieves in his portrayal of the canny M'Coul, was subsequently
discredited as obscene.[13]

In 1798 E. J. Smith of Dumfries had his political satire, *Sir John Butt*,
privately printed in Edinburgh. This exhortation to avoid all inter-
course with Gallics, "Timothy Plain" might well have described as
replete with indecency. The play begins with ale house habituées
exchanging vulgarities. Their small street talk is interrupted by the
entrance of Sir Luisdore Frisky (France),[14] who has come to wed the
daughter of Sir John Butt (Scotland) and Lady Butt (England). After
raillery about French customs, which includes suspicion of the acco-
lade, Frisky departs for the house of his fiancée. The Frenchman offers
to sleep with his future mother-in-law, then marry Grecy (Ireland), as
Sir Sodom Shittle-cock (Austria-Prussia) enters with a clyster pipe to
clear Sir John's "rough places." The *double entendres* of those who

13   *Scots Chronicle* 2 February 1798. Dibdin, *Annals of the Edinburgh Stage*,
p. 233.
14   James Maidment wrote the key in his copy of *Sir John Butt* (NLS).

would evacuate Britain are as gross as they are politically extreme, and become more outlandish with the entry of Sir Pompey Battle-dore (Russia). In the final scene, the cuckolded Sir John learns his lesson from the mercenary foreigners; he sees isolationism as preferable to alliance.

Distrust of the French provided Smith with a source of departure for his nationalistic squib, and also factored in Gideon Duncan's romantic comedy, *The Constant Lovers; or the Sailor's Return* (1798). Duncan, a former navy man, had forty years of nautical experience with which to salt his closet play. Unfortunately, he had less familiarity with the boards than the deck, which becomes painfully evident in the long expository speeches and strings of coincidences. The action commences when Crawford begins courting Ann. The heroine still pines for Hardy, who has been at sea for a decade fighting the French. Sir John Squire thinks the sentimental notions of his daughter Ann and Crawford foolish, for although he admits he and his wife never won the Dunmon flitch at New Year's for compatibility, their old-style marriage sufficed.

The author's idealistic vision of love and marriage, which is as idyllic as David Morison's, parallels his description of life at sea. On one level *The Constant Lovers* functions as a plea for men to sail King's ships rather than merchant vessels. Hardy, the gentle, perfect tar, puts into Scotland. He leaves His Majesty's ship disguised as a doctor, because he suspects that Squire was instrumental in his being "Japanned" in Grennock. The "doctor" and Squire meet and agree that revolution and rotten boroughs are "idle ideas." They are also in accord that Parliament will protect the people. Such upper-class views are diametrically opposed to the sympathies of the author. Before the lovers are united in the fourth and final act, supporting characters' love affairs are introduced. Duncan settles the various domestic complications predictably, and he ends the piece with a familiar moral, spoken by the repentent Sir John Squire: "And after all our troubles, pain and care, / The constant and the brave will gain the fair."

Duncan and other writers tried to assuage anxiety caused by the French Revolution through effusive professions of loyalty. Historically oriented authors drew from the national past. The turmoil of the revolution reminded many of the Caroline period. This interest sparked the 1794 revival of *The Royal Martyr; or Life and Death of Charles I*, which caused a riot in the Edinburgh Theatre Royal. The fight started by university students, who favored the French Revolution and cheered the democratic lines of this tragedy, was taken up by the Tory members of the audience.[15]

A less feverish reaction than that which provoked the 1794 melee caused Colin MacLaurin to write *Hampden* (1799). This treatment of Caroline events, colored by the violence of the day, contains speeches about popular rights and freedom, but seeks a more moderate means of extending liberty while preserving the status quo. The play opens shortly after Hampden has been accused of treason. Hampden does not agree with Lord Holland, who seeks bloodless change:

> Reason you have thus to reproach our laws,
> But the time's now come, you ought to know
> When these, our country's laws, its former boast,
> The pride of us, the envy of the world,
> Have been wounded even to the vitals,
> And by the power supreme that makes them.
>
> (I. 1)

Hampden is in favor of a *coup d'état*, but does not wish the ensuing chaos which accompanies violent change. The protagonist's love, Lady Sophia Russell, pleads with him to escape the dilemma and go away with her. Hampden orders her not to "unsex" him. Lady Russell answers the objection in extravagant rhetoric:

> What! drive me thus from thee? No, thou shalt not:
> Still to thee I'll cling, like the fond ivy
> To the aged oak; to whose kind embrace
> The creeping plant as to a parent's arms
> Flies at first for aid; then, with its texture
> Shields its aged fire, clasps him in its arms,
> As I now thee. Come do proceed with me.
> For ought I know they now pursue thee.
>
> (III. 4)

She cannot tempt Hampden to run away and he is imprisoned. In jail he soliloquizes about his psychological states. The first three acts contain many romantic estimates of feelings; these assessments summon sympathy for the lovers and serve to humanize the historical figures. The Byronic Hampden's reflections on solitude as a distorting factor on the mind are astute.

---

15 Dibdin, *Annals of the Edinburgh Stage*, p. 224, gives a more objective account of the theatre riot of 1794 than does Walter Scott in *Memorial for Donald Maclean Writer in Edinburgh Against Joseph Mason Carpenter of Bradford in Wiltshire.*

The last two acts dash to a melodramatic conclusion. Lady Russell visits Hampden's cell and informs him that she can obtain his release, if she will make love with Stafford. Hampden is outraged at the prospect of an unfaithful mistress. Lord Russell returns home, kills Stafford, and is thrown into the cell next to Hampden's. The council releases both prisoners; finally the Russells are reunited. *Hampden* has faults common to many melodramatic closet dramas, but it possesses a character, which is best described as drive. This thrust permits the reader to disregard a number of improbabilities in seeking the outcome of a hero who has more vitality than the sensible paragons found in many late eighteenth-century plays.

Colin MacLaurin exhibited this verve in his second tragedy written late in the 1790s. *Laura, or, the Punishment of Perfidy* remained unpublished until 1812, when it was included in *The Poetical Works of Colin and George MacLaurin*. This melodrama begins with Lord Albert's confession to Valmond that he has an illegitimate child by his ward Laura, whom he seduced by promising marriage. "Perfidious wretch," exclaims Valmond, for Lord Albert is married. Lady Eugenia Albert receives evidence of her husband's extramarital activities when Albert storms out after a domestic quarrel saying: "What think you of me now? there, there, is food / For jealousy—let now your fancy range, / Can you discover what that letter means?" It takes Eugenia longer to uncover the meaning of the letter than it should—perhaps because of the other hand in the play.

The first scene of the second act is not Colin MacLaurin's, for the style is entirely different. The gusto is missing. In this inserted scene the ghost of Madam De Courcy, Laura's mother, armed with a dagger, appears to Albert and tells him of her death giving life to the girl he has ruined. The scene tries to be ethereal, but it suffers in comparison to the second scene in this act which is a more vigorous example of a similar device. In Act II, scene 2, Laura tells Albert of her apparition. Laura's father appeared to her, and has threatened to avenge his daughter. Laura begs the womanizer to marry her and to give her son a name. De Courcy is no ghost, and when Albert discovers this, he makes plans to run away.

In the third act De Courcy confronts Lord and Lady Albert; the coward then flees. The fourth act is a rehash of the wrongs done innocent parties. The fifth act consists of the meting out of the punishment for perfidy. Albert is about to shoot himself, but De Courcy prevents him from pulling the trigger. Laura rushes in and stabs the father of her child, then kills herself. MacLaurin executed this melodramatic

surprise with *éclat*. What makes the play distinctive is its treatment of
Albert. He is antihero rather than villain. The weak and foolish noble
is not entirely unsympathetic. As a man with a past which destroys
his present, Lord Albert may be considered a relative of the Byronic
protagonist.

Colin MacLaurin possessed skill as a story teller, but his chief talent
may have been comedy rather than cliff hangers. (Also, MacLaurin
collaborated with Sir Alexander Boswell on *The Songs in the Justiciary
Opera. Composed Fifty Years Ago*, which was published in 1816 at the
new press at Auchinleck. The script, an antiquarian imitation of early
ballad opera, deals with a trial for theft. The courtroom proceedings
may have been based upon James Boswell's winning an acquittal for
John Reid, a sheep thief who was tried before the Justiciary in 1767.)[16]

James Grahame, like Colin MacLaurin, was an advocate who pursued literary interests. Grahame left law to become an Episcopal
minister. Today, Grahame is better known as one of the authors at
whom Byron sneered in *English Bards and Scotch Reviewers* than for
the poetry he modeled after Thomson.[17] In 1799 Grahame had six
copies of *Wallace* printed. The play is a good example of the nationalist
theme lightened gracefully by tender romance. As the play opens Wallace admonishes the Scottish chiefs to unite against the common foe.
Tension mounts in the ranks of the clans for some feel that siding with
England is expedient. In the love affair of Margaret with Wallace there
is accord. They profess their affection while outside the tent of Monteith, the leader who also loves the maid of Hexeldham. Monteith
capitulates to the English side at Comyn's suggestion, for Monteith is
as power hungry as he is jealous of Wallace.

The second act opens at Edward's camp, where Bishop Durham, a
warmonger, assures the monarch of victory. In the first of a series of
short scenes of the Shakespearean panoramic order, two English senti-
nels express their lack of sympathy with the fight, and mention episcopal coercion of tenants who were made to send one son to battle. The
third scene shifts to the Scots' encampment, where Rougecroix delivers
Edward's offer of clemency for all but the leaders. Wallace gives his
permission for the messenger to spread the news through the camp,
but Rougecroix leaves after Highlanders insult him. The remaining five
scenes of the act flash with actions in the field. Wallace is wounded;
Comyn withdraws; De Graham is killed.

16   Pottle, *James Boswell, The Earlier Years 1740–1769*, pp. 308–09.
17   W. L. Renwick, *English Literature 1789–1815*, vol. 9, *Oxford History of English Literature* (Oxford, 1963), pp. 225–27, considers James Grahame's poetry.

The Reverend James Grahame (1765–1811).

Suspense slackens after the second act, for the Scottish cause is lost. A notable exchange between Robert De Bruce and the hero does occur, which makes the hero more human. De Bruce suggests that ambition rather than Edward's tyranny drives the leader to carry on a hopeless cause. Later in the third act, when Eleanor pleads for De Graham's corpse, Edward is indifferent. Eleanor then leaps from a cliff. Bishop Beck, who denies the woman last rites and recommends burial "in a public way with stake transfixed," shows greater cruelty than the King, who has Eleanor properly interred.

In the fourth act, Monteith betrays Wallace to the English, and in the catastrophe the fettered lovers, Wallace and Margaret, die in the Tower of London. The denouement, the death of Monteith, is the kind of touch which exhibits Grahame's strength. Monteith despairs upon hearing Scottish music, because the traitor can never again return to the land of the bagpipes. While he is disconsolate, the people who have watched the execution of the lovers are so moved that they go after the Judas responsible for the decapitations. Monteith, still concerned with power and panoply, mistakes the mob for the King's entourage, and the play ends as he runs to meet the crowd.

In 1801 Grahame published *Mary Stewart, Queen of Scots*, a second dramatic popularization of Scottish history. He added fictitious characters, such as the burgesses who speak broad Scots, and juggled the order of historical events to focus upon Elizabeth's cruelty to Mary. To substantiate his treatment of historical material, Grahame cited a number of sources at the end of this play, many of which he included to defend his portrayal of Knox as dour and unbending.

There are a number of human touches in the drama. Cecil convinces Elizabeth not to free Mary before Melvil pleads for her release. Mary's ambassador is less than diplomatic in his request for her freedom. His love for the Scots Queen clouds his perceptivity. Melvil praises Mary's beauty and abilities to the obvious annoyance of the vain Elizabeth.

Grahame was equally adroit in treating Mary's effort to save her companion's love, Douglas. After the Queen fails and Adelaide dies at the news of the death of Douglas, Mary expresses her disappointment with regal reserve:

> Bereave me miserable, if not of life,
> Of reason, dash down the conscious power and make
> My soul a dream without an interval.

> (V. 4)

Professor William Richardson read his pseudo-historic drama *The Maid of Lochlin* to a Glasgow College literary society several years before the play taken from *Fingal* was published in 1801. The description of the lyrics in the advertisement as expressions of "extreme emotion, marking, the diversity of their structure, the great earnestness or agitation of the speaker," indicates the concern with psychology. This introspective penchant is more observable in the works of Joanna Baillie, yet it manifested itself in plays by Scottish romantics years before the spinster wrote *Plays on the Passions*.

The Maid of Lochlin, Agandecca, is the central figure in Richardson's Ossianic play, which owes something to French neoclassic tragedy in its preoccupation with love versus honor. In her anguish over the options of marrying the noble Fingal or the vengeful Starno, Agandecca loses passion. Rather than a tragic flaw inherent in her character, this amatory deficiency is a temporary state. Richardson expresses the psychological dispositions in poetic interruptions inspired by Shakespeare, whom the humanities professor at Glasgow was more adept at criticizing than imitating.[18]

Richardson was proficient in his use of pageantry. The grand scene, incorporating banner waving, martial music, and choruses, had been used by other Scots, among them Mylne and Logan, but Richardson possessed a better sense of timing, and his grand entrances are as dramatic as they are spectacular. The confrontation of Fingal and Starno, which precipitates Agandecca's suicide, is weak. Richardson's expansive displays are superior to his presentation of intrigues that bring about the heroine's death. *The Maid of Lochlin* is derivative, but it is more mature in concept than his earlier dramatic poem *The Indians*.

In 1799 Walter Scott published the fifth German play he had translated, *Goetz of Berlichingen With the Iron Hand*.[19] Goethe's tragedy had unleashed *Sturm und Drang* in European theatre. The translation of the play, about the historical character who lost his right hand for violation of Maximillian's ordinance against dueling, earned Scott his first twenty-five pounds as a writer.

18 William Richardson's moralizing psychological analyses *Essays on Shakespeare's Dramatic Characters of Mac Beth, Hamlet, Jaques, and Imogen* (1785), and *Essays on Shakespeare's Dramatic Character of Sir John Falstaff and on His Imitation of Female Characters* (1789), are exercises "no less adapted to improve the heart, than to inform the understanding." The frame of sensibility in which Richardson places all of his criticism does not impede his recognition of the characters he treats as unique individuals. It is his emphasis upon the personal that distinguishes his criticism.
19 Paul M. Ochojski, "Sir Walter Scott's Continuous Interest in Germany," *Studies in Scottish Literature* 3 (1966):164–66.

Scott's later contribution to the theatre consists of providing material which was adapted from his novels for theatrical presentation. The most notable of the Waverley novels recast for the stage was *Rob Roy*. The author's actor friend, Daniel Terry, had written a dramatic version of *Guy Mannering* in 1817, and he also wrote a version of *Rob Roy*. The Isaac Pocock treatment of *Rob Roy MacGregor, or Auld Lang Syne*, which opened on 15 February 1819, was so popular that it filled the Edinburgh Theatre Royal for forty-one consecutive nights. The play and the concern for national identity coincided. The reviewer in the 20 February 1819 issue of *The Scotsman* asked rhetorically: "Why should we not be proud of our National genius, humour, music, kindness and fidelity?—*why not be national?* We found ourselves pre-eminently so on Monday evening."

Scott's novels and poems provided inspiration for composers as well as dramatists.[20] Musicians as diverse as Donizetti and Berlioz strove to interpret the feeling of the mist-shrouded hills. Robert Schumann in a review of Berlioz's *Grand Ouverture de Waverley* in *Neue Zeitschrift für Musik* described the master of program music as the "Mephistopheles of music at the crackling fire of a Scottish manor house among hunters, hounds and smiling country maidens." Few of the Waverley adaptations for the stage and concert hall retain the native heath quality which made Scott's novels popular.

The manifestation of national consciousness which Scott epitomizes had its beginnings in the eighteenth century. The Scottish accomplishment made Edinburgh a center of the Enlightenment. This contributing factor in the upsurge of national pride resulted from the realistic attitude that characterizes the Common Sense School. The canny faculty in the native temperament contributed feats of engineering and architecture, as well as sagacity in philosophy and economics. It was the untamed romanticism, which coexists in the national temper, that manifested itself in serious drama in the eighteenth century. When the realistic strain appeared it was in the lighter vein.

Scottish dialect and custom were invariably used for comic purposes, and followed the Southern practice of exaggeration. In urging Joanna Baillie to see Charles Mackay play Baillie Nichol Jarvie in a Covent Garden production of *Rob Roy*, Sir Walter Scott, who thought Mackay's characterization possessed "truth and comic effect at the same time," advised: "I pray you collect a party of Scotch friends to see it. . . .

---

20   See Henry A. White, *Sir Walter Scott's Novels on the Stage* (New Haven, 1927); Terence Tobin, "Scott's Plaid at the Opera," *Music Journal* 27 (1969):48 ff.

I doubt whether the exhibition will prove as satisfactory to those who do not know the original from whom the resemblance is taken. I observe the English demand, as is natural, broad caricature in depicting of national peculiarities."[21]

21   *The Letters of Sir Walter Scott* (London, 1934), 6:465. Dibdin, *Annals of the Edinburgh Stage*, p. 89, provides a number of interesting documents connected with the Edinburgh performances of *Rob Roy*.

SECOND NIGHT.

THEATRE CANONGATE,
THIS EVENING,
Being 15th DECEMBER 1756,
A CONCERT OF MUSIC.

After which will be prefented (*gratis*)

The NEW TRAGEDY

DOUGLAS.

Taken from an Ancient *SCOTS* STORY,

AND

Writ by a GENTLEMAN of SCOTLAND.

The Principal PARTS to be performed

By Mr. DIGGES;
Mr. LOVE,
Mr HEYMAN,
Mr YOUNGER,
Mrs. HOPKINS,
And Mrs. WARD.

With NEW *DRESSES* and *DECORATIONS*.

A PROLOGUE to be fpoke

By Mr. DIGGES,

And an EPILOGUE to be fpoke

By Mrs. HOPKINS.

Between the ACTS will be performed Select PIECES of

OLD *SCOTS* MUSICK.

AS fome Rows in the Pit were let for the firft Night of this Play, before the Inconveniencies were properly confidered, of admitting Places to be taken there, when a Number of Perfons might reafonably expect the Chance of Seats. It is thought proper to advertife, that in the Run of this Play, no Benches in the Pit will be allowed again to be kept for any particular Company.

This Play will be prefented every Night this Week, and NO MORE THIS SEASON: And as a Report has prevail'd that there are no Places in the Boxes to be had, this Notice is given, that there are Upper Boxes to be let for this Night and *Thurfday*, and fome of the Lower Boxes, as well as Upper, are unlet for *Friday* and *Saturday*.

As many Gentlemen have at Times requefted Entrance into the two fmall Balconies upon the Stage, over the Stage Door; Notice is hereby given, that the Decency of the Drama abfolutely obliges fuch Liberty to be refufed to any one, fince by it the Scenes may poffibly be interrupted.

None but Tickets printed for the Occafion will be taken at the Door.
The Doors to be opened at Five, and to begin precifely at Six o'Clock.

To-morrow, The THIRD NIGHT, DOUGLAS.

Douglas. Second Night Playbill, 15 December 1756.

The Edinburgh Theatre

Whether drawing from past glories in national history or concocting farces about Jemmy and Jenny, Scots rarely intended their plays for Scottish theatrical production. Home, Marshall, Mackenzie, Mickle, and others settled for local production or publication as a last resort. In a period when a successful drama was synonymous with a London premiere, the more able writers submitted manuscripts in England. Consideration of the management of the Scottish stage during the Restoration and eighteenth century, when players rather than playwrights dominated, aids our understanding the propulsion to seek London production.[1] *Qualis rex talis Græcs* applies as a criterion when managers solicit manuscripts. Few managers of the Edinburgh theatre evinced taste that approached the discriminating, and no evidence substantiates that the management ever actively sought new plays from Scottish writers. Those in charge usually relied upon material which had been commercially rewarding in the South. Voluminous litigation underscores the financial troubles which plagued the Scottish stage. In 1768 the Theatre Royal in Shakespeare Square realized only £140 from a full house. The Canongate house brought in £80. Managers relied upon favorites such as *Macbeth*, *The Beggar's Opera*, and *Venice Preserved* to cover costs. Several plays by Scots did enter the Northern repertory, but these pieces were also popular in London.

Cryptic notices indicate that Clerke's *Marciano* was an amateur production. Thomas St. Serfe, who staged his own comedy, *Tarugo's Wiles*, managed an acting group. Robert Clerk, Stephen Grege, and James Underwood probably handled troupes during the seventeenth century. Prior to 1678, when T. Gray, C. Goodman, and other actors from the London Theatre Royal came North, no record of performers exists. Actors who achieved fame did not journey to Scotland until the

1 Jack Mackenzie, "A Study of Eighteenth Century Drama in Scotland (1660–1760)," (Ph.D. diss., University of St. Andrews, 1955), updates and amplifies source material on the management of the Edinburgh theatre found in Dibdin's *Annals of the Edinburgh Stage*.

eighteenth century. Dramatic presentations by strolling players were occasional and haphazard.

Theatrical activity which can be dignified with the term *season* occurred when Anthony Aston brought a road company to Edinburgh from England about 1724. Aston, who battled intermittently with the magistracy, departed shortly after he took his actors on tour to Glasgow in August 1728. Some of these thespians may have remained there or returned to England. The *Edinburgh Courant* of 13 March 1729 reports: "The Scots Company of Comedians, as they call'd themselves, have all on a Sudden, elopt, without counting with their Creditors." Financially unprofitable visits to Scotland caused many actors to exit the country stealthily, leaving rock-filled trunks behind to the consternation of irate landladies.

Allan Ramsay managed the Edinburgh Players from 1730–37. During his often frustrating term he was forced to combat countrymen convinced that he was involved in the "deil's wark." Ramsay presented dramas which had been hits in London. Restoration plays, contemporary pieces, and Shakespearean revivals comprised the bulk of the repertory throughout the eighteenth century. Ramsay probably produced Thomson's *Disappointed Gallant*, since the cast list printed with the play contains names known to have been those of Edinburgh Players. After the Licensing Act, Ramsay tried to present shows during 1738–39, but he was stopped by the authorities.[2] Thomas Este was more adept at evading the law. He managed the Edinburgh theatre from 1741–45, and used the admission-for-concert-free-play technique.

Este's obituary in the *Caledonian Mercury* for 12 February 1745 states that he was one of the managers of Taylors Hall. The *Edinburgh Courant*, 3 August 1747, lists Concert Hall managers: Henry Thomson,[3] John Hamilton, William Lyon, Henry Ward, Edward Huide, Edward Davenport, and William Berry. This group produced Lyon's *Wrangling Lovers*, mounted the first Scottish production of Thomson's *Tancred and Sigismunda*, and incorporated Ramsay's *The Gentle Shepherd* in the repertory.

Multiple management by actors gave rise to squabbles. Salmon,

2   The Yule Collection, Ms. 3134 (NLS), contains letters which indicate that Ramsay's troupe played Newcastle and probably Scarborough in 1738. Ramsay applied for a patent in 1739; he ran into financial problems resulting from his efforts to make his theatre a legal operation. See *Caledonian Mercury* 4 April 1739.
3   Henry Thomson is also referred to as Alen or Ben Thomson in documents of the period. Alen Thomson proposed a subscription publication in an *Edinburgh Courant* advertisement 3 April 1759: "An Historical Account of the Stage in Edinburgh and the Management thereof from the building of the theatre in Carrubber's Close in 1736, (being then under the direction of the late ingenious Mr Allan Ramsay) to the conclusion of the season." This project was never completed.

a performer who had been turned out of the Concert Hall group, resumed his craft at Taylors Hall. The others built a better theatre in the Canongate. John Ryan of Covent Garden played Edinburgh from 10 July to 14 August 1747. Ryan, who laid the cornerstone of the new playhouse on 3 August was the first of a series of well-known visiting players who came from London in the off season and provided variety in theatrical offerings. Salmon had financial difficulties maintaining Taylors Hall; in 1748 he reconciled with the Canongate company.

Thomas Davies, who introduced Boswell to Johnson, purchased title to the Canongate Concert Hall on 24 September 1750. Davies and Thomson brought in better actors, but they demanded more money than the operation could bring in from ticket sales. In 1752, Thomson disposed of the management to Charles Storer, who took over the operation for several months. Then in the summer of 1752 John Lee of Covent Garden became manager.[4] Lee, who ran the playhouse from

4 John Lee may have tried out some of his pieces in North Britain during the 1750s, but no recorded performances have been discovered. The *Biographia Dramatica* describes Lee's Shakespearean adaptations as literary murders.

It was unusual for a writer who was not Scottish to have a play open in the Northern capital. David Erskine Baker, whose translation of *La Serva Padrona*, presented 21 June 1763, introduced Italianate musicals to the North, wrote a three-act drama based on Macpherson, which did open in Edinburgh. *The Muse of Ossian . . . Selected from the Several Poems of Ossian the Son of Fingal* premiered in December 1763. The play deals with a sentimental princess involved with warriors who prowl about a setting of supposititious antiquity. All declaim love of solitude and portray "elemental" emotions. George Anne Bellamy explains how this rare presentation occurred: "Whilst I was at Edinburgh, I had prevailed upon a gentleman, who was possessed of some talents, to compile a little piece from the celebrated poem of Ossian; and I appeared in the character of Commela, there, with great success. But at Glasgow the applause I received was beyond all bounds. This little piece alone, tacked to any indifferent comedy, would fill the house." From *An Apology for the Life of George Anne Bellamy* (London, 1785), 4:18. See 3:208–16 for Mrs. Bellamy's entertaining account of her first experiences in Scotland.

John Shomberg, a physician, bled *The Rival Queens* for a two-act burlesque, *The Death of Bucephalus*. This unsuccessful piece, which concluded with "a funeral procession, accompanied by a solemn dirge," opened 2 March 1765, the night after Edinburgh witnessed Dryden's portrayal of the triumphant entry of Alexander into Babylon. Baker and others who note the existence of Shomberg's comedy are scathing.

William Woods, an English-born actor who played character roles during his many years at the Edinburgh Theatre Royal, wrote plays for the company. These include: "The Highlander's Return," an interlude presented 31 March 1777 (*Edinburgh Courant* 26 March 1777); "The Volunteers," a farce presented 19 March 1778 (*Edinburgh Courant* 11 March 1778). The title was expanded to "The Volunteers; or, Britons strike Home" when the piece was staged at Hull in 1778. *The Twins; or, Which Is Which? . . . Altered from the Comedy of Errors by William Shakespeare* opened 27 March 1780 (*Edinburgh Courant* 20 March 1780), and was published in Edinburgh the same year. Woods probably wrote other light works which have yet to be identified.

1752–56 found the management poor on his arrival. In *Mr. Lee's Address to the Public* (1767), and *A Narrative of a Remarkable Breach of Trust, etc.* (1772), Lee is scathing in his estimation of his predecessors. The disgruntled state of the writer may have biased his judgment, for he was narcissistic and hot-tempered. Difficulties with Garrick had prompted his relocation to Scotland. The strong-willed manager determined to upgrade the company at Canongate Concert Hall. To entice strong performers—Mr. and Mrs. Love, Mr. and Mrs. Stamper, Mr. Griffith and Mrs. Ward—Lee offered year-round salaries. The theatre season ran November through March, and for several weeks in summer. To make this arrangement financially feasible the players had to go on tour.[5] This aided actors who advertised continually in newspapers for elocution students, in order to supplement their incomes when the theatre closed.

Lee remodeled the Canongate Concert Hall, refurbished the sets, and improved the stock of costumes and props. The expenditures exceeded the profits. The summer tour of 1754 lost £500. To prevent vendors' foreclosures, Lee extended partnership to a group of patrons: Lord Patrick Elibank, Andrew Pringle of Alemoor, Thomas Miller, George Brown of Coalston, James Burnett of Monboddo, James Veitch of Elliock, Patrick Home, David Ross, David Stuart Moncrieffe, David Kennedy, Sir John Dalrymple, George Morison, William Alston, Alexander Maxwell, and James Callender. The backers were skilled at financial maneuvers and determined to realize profits. Lee was concerned with the stage rather than the box office. The manager produced Hart's *Herminius and Espasia,* revived *Tancred and Sigismunda,* and *The Gentle Shepherd.*

Lee prohibited on-stage seating, refused to reduce admission for part of the performance, and experimented with staging. He kept running into debt. The patrons hired West Digges to replace him as manager. They then took possession of the playhouse on 23 February 1756, confiscated Lee's goods, turned his two children out of their home, and imprisoned the hapless actor.

Digges, who served as manager from 1756–59, was a handsome

---

5   When playing Scottish towns outside the capital the company, on occasion, offered plays by native authors. *Tancred and Sigismunda* was presented in Glasgow on 25 May 1751 (*Glasgow Journal* 14 May 1751); *The Gentle Shepherd* was performed in Berwick in 1761 (Jack MacKenzie, p. 336); Archibald MacLaren's *Siege of Perth* was given by Sutherland's company in Glovers Hall Theatre, Perth, in 1792 (Lawson, p. 251). Road performances were mainly London successes, for small town audiences usually prefer to see entertainments which are popular in cities.

descendant of gentry. He possessed an engaging personality, few moral scruples, and less business sense. Lord Elibank and company engaged Callender, a merchant in their circle, to handle the business details of the theatre. Digges was attuned to theatrical advertising and promotion, and the announcements he placed in newspapers indicate that he followed the London trend toward more authentic costuming. Samuel Foote described Digges, who played Wolsey in a 1758 production, attired in black and gilt leather, as "a Roman chimney-sweep on Mayday."[6] Digges hired William de la Cour to paint sets. He launched *Douglas*, and gave the Scottish productions of *Agis* and *The Reprisal* as well as the popular *Tancred and Sigismunda* and *The Gentle Shepherd*.

During his Edinburgh management tenure, Digges formed a liaison with Sarah Ward. *Letters which passed between Mr. West Digges, Comedian and Mrs. Sarah Ward, 1752–1759* (1833), indicates that the more shabbily the manager treated his mistress the more affection she displayed. The letters illumine Digges's dismissal from the Canongate in August 1758. Digges had fallen behind on salary payments, as the musicians' strike of 1758 illustrates. He fought continually with James Callender and David Beatt (Beat? Bates?), who had joined the management team; usually the differences arose over money. Beatt became sole manager in 1759, and he and James Dawson handled the commercial aspects of the enterprise until 1767. This management produced Lady Houston's *The Coquettes*. Tate Wilkinson, who played Edinburgh, notes in his *Memoirs* (1790), that Beatt and Callender engaged mediocre performers. They did, however, hire Samuel Foote to act from 15 March to 7 April 1759. The playwright-comic appeared in his own farces, which treat Scots characters kindly, as well as in repertory pieces. Foote realized such a full purse that he returned for several seasons.

Mr. Digges's Case, in regard to his present Dismission from the Theatres of Newcastle and Edinburgh (1759), substantiates the former manager's return to perform in the North. Digges who left again during the summer of 1760, clashed over contracts. Beatt, who feared that Digges would resume his post, made James Love, a member of the company, general manager. With the departure of Digges, Lee

---

6   William Donaldson, *Recollections of an Actor* (London [1865]), p. 166, reports seeing an 1805 performance of *Macbeth* in which the Thane of Cawdor dressed in a red coat, blue pants, Hessian boots, and a cocked hat. Anecdotes about makeshift and bizarre costumes abound in Scottish theatrical lore.

returned to play leading roles. Love produced Erskine's *She's Not Him*, and revived *The Gentle Shepherd* and *Douglas*.

The *Edinburgh Courant* for 1 May 1762 announced the arrival of George Anne Bellamy, whose first appearance in Scotland was in *Tancred and Sigismunda*. The actress's notoriety filled seats. Edinburgensians were treated to the kind of scandal that sells tickets to those who do not regularly attend performances. Digges returned for the 1762 season, took up residence with the actress, and shortly thereafter was billed as Mr. Bellamy. When Mrs. Bellamy left in 1764, the pair had run up sufficient debts to keep the name resounding in the law courts.

George Stayley, an actor who was popular with the small core of regular theatrophiles if not the management, supported John Lee in applying for the theatrical patent. Dawson and other solicitors supported David Ross, who obtained it. The patentee came from Covent Garden; he modeled administration of the Theatre Royal, Edinburgh, on the London patent houses. Under his management the theatre in Shakespeare Square was constructed. Ross, who ran the theatre from 1767–81, first produced Mackenzie's *Prince of Tunis*, and Woods's farces. He also staged *The Gentle Shepherd* and the reliable *Douglas*.

Ross tried to make the theatre pay by bringing in famous actors and actresses, and by leasing the playhouse. For the Edinburgh Race Week in 1773, Ross presented Ned Suter, the comedian. Because the London season was slack in July, Miss Young ventured from Drury Lane for race week in 1775. Despite engagements by players such as Mrs. Hartley, Mrs. Inchbald, and the Barrys, the Theatre Royal remained in financial trouble. In 1770 Ross leased the playhouse to Samuel Foote, who brought his Haymarket company North for the winter when the London house was closed. Ross rented the premises to George Stayley in 1771, who presented *Metraphrastus, or the Wrangling Lovers*. Tate Wilkinson was tenant for the summer of 1780, and Ross entered into partnership with Mr. Heapy for the winter season. In 1781 Ross fled to London with the receipts. Wilkinson took charge of the theatre for race week, when John Kemble was the featured player.

John Jackson, who first appeared in Edinburgh in 1761, claims to have purchased the managerial rights from Ross on 10 November 1781. Lee Lewes in his *Memoirs* (1805), says that Jackson obtained a judgment against Ross for back wages and settled with the bankrupt proprietor by securing the managership. Jackson, who managed the Theatre Royal from 1781–92 and from 1801–09, reveals himself in his *History of the Scottish Stage* (1793) to be an individual who made up in ego what he lacked in talent, but he did contribute to the theatre he

La. RAN. Eternal providence ! What is thy name ?
My name is NORVAL : and my name he bears.

Mrs. Woods, Mrs. Siddons, and Mr. Sutherland performing in *Douglas* at the Theatre Royal, Edinburgh, 1 June 1784.

managed. He repaired the structure and replaced properties. The year after he took charge, Jackson opened the Theatre Royal in Glasgow's Dunlap Street on 9 January 1782. This first link in a chain of theatres was to provide actors work for the full year. He tried to extend the circuit but failed because he lacked capital.

Jackson produced Logan's *Runnemede*, his own *Eldred*, "Wallace" and "Tony Lumpkin's Rambles Through Edinburgh." He staged a number of original farces and afterpieces, mounted MacDonald's *Vimonda* for the first time in Scotland, and treated Edinburgh to a production of *Douglas* starring Sarah Siddons as Lady Randolph.

From the audience's point of view Jackson's greatest achievement was engaging Mrs. Siddons for a nine-performance run in 1783. Her first visit to the Scottish capital was so triumphant that the General Assembly reputedly had to reschedule its hours of meeting to draw members to the sessions. Such crowds flocked to see the greatest actress of her generation that London thieves trekked North to pick Scottish pockets. The spectators were enthusiastic in a peculiarly Scottish fashion. Thomas Campbell recounts the opening night performance of Mrs. Siddons in *Venice Preserved:*

> The grave attention of my Scottish countrymen and their canny reservation of praise till they were sure she deserved it, had well nigh worn out her patience. She had been used to speak to animated clay; but now she felt as she had been speaking to stones. Successive flashes of her elocution, that had always been sure to electrify the south, fell in vain on these northern flints. . . . she coiled up all her powers to the most emphatic possible utterance of one passage, having previously vowed in her heart that if *this* could not touch the Scotch, she would never again cross the Tweed. When it was finished, she paused, and looked to the audience. The deep silence was broken only by one voice exclaiming, *"That's no'bad!"* This ludicrous parsimony of praise convulsed the Edinburgh audience with laughter. But the laugh was followed by such thunders of applause that, amidst her stunned and nervous agitation, she was not without fear of the galleries coming down.[7]

Mrs. Siddons returned to Edinburgh for two other engagements during Jackson's first term as manager, but patronage of the playhouse was generally poor. Deficit spending soon bankrupted Jackson. The first patent expired on 29 September 1788. Jackson applied for the new patent as sole proprietor. Twenty-five people declared themselves joint

7 Thomas Campbell, *Life of Sarah Siddons* (London, 1834), 1:259–60.

shareholders. The Duke of Hamilton and Henry Dundas became trustees of the patent with Jackson. By 1792, the manager was forced to rent out the theatre to Stephen Kemble, who then refused Jackson the premises. During his first year as proprietor, Kemble assembled a good cast and produced a number of new dramatic pieces. He employed Alexander Nasmyth, the most competent artist to work in eighteenth-century Scottish theatre, to do the scenery.

Jackson arranged to lease the Theatre Royal to Mrs. Esten in 1793. Kemble was forced to move his troupe to the newly built Royal Circus in Leith Walk. Authorities shut the Circus down on 6 February 1793 on the grounds that it violated the Licensing Act. Kemble reopened the theatre on 2 March; he used the concert ploy and even staged a ridotto and a *fête champêtre* to keep receipts coming in. On 11 January 1794, Kemble moved back to the playhouse in Shakespeare Square. He included *Douglas* in almost every season of the 1790s, revived Smollett's *Reprisal*, and staged local comedies, among them Heron's *St. Kilda in Edinburgh*. Kemble presented Sarah Siddons, the Northern debut of Henry Erskine Johnston, the Scottish Roscius, and other players of note, but his casts weakened with each season. During Kemble's farewell speech, 30 July 1800, he was hissed off the stage. Jackson in partnership with Aickin resumed management the next season.

Professional characteristics increased markedly during the late 1700s, but the Scottish stage remained a provincial operation. For playwrights, the greatest opportunities for recognition waited in London. James Barrie, in "Courage: Rectorial Address at St. Andrew's," on 3 May 1922, said: "The greatest glory that has ever come to me was to be swallowed up in London, not knowing a soul, with no means of subsistence, and the fun of working till the stars went out. To have known any one would have spoilt it. I did not even quite know the language." He expressed the dreams of many antecedent dramatists.

SCOTS ABROAD

1660-1800

SCOTS ABROAD   1660-1725

In a land so devoid of entertainment that the first masters of revels resorted to requiring licenses for dancing school socials, kyle allies, and tavern card games to recoup the expenditure of the patent,[1] Scottish playwrights were well advised to go to England. During the Restoration and early eighteenth century, rigid Northern laurels who transplanted bent to Southern willows. A Scot abroad in the theatrical world was an anomaly. His speech was strange. Both established and obscure authors endured much abuse for their craft. The light pieces Scots contributed to the London stage were imitative of more popular English comedies of the day. Whatever quality the play, Southern audiences were disposed to scoff at the work because of the writer's origin, for Samuel Johnson was not singular in his prejudice against the hyperborean "barbarians."

During the reign of Charles II, Thomas St. Serfe was the only Northerner who contributed to the London stage. Samuel Pepys went to Lincoln's Inn Fields for the opening of *Tarugo's Wiles, or the Coffee House* on 5 October 1667, but the playhouse was so crowded he was unable to obtain a seat. Pepys saw a later performance and he thought the comedy insipid. John Downes also gave the play, which "expir'd the third day," an unfavorable notice.[2]

St. Serfe's comedy is indebted to Spanish romance, a genre popular with his audience, but the author was not adept at creating scathing witticisms theatre patrons could remember for future use in devastating conversation. *Tarugo's Wiles* is silly rather than scintillating.

1 Terence Tobin, "The First Scottish Masters of Revels: Comptrollers of Popular Entertainment," *Theatre Survey* 9 (1968):65–71.
2 John Downes, *Roscius Anglicanus, or an Historical View of the Stage*, ed. Montague Summers (London, 1928), p. 31. E. L. Avery, et al., *The London Stage, 1660–1800*, 11 vols. (Carbondale, 1965), is the source for all London performances, unless otherwise recorded.

Augustin Moreto y Cabaña's *No puede ser* is St. Serfe's source. *No puede ser*, a more polished version of *El Mayor impossible* by Moreto's patron Lope de Vega, has the sophistication Restoration crowds loved. Charles II advised John Crowne to use *No puede ser* as a point of departure. He followed the monarch's suggestion and wrote *Sir Courtly Nice* (1685). The English writer did not realize that the Scot's play existed until he had completed three acts of his most famous comedy.[3] Crowne did not have to worry about duplication because his invention is far superior to that of his predecessor. The imitative English coffee-house scene St. Serfe inserted in the midst of his comedy set in Spain exhibits the dramatist's limitations. When compared to Sir George Etherege's *The Comical Revenge; or Love in a Tub* (1664), which incorporates the London parade skillfully, the Scot's attempt to put town types on review is ragged.

Tarugo's Wiles involves two pairs of lovers, Lavinia and Horatio and Patrucio and Sophronia, whom Tarugo, the catalyst, helps by disguise and puckish trickery. After the wily one poses as Hurtante the tailor in order to further Horatio's pursuit, the coffeehouse scene intervenes. Ladies and their maids, swains, tradesmen, and scholars provide a panorama of fashions and foibles. The coffee master exchanges remarks with these characters on items in the gazette which are topical but not incisive. The scene ends with a feeble debate on art versus science.

After the coffeehouse intrusion Tarugo once more dons a disguise to aid Lavinia. Posing as Don Crisanto, a Peruvian merchant, Tarugo plots against Lavinia's brother, Patrucio, who has chosen Roderigo to be his sister's husband. In the final scene Patrucio is reconciled to the union of Lavinia and Horatio. Sophronia will marry Patrucio, and the instigator of the happy matches will receive an army commission for his efforts.

When *Tarugo's Wiles* was printed in 1668, the Earl of Dorset composed an adulatory poem in honor of the occasion:

> Tarugo gave us wonder and delight,
> When he obliged the world by candle-light.
> But now he's ventured on the face of day,
> T' oblige and serve his friends a nobler way!

3 Montague Summers, *The Playhouse of Pepys* (New York, 1964), p. 380. Also see Montague Summers, "Introduction," *Restoration Comedies* (New York, 1962), pp. xxxviii–xliii.

Make all our old men wits, statesmen the young,
And teach ev'n English men the English tongue . . .[4]

Rather than following the noble's advice, St. Serfe did not remain to teach Englishmen; he returned home and pursued a career as a manager of theatricals.

George Lesly,[5] the Vicar of Olney, put religious instruction into dramatic structure. *Abraham's Faith* (ca. 1675) which the minister labeled a tragicomedy, is a morality. Faith, Flesh, Despair, a Devil, and a Midwife appear in the story of the prophet's dilemma, which arises when God commands Abraham to sacrifice Isaac. Lesly's *Fire and Brimstone; or, the destruction of Sodom* (1675), was revised as was *Abraham's Faith;* both were reprinted in *Divine Dialogues* (1684). This book also contains *Dives's Doom,* which recounts the antagonism of the rich man for Lazarus.

Robert Fleming the Younger published *The Monarchical Image: or, Nebuchadnezzar's Dream,* a "Dramatique Poem" in heroic couplets, based upon the second chapter of Daniel. Fleming included this religious work with Jacobite undertones in *The Mirrour of Divine Love Unvail'd* (1691).

In the last year of the century, David Craufurd (Crawford) succeeded in having *Courtship A-la-mode* accepted for presentation. The comedy, which premiered at Drury Lane on 9 July 1700, contains a preface in which the author recounts the tribulations that arose when he submitted his comedy to Thomas Betterton's company at Lincoln's Inn Fields before he eventually took his work to Christopher Rich at the more reliable playhouse in Drury Lane. Craufurd does not berate Betterton, but laments the substandard quality of other members of the troupe. According to the author, John Bowman, who was to play the lead, had the part six weeks and "then cou'd hardly read six lines on't." Bowman and others were negligent in attending rehearsals, which must have been chaotic, since "six or seven people cou'd not perform what was design'd for fifteen." Colley Cibber in his *Apology* corroborates Craufurd's low opinion of Lincoln's Inn Fields. Cibber alleges that Betterton's players had become lax, and that the manager

---

4 "To my Friend Master Thos. St. Serfe," in Montague Summers, ed., *Covent Garden Drollery* (London, 1927), pp. 65–66. Summers attributes this poem, which appeared anonymously in J. Tonson's *Miscellanies* (1703), to the Earl of Dorset.
5 An untitled paragraph in *Notes and Queries,* 5th ser., 7 (1879):308, establishes the Scottish heritage of the divine, who pleads in the preface to *Divine Dialogues* for the Earl of Westmoreland's patronage "not that I think it worthy your lordship's acceptance, being the frozen conception of one born in a cold climate . . . ."

unsuccessfully turned to novelties in an attempt to compensate for his group's inadequacies.[6]

Less than twenty days after Craufurd took his script to Rich, *Courtship A-la-mode* was on the boards. Fledgling playwrights frequently try to emulate the offspring of established dramatists. Craufurd's treatment of youth struggling against age and emerging victorious in love is reminiscent of Dryden and Etherege. As *Courtship* opens, Sir John Winmore, like Dorimant, is tiring of Lucy, his stale mistress. Sir John converses with his man Scowrer on love and the ladies. The clever servant is quicker than his master. Dismissing the prurient Scowrer, Sir John greets Captain Bellair, who has come from the country to win Flora, the daughter of Sir Anthony Addle. Winmore promises to abet Bellair by introducing him to Decoy, the matchmaker, "a Medea whose cunning Arts shall blind the old Dragon." Testy old Alderman Chollerick's nephew Ned enters to discuss with Bellair the conquest of Flora. They are joined by Freelove who tells of his latest amorous mishap. Ned warns Bellair of the dangers in courting Flora, which he says is "a voyage into *terra incognita.*"

The next scene, a distaff conversation about love, parallels the preceding. Sophisticated Flora chats with naive Melintha, who praises Bellair. In the tradition of Restoration heroines, Flora is noncommittal. Sir Anthony interrupts the *tête-à-tête* to express his desire that Flora marry Alderman Chollerick. Decoy enters to tell Sir Anthony of Bellair's suit. As the first act closes, the matchmaker whets Freelove's appetite for the rejected Lucy.

Act two further complicates the romantic antics with the introduction of Timandra, Chollerick's niece, whom Decoy wishes to pair with Winmore. By mutual paternal consent Sir Anthony's doltish son, Dick, will court Timandra.

The last act begins with Sir John's admission that he'll "abandon his darling sins" and marry. Freelove too is matrimonially minded, because of his newest quest "Lucinda," who is really Lucy. Since he is to court the rich, witty, and beautiful Lucinda, the beau borrows Bellair's pawky footman Willie:

> *Willie*, honest *Willie*, come along *Willie*.
> WILL. Ay Sir, whaun I hae tasted the Wine, aun drunken tea yer good health.
> *Drinks.*

6   R. W. Lowe, ed., *An Apology for the Life of Colley Cibber* (London, 1888), 1:315–19.

FREE. This is unsufferable Ignorance.

Kicks him.

CAPT. Down stairs ye mangee Rake—use him thus, and then expect the effects of good breeding from him.

Exit Freelove.

WILL. Wuns whaut the maun be aut, my arse is na made of Wainscoat, baut gin I haud ye—I ken whaur, Sir—I soud mauke your head as sauft aus an—

Exit, muttering.

(III. 1)

Old Chollerick schemes to marry off his niece to the man of his choice, Dick Addle. The ill-at-ease, pedantic Dick alleges that he is a swain, using diction which parodies heroic drama. Dick prefaces his remarks with "Uds so," recalling Old Bellair's eternal "A dod."

Willie and Freelove arrive at his new master's place of assignation. Willie, who makes up in shrewdness what he lacks in finesse, cautions Freelove not to pay for Decoy's services, because "in our Kintry we never buy au meer till eans we ride upon her; pay Sir, I saw whun ye get the Lady aun be hang'd till her." Provincial though Willie may be, he is wary of Decoy's proposition that Freelove pay her ten per cent fee in advance of the marriage that promises a dowry of ten thousand pounds. The earthy servant warns Decoy: "Aun the muckle deel thuank ye for yer well pay'd for yer pains; hark ye aul woman, I hope me Maisters siller sall burn the arse out o yer purse before night, an be me saul aun ye pit au trick upon him this bred Sword sall let the Sun and Moon shine through ye like a glass-window."

Flora disdains Captain Bellair's expression of love. Freelove confesses his roguery to Lucy, and promises to be faithful in marriage. In contrast to these love scenes Willie asks Betty, Lucy's servant, if she will warm his bed and let him get bairns on her. Lucy inquires if Willie has acquired a mistress since he came to England. Their ensuing exchange has a freshness lacking in the dialogue of madcaps and repentant rakes:

WILL. Nau, Madam; baut I hea gotten ean here aun she aun I caun agree, we may come tea confirm the bargain between a pair of blankets.

BET. And what wou'd you think of making the bargain there, and confirming on't afterwards? I've a Maidenhead to dispose of, I assure ye.

WILL. Wau thaun we sall save the expences o' Kirk-fees, aun make the bargaun like our for-bearers; I sall gang in to ye aun be acquainted we ye and sua forth, we cau thaut only playing a tune without a prelude.

BET. Ay, but *Willie*, 'tis necessary the Church shou'd give us liberty to play, else we may come to pay too dear for our Musick.

(IV. 1)

The intrigue, which occurs before the ending in which the correct couples are paired and an older generation's plans are thwarted, is less heartless than Restoration antecedents. Lucy is discarded, because of Decoy's misrepresentation rather than through her own deception. The cruelty is absent, but unfortunately the vivacious repartee is missing too. With the exception of the servants' banter, the dialogue, much as it tries, lacks sparkle. Craufurd seems to have followed advice which Freelove gives the Northern servant: "Willie, you must forget Scotland, and conform yourself to the Customs of England." Craufurd's conformity did not please his audience.

RAMBLE: *Courtship Alamode,* the author, one Crawford, a Caledonian.
SULLEN: I remember it, and its Adventures; it was enter'd into the New-House, at the Recommendation of a certain Scotch Lord, and sojourning there six Months to no purpose, it travell'd afterwards to the Old-House, where it was with much ado Acted.
RAMBLE: And Damn'd—there I was in with you.[7]

In *Love at First Sight,* Craufurd repeats the expository device he used to introduce *Courtship A-la-Mode.* The master, Mr. Courtly, divulges information to his man. Mr. Courtly in his opening speech gives the play's theme, and sets the tone of Cibberesque sentimentality:

Heaven defend us! of all Plagues that attend us Mortals, this Love, this Damned Vertuous Love is sure the first; 'tis the very Cut-throat of our Ease and Pleasure, and the Highway to Ruin. For whilst we Travel in Vertue's Road, we are hiss'd at by those that think themselves Wise;— What a Miserable Age do we Live in then? when to be Lewd is to be Witty; and Vice is become the Honourable Badge of Quality.

(I. 1)

Mr. Courtly, after delivering much pseudo-epigrammatic dialogue interspersed with allusions to plays and fashions of the town, wins the sensitive Melissa, who finally sees him in his true radiant light. Courtly's friend, Mr. Lovewell, another epitome of bourgeois goodness, overcomes romantic difficulties and earns fair Fidelia. Sir Nicho-

7 S. B. Wells, ed., *A Comparison Between the Two Stages: A Late Restoration Book of the Theatre* (Princeton: 1942), pp. 104–05.

las Empty and Mr. Gripeall are foiled, and as the last homily in doggerel suggests, virtue is practical.

> All Men with equal Strength the Race begin,
> O're Toyls and Cares all Drive, all hope to Win,
> But he who constant Virtue guides comes always soonest in.
>
> (V. 2)

Craufurd's second comedy has less to offer than his first play. *Love at First Sight* premiered at Lincoln's Inn Fields on 25 March 1704 and closed after one performance. The unprepossessing reception his theatricals received caused the playwright to give up writing comedy. Craufurd became Historiographer Royal of Scotland during the reign of Queen Anne.

Newburgh Hamilton wrote two comedies for the London stage, but he is better known as the librettist for Handel's oratorio *Samson*. Hamilton's first play, *The Petticoat-Plotter*, like Craufurd's comedies, is more familiar than arresting. Hamilton uses youth versus age, disguises, and horseplay by menials, all standard ploys to provoke laughter. From these stock situations, the writer fashions rather entertaining fluff because of a penchant for physical comedy and a good sense of farcical pace.

Thrifty refuses to give his daughter Isabella's hand to True-love; he wants her to marry the aged Sir Simon Scrape-all. The petticoat plotter is Plotwell, True-love's servant. This retainer disguises as a Spanish woman to gain entrée to Thrifty's house. The materialistic father believes Plotwell to be Theodosia, who has lived with Thrifty's late brother.

True-love also covers his identity. He poses as Ananias Scribe, but is unmasked when the real Scribe arrives on the scene. True-love and a parson gain entry into the Thrifty household by having themselves delivered in two chests. Once inside Plotwell ties Sir Simon and Nicompoop, a dull servant, together and puts them out in the street. This machination enables the lovers to be married.

The Petticoat-Plotter opened at Drury Lane on 5 June 1712. Six years later Susan Centlivre borrowed some of Hamilton's brisk business for her 1718 hit, *A Bold Stroke for a Wife*.

Hamilton's next contribution to the theatre, *The Doating Lovers, or the Libertine Tam'd*, premiered at Lincoln's Inn Fields on 23 June 1715. According to the *Biographia Dramatica*, the comedy "met with no approbation from the unbiased part of the audience, but was sup-

The Doating Lovers (1715) by Newburgh Hamilton.

ported to the third night, when, for the author's benefit, the boxes and pit were laid together at the extraordinary price of six shillings each ticket."[8] Hamilton's friends were entertained by another tale of a rogue subdued by an understanding and persistent woman; there is some interesting naughtiness before the abrupt reformation in the final minutes of the last act. Lord Gaylove and Cosmelia engage in a battle of the sexes. They banter as a madcap couple should, as do their inferiors, Prate and Decoy. The contest rages by the familiar parallel scene device in which members of the same sex discuss their paramours. The merriment of the fracas is heightened by Sir Butterfly, a fop who is infatuated with Cosmelia. A remarkable fellow, Butterfly drank four bottles and then "had 7 young plump Partridges and 2 old Ducks" at a brothel. Hamilton provides further insights into Butterfly's character in an amusing toilet scene in which the fop primps, while his man, Haircut, paints his master's vain face. Stamina and beauty he may have, but Butterfly is no match for Cosmelia. During the third scene of the second act, in one of the most humorous moments of the play, Cosmelia tricks Butterfly, who is ready to bed down with the heroine, by having her servant, Prate, tie her amorous caller to his chair. When she consents to Butterfly's proposition, he finds that he is immobile. The obtuse Butterfly continues to plead for her favors, but is rebuked by the soubrette who flounces off stage saying that she'd rather "lie with a marble Man from Westminster Abbey."

Deception is the watchword in *The Doating Lovers* until the unrepentant rake, Gaylove, capitulates at the last minute. In this comedy of intrigue, Hamilton employs physical apparatus advantageously to put across his point. Gaylove interviews members of a funeral procession. He is astounded that the casket is for him. When the cortege reaches Cosmelia's house, the heroine tells Gaylove that she ordered it for him because he is dead to virtue. This measure prompts his reformation.

Hamilton is competent in handling masquerade, which he uses to underscore the moral. Butterfly in a transvestite garb meets Lady Youthful, who agrees to marry him. As they go to the priest, Butterfly observes, "Now we shall deceive Cholerick," Winfield's father and Clorinda's trustee. When they unmask and Cholerick discovers that he has a daughter-in-law, he is furious, as are all duped parents in comedy. Age is impotent, however, and Cholerick's threats of disinheri-

8 David Erskine Baker, Stephen Jones, and Isaac Reed, eds., *Biographia Dramatica, or a Companion to the Playhouse* (London, 1813), 2:89.

tance are futile, for the estate the old man refuses to give, does, in fact, belong to Clorinda. Cholerick has been holding it in trust. Giddy then unmasks to reveal she has married Sir Tim. In this confusion of different costumes and duplicity, Hamilton makes a distinction. Butterfly's is the only doomed alliance. Although all are involved in deception, only the fop refuses to reform. Lady Youthful admits that she has married Butterfly out of spite and promises to make him a cuckold.

In his adaptation of *Samson Agonistes* for Handel's *Samson*, as well as in his comedies, Hamilton shows himself to be a man of his time. Hamilton's lyrics follow Milton's tragedy closely in general outline. The lyricist had an impossible task of condensing 1,750 lines of poetry to an oratorio libretto. Hamilton's method was cut-and-paste. At times the technique is ingenious, but it ruins the original. "Therefore God's universal law / Gave to the man despotic power / Over his female in due awe, /" is transformed to a banal couplet: "To man God's universal law / Gave pow'r to keep his wife in awe." Such scrutiny is unfair, considering the horrendous task Hamilton attempted. Julian Herbage considers Handel's *Samson* to have the best oratorio text, and the one which became the archetype of his future productions in this form.[9]

Hamilton also fit Dryden's "Alexander's Feast" to a musical setting by Handel. The librettist confined himself, as he says, "to a plain division of it into airs, recitatives, or choruses, looking upon the words in general so sacred as scarcely to violate one, in the order of its first place."[10] Hamilton did add some of his own lines to the end of the Dryden ode, in order that the cantata could end with the conventional chorus in minuet time. Handel accepted the additional chorus, but later deleted Hamilton's emendation.

In a discussion of the Scots writing for the London stage, it is necessary to mention Dr. John Arbuthnot, who collaborated with fellow Scriblerus intimates Pope and Gay, on *Three Hours After Marriage*. It is not certain to what extent each writer contributed to the comedy which premiered at Drury Lane on 16 January 1717, but it is generally conceded that John Gay did most of the work. This piece, in which main characters are patterned after well-known figures of the day, occasioned attacks because of the personal nature of the satire.[11] One of the criticisms, Captain John Breval's *The Confederates* (1717),

9 Julian Herbage, "The Secular Oratorios and Cantatas," in *Handel: A Symposium*, ed. Gerald Abraham (London, 1963), p. 101.
10 Cited in Herbage, "The Secular Oratorios and Cantatas," p. 132.
11 Allardyce Nicoll, *A History of English Drama 1660–1900* (Cambridge, 1966), 2:14, 213. *London Stage*, Part 2, 1:clxxi.

issued under the pseudonym "John Gay," contains a frontispiece which shows Arbuthnot in Highland dress, Pope as an insignificant little gnome, and Gay in a fool's cap. The kilt functions as an object of ridicule. This cartoon, as well as a number of other satires of the period such as *Caledonia; or the Pedlar Turned Merchant* (1700),[12] indicate that a Scot in London had to live down his native origins.

Scottish dance enjoyed a London vogue during the 1720s. Mrs. Bullock, who performed frequently at Drury Lane and Lincoln's Inn Fields, was a leading exponent of jigs and reels. These specialties were inserted between the acts of *Othello* or after a presentation of *Sophonisba*, for example. The variety acts were determined by the ability and the availability of members of theatre companies. Clusters of Scots dances and songs appear in London stage bills, but there is no apparent correspondence with ethnic motive or political event. Highland dance had a revival in the late 1740s. One would not expect performance of the Scots measure or the sword dance on the heels of the Forty-five. Northern dancing waned during the last quarter of the century. On occasion, pieces such as "A Scottish Dialogue," first presented at Tottenham Court on 4 August 1740, were included in programs. Scots songs, particularly traditional ballads, were more popular than playlets. Scottish songs by Beard, Lauder, and Froment entered the repertory during the 1750s. Scottish airs were popular with Scottish and English playwrights as ballad opera melodies. Ironically, Joseph Mitchell, a pioneer in Scottish ballad opera, felt it necessary to tamper with the traditional tunes.

Mitchell, conscious of the consternation which the Old Pretender had aroused, established himself in the British capital under the patronage of Sir Robert Walpole. He was known to contemporaries as Walpole's poet, and was bold enough to set one of his dramas in the braes between the Highlands and the Lowlands, perhaps because of his powerful backing. More likely he was inspired by Theophilus Cibber's version of Allan Ramsay's *The Gentle Shepherd,* which had appeared at Drury Lane the year before Mitchell's ballad opera opened.

The first play which bears Mitchell's name is considered traditionally to have been written by Aaron Hill. Hill is supposed to have given his one-act play, ironically titled *The Fatal Extravagance,* to ease the continually improvident Scot out of a financial scrape. Recent scholars

---

12 *Caledonia: or The Pedlar turned Merchant. A Tragi-Comedy, as it was Acted by his Majesty's subjects for Scotland in the King of Spain's Province of Darien* has been listed as a drama, but it is a verse satire. See Terence Tobin, "*Caledonia:* a Satire of the Darien Disaster," *Notes and Queries* 15, n.s. (1968):106–07.

The Highland Fair (1731), A Scots Opera by Joseph Mitchell.

believe that Mitchell and Hill collaborated on this drama.[13] The declamatory extravagances of the tragedy, first performed at Lincoln's Inn Fields on 21 April 1721, point to the bombast Mitchell was to strew through his comedy. Mitchell's name appeared on the title page when the drama was published after its initial production. Five years later Hill reworked and enlarged *The Fatal Extravagance*. The 1726 version was more popular.

Mitchell's ballad opera, *The Highland Fair, or, Union of the Clans* premiered at Drury Lane on 20 March 1731. The introduction consists of a dialogue between poet and critic which defends the idea of a Scottish opera. This debate, which ends with the line, "Let the Overture begin," may have been presented in the playhouse. The preamble did not convince the commentator in *Biographia Dramatica*, who thought the subject "too local for Drury Lane." Mitchell did not treat his subject in a highly ethnic way. Some of the Scots airs he uses were altered with melismatic furbelows to fit the lyrics or perhaps to make the folk tunes conform to the style of English opera. In English dialogue, Mitchell inserts ingratiating sentiments to please his audience. Charles, a swashbuckling Highlander who despises clannishness, is a veritable Esau:

> Tell me not of a Woman's Mind. Give me her Person, if 'tis but tolerable. I wish this plaguy Negotiation was fairly ended, that I might have time to ramble among the Sex. I can't have an Hour's Pleasure for Business. But what makes the Case much worse, 'tis dangerous in this Country to use one's Freedom; on the one Hand, the Girls are shy, and their Kindred watchful; on the other, there's the Kirk Discipline so rigid and affronting: Wou'd I were in *Westminster* again! Dear *Covent-Garden!* I shall never forget thee. Why was I a *Caledonian* born, or why confin'd at Home? Happy Soldiers about St. *James's.*
>
> (II. 2)

The plot of *The Highland Fair* is set in motion when rival clans meet at a fair. The feuding of the Colins and Euens ends when a match is arranged between Nan and Davy. This solution to the quarrel is complicated by Kenneth, who loves the girl assigned to his rival by treaty.

> NAN. Pray be Friends. You shall not quarrel about me. I'll renounce you both for ever, if you do.

13 Paul S. Dunkin, "The Authorship of *The Fatal Extravagance,*" *Modern Language Notes* 61 (1945):328–30; P. P. Kies, "The Authorship of *The Fatal Extravagance,*" *Research Studies of the State College of Washington* 8 (1945): 155–58.

DAVY. You are mine by Treaty—

KEN. A Treaty that may never be concluded.

DAVY. Then 'tis War. No Peace, no Marriages; and no Marriages, no Peace. We shall be, as we were, mortal Foes.

KEN. With all my Heart, so *Nanny* be mine.

DAVY. I shan't be at a Loss in seeking a Wife, if I want one.

NAN. I thank you, Sir, for that.

KEN. Be it Peace, or War, I'll hazard all for my Love.

DAVY. I stand to Bargain. Honour's the Word. If 'tis Peace, she's mine; if 'tis War, take her and be d——n'd.

NAN. A rare Lover!

DAVY. Lover! Look-ye Sweet-Heart, I like you very well, and cou'd couple with you as heartily, as with any Woman. But things must take their Course, and my Honour not be touched.

"Be Valiant Still"

Affronted, I
My Foes defie,
And will have Satisfaction too.
Who me provokes without a Cause,
Against true Honour, and the Laws,
Had better fall in Lion's Paws,
Than meet from me Chastisement due.

(II. 4)

Despite the much discussed treaty, Davy does not marry Nan, but a widow of his choice. In the final moments of the opera, the couples who love truly are brought together. Davy's admission that his long insistence upon Nan and the treaty has been in fun is such a pat solution that the ending is dishonest. Mitchell's lack of dramatic sense reputedly won him a place in the first draft of the *Dunciad*. Pope is supposed to have deleted the Scot's name from the list of "Peel'd, patch'd, and piebald, linsey-woolsey brothers" at Mitchell's request.[14]

According to Fielding, Mitchell's ballad opera was laughed off the stage:

A certain comic Author produced a Piece on Drury-Lane Stage, called *The Highland Fair*, in which he intended to display the comical Humours of the Highlanders; the Audience, who had for three Nights together sat staring at each other, scarce knowing what to make of their Entertainment, on the fourth joined in a unanimous exploding Laugh. This they had continued through an Act, when the Author, who unhap-

14 James Sutherland, ed., *The Dunciad*, vol. 5, *The Poems of Alexander Pope* (London, 1943), pp. 162–63, 448.

pily mistook the Peals of Laughter which he heard for Applause, went up to Mr. Wilks, and, with an Air of Triumph, said *Deel o' my Sal, Sare, they begin to tauk the Humour at last.*[15]

Genest thinks Fielding's observation dubious, but the portrayal of a Scots dramatist as an incongruous figure is more significant than the accuracy of the anecdote. The mere presence of a Scot in London writing for the stage struck a number of Englishmen as a source of amusement.

Mitchell's *Highland Fair* was probably inspired by Theophilus Cibber's ballad opera, *Pattie and Peggie; or the Fair Foundling,* produced at Drury Lane on 20 April 1730. Cibber reduced the Ramsay pastoral to one act, changed the dialect to English, and added inferior songs. In his preface Cibber says that his work is a one-day alteration. *Pattie and Peggie* is the first and best known of a number of adaptations which *The Gentle Shepherd* spawned. Cornelius Vanderstop, Thomas Linley, Richard Tickell, W. Ward, Andrew Shirrefs, Margaret Turner, Charles Bonner, and Archibald MacLaren all produced versions of the Scottish pastoral.[16]

Translations and imitations appeared in the late century because *The Gentle Shepherd* had proven durable. The original was frequently revived; often new business and songs were inserted. Apparently the most popular addition was "The Cries of Edinburgh," a song which Lauder introduced. This actor, noted for his portrayal of Sir William Worthy, promoted *The Gentle Shepherd,* and the play, advertised under an assortment of titles, e.g., *Pattie and Peggie, Patie and Roger,* became one of the staples of the Little Theatre in the Haymarket during the third quarter of the eighteenth century. The play enjoyed

15 Henry Fielding, *The Covent-Garden Journal,* ed. G. E. Jensen (New York, 1964), 1:249–50. John Genest, *Some Account of the English Stage from the Restoration in 1660 to 1830* (New York, n.d.), 3:90.
16 Cornelius Vanderstop, *The Gentle Shepherd, A Dramatic Poem* (London, 1777). See *Monthly Review* 57 (1777):82; Thomas Linley, *The Overture, Songs and Duetts, in the Pastoral Opera of the Gentle Shepherd* (London, 1781); Richard Tickell, *The Gentle Shepherd* (London, 1781); Charles Bonner, "The Gentle Laird, or A Sequel to The Gentle Shepherd" [This latter piece was presented at the Theatre Royal, Bath, 1783.]; W. Ward, *A Translation of the Scots Pastoral Comedy, The Gentle Shepherd Into English . . .* (London [1785]); Andrew Shirrefs, *Jamie and Bess Or The Laird in Disguise, A Scots Pastoral Comedy. In Imitation Of The Gentle Shepherd* (Aberdeen, 1787), [Burns Martin, *Allan Ramsay, . . .,* pp. 94 and 160, compares Shirrefs's play to Ramsay's.]; Margaret Turner, *The Gentle Shepherd. A Scotch Pastoral Attempted in English . . .* (London, 1790); Archibald MacLaren, *Spite and Malice Or, A Laughable Accident: A Dramatic Sketch. To Which is Added, An Humble Attempt to Convert The Gentle Shepherd Into English Prose* (London, 1811).

a vogue at the patent theatres throughout the last quarter of the century.[17]

The Gentle Shepherd went through numerous editions.[18] *The Assembly* by Pitcairne was the only other comedy by a Scot published during the early decades of the eighteenth century later considered worthy of more than one printing.

For nearly seventy years after the Restoration, the Scots whose plays were presented or published in London worked almost exclusively with comedy. In 1725 a young man, then just twenty-five, went to London. Soon after the advent of James Thomson, Northerners changed allegiance from Thalia to Melopomene. Comedies, farces and ballad operas were popular in London theatres, but neoclassical tragedy was favored by Thomson and his circle. In the days before the Licensing Act, drama acquired a political tinge. Scots in London almost unanimously supported the Whigs. Comedy is the weapon of the establishment rather than the aspirant. A faction in ascendency is far more apt to gain supporters by serious and positive treatment of the virtues of its cause, than by negative ridicule of opponents' follies. From the standpoint of effectiveness, Thomson's *Agamemnon* is better propaganda than Pitcairne's *Assembly*.

1725-1750

A number of Scots whose dramatic works appeared in London during the second quarter of the eighteenth century had gained recognition for other literary endeavors before they contributed to the stage. As difficulty in having a play accepted for presentation increased, reputation became more important than patronage. In addition to evading politically oriented censorship enforced by the Lord Chamberlain after 1737, playwrights were faced with more competition, for dramatic form was in the vanguard of creative expression. Theatre managers could afford to be more selective in choosing vehicles. Alexander Gordon had a reputation as a writer before he submitted his comedy to London

17 *London Stage*, Part 4, 1:lxxi, 284 et seq.; 2:538 et seq.; 3:1312 et seq.; Part 5, 1:17 et seq.; 2:644 et seq.; 3:1485 et seq.
18 For a list of editions of *The Gentle Shepherd* see *Cambridge Bibliography of English Literature* (Cambridge, 1941), 2:970–71.

James Thomson (1700–1748).

playhouses. His *Itinerarium Septentrionale* (1726), was a *vade mecum* for antiquarians. His *Lupone, or the Inquisitor* (1731) was a *vae mihi* for Haymarket comedians on 15 March which was the reason several theatre managers had rejected the play on the grounds that it was too classical for presentation.[1] The pseudo-classic story had come into vogue with Joseph Addison's 1713 success, *Cato*. Scottish playwrights favored the antique trappings of neoclassic tragedy to clothe assessments of the political events of Hanovarian England.

James Thomson, the leader of the pre-romantics who espoused the Whig ascendency, embarked upon his theatrical career the same year the first collected edition of his influential poem, *The Seasons*, appeared. "O Sophonisba, Sophonisba, O," echoed in Drury Lane on 28 February 1730. *Sophonisba* ran ten performances. Thomson dedicated this first play to Queen Caroline. Although correspondence to contemporary political events is less apparent in this tragedy than in his later dramas, the play can be interpreted as a plea for the Queen to disengage herself from French influence. The heroine's dominant passion is to prevent her native Carthage (Britain) from becoming subservient to tyrannic Rome (France). The tragic Queen sacrifices Masinissa for her country, and agrees to marry Syphax, who has defended Carthage. When Syphax is captured, Masinissa persuades Sophonisba to resume their love, which she does, again for patriotic reasons. To prevent the Queen from falling into Roman hands, Masinissa gives her poison. One of Scipio's lieutenants delivers the heroine's epitaph, which is also the moral of the tragedy:

> She had a *Roman* soul; for every one
> Who loves, like her, his country is a Roman.
> Whether on *Afric's* sandy plains he glows,
> Or lives untam'd among *Riphoean* snows.
> If parent-liberty the breast inflame,
> The gloomy *Lybian* then deserves that name,
> And warm with freedom under frozen skies,
> In farthest *Britain Romans* yet may rise.
>
> (V. 9)

The plot of *Sophonisba* is as simple as its diction is ponderous. Baroque circumlocution, particularly in reflective and descriptive passages, strains for elegance. The bravura effects lend themselves to par-

---

1   *Biographia Dramatica*, 1:292; 2:404.

ody, and, in an age given to ludicrous imitation, Thomson's maiden tragedy provided a number of satirists with material.[2] Fielding's burlesque of Masinissa's exclamation, "Oh Huncamunca, Huncamunca, oh," in *The Tragedy of Tragedies* is the best-known example of the caricatures.

The mirth which Thomson's first play provoked shook the dramatist's confidence in his next effort. On 6 April 1738, the evening *Agamemnon* opened at Drury Lane, the author was not as cool as the lofty characters he created. Dr. Johnson recounts Thomson's nervousness the night of the premiere. The playwright arrived late for supper with friends, and "excused his delay by telling them how the sweat of his distress had so disordered his wig, that he could not come till he had been refitted by a barber."[3] The play had a respectable run of ten nights.

Alexander Pope was in the audience the first night of *Agamemnon*. Although not captivated with the drama, he was favorably impressed with certain aspects of the tragedy. According to Benjamin Victor who wrote Nathaniel Wood of the first night, Pope had a vested interest in Thomson's second play:

> . . . As to Agamemnon, I can promise you an excessive deal of pleasure from the reading it; I take the first three acts to be equal to any thing that ever was written; they were excellently performed, and with the loudest, and most universal applause! after this (such is the uncertainty of human affairs) the two following acts, (particularly the last) were deservedly hissed and cat-call'd; and the reason of all this proceeded from a palpable defect in the plan. —The hero, *Agamemnon*, dies in the fourth act,—and in the fifth, which, you know, is the act for catastrophe, and should be fullest of business, you are chiefly entertain'd with the prophetic strains of *Cassandra*, whom *Agamemnon* brought with him from Troy; and the distresses of young lovers, children to the depar[t]ed heroes, characters that generally fall into the hands of young, weak actors, and therefore the consequence of such bad conduct in the author, as well as bad acting, might have been foretold without the gift of prophecy. But a club of wits, with Mr. Pope at the head of them, met at the theatre the next morning, and cut, and slash'd, like dexterous surgeons—the lovers are no more—and they have brought a fine scene, that finish'd the fourth act, into the fifth. If the play is printed,

---

2   Genest, *Some Account of the English Stage*, 3:255–57, treats the parodies of *Sophonisba*.
3   Samuel Johnson, *Lives of the English Poets*, ed. George Birkbeck Hill (Oxford, 1905), 3:291. See also Thomas Davies, *The Memoirs of David Garrick* (London, 1781), 1:34–35.

after these necessary alterations, it will be better for the reader, as well
as spectator—But the work must for ever remain maim'd and defective.[4]

Aaron Hill wrote Alexander Pope and David Mallet identical lengthy
letters criticizing *Agamemnon*. Pope wisely refrained from forwarding
Hill's remarks to Thomson.[5]

In Thomson's romantic version of the Greek drama, Agamemnon has
been away from Clytemnestra for a decade. The heroine resists Egisthus' advances, but finally succumbs. Agamemnon excoriates Egisthus
for defaming Melisander, which motivates Clytemnestra's lover to plot
the King's death, but the Queen will have no part of the murder.
Although Clytemnestra bears her husband ill will, when Egisthus suggests that Cassandra may be queen, the heroine continually pleads
with her paramour to desist in his "fell designs on Agamemnon." Such
diminution of heroic flaws is characteristic of Thomson's portrayal of
tragic figures. Cassandra's prophecy of doom comes to pass: Agamemnon's corpse is displayed; disaster awaits Egisthus.

Thomson inserts his political philosophy in *Agamemnon*. The basis
of the vague concepts is analogous to the Aristotelian-Thomistic defini-
tion of law—the ordination of reason for the common good. Agamemnon's reply to the hypocritical Egisthus, who complains that he has not
participated in the glory of war, exemplifies a recurring pacific theme
in the poet's recondite thought.

> That ruling a free People well in Peace,
> Without or yielding or usurping Power;
> Maintaining firm the Honour of the Laws,
> Yet sometimes softening their too rigid Doom,
> As Mercy may require; steering the State,
> Thro' factious Storms, or the more dangerous Calms
> Of Peace, by long Continuance grown corrupt;

4 Allan Dugald McKillop, ed., *James Thomson (1770–1740) Letters and Documents* (Lawrence, Kans., 1958), p. 120.
5 *The Works of Aaron Hill* (London, 1753), 2:42–43. The following excerpt
from Hill's letter to Pope, 8 November 1738, indicates the tone of his criticism:
  If the design of that Tragedy is, what I suppose it to be, to derive from
  Agamemnon's impolitic rambling, his disappointment in domestic felicity,
  the alienation of his subjects affection, and his becoming a property to an
  ill-trusted rogue, in his absence. [*sic.*] The *Agamemnon*, who gives *moral*
  and *name* to the Play, ought to have animated, and stood obvious in every
  part of it. All the evil he *suffers*, should be an effect of some act which
  he *does*. For, whenever he ceases to sustain the chief weight of intention,
  his character, sinking at once, our passions, which took rise, but from the
  activity of his dramatical virtues, must, of course, become languid, in
  defect of their motive.

Besides the fair Career which Fortune opens,
To the mild Glories of protected Arts,
To Bounty, to Beneficence, To Deeds
That give the Gods themselves their brightest Beams:
Yes, know that these are in true Glory, equal,
If not superior, to deluding Conquest:
Nor less demand they Conduct, Courage, Care, and
    persevering Toil.

(II. 5)

Agamemnon was dedicated to Augusta, Princess of Wales. It is likely
that Thomson intended his audience to see the effort to depose Orestes
(Frederick Maurice, Prince of Wales) by Clytemnestra (Queen Caroline) and Egisthus (Robert Walpole) in the light of the power struggle
of the day. The characters' relation to political personages is more pro-
nounced in *Edward and Eleonora*. This story of Edward I and his
consort, which went into rehearsal at Covent Garden in 1739,[6] was
censored by the Lord Chamberlain, but it was published, with a dedication to Frederick, for as Thomas Edwards observed "prohibition
alone piques public curiosity to subscription."[7] The Earl of Gloucester's
speech to the crusading Edward, urging him to accept Sultan Selim's
peace offer, is a commentary on the "holy war" involving George II,
Walpole, and the Prince of Wales.

A nobler Office far! on the firm Base
Of well-proportion'd Liberty, to build
The common Quiet, Happiness and Glory,
Of King and People, *England's* rising Grandeur.
To you, my Prince, this Task of right belongs.
Has not the Royal Heir a juster Claim
To share his Father's inmost Heart and Counsels,
Than Aliens to his Int'rest, those who make
A Property, a Market of his Honour?

(I. 1)

6 While the play was being prepared the following compendium appeared: *The
History of the Life and Reign of the Valiant Prince Edward Afterwards King Ed-
ward the First of England, Son to King Henry the Third; and his Princess Eleonora.
On which History, is founded a Play, written by Mr. Thomson, call'd, Edward and
Eleonora, Now in Rehearsal at the Theatre in Covent-Garden. Extracted from the
Best Historians. With a Geographical Description of that Princes Expedition to
the Holy-Land &c.* (London, 1739).
7 Letter of Thomas Edwards to Lewis Crusius, 8 June 1739, in McKillop, ed.,
James Thomson Letters, p. 129. See Jean B. Kern, "The Fate of James Thomson's
Edward and Eleonora," *Modern Language Notes* 42 (1937):500–02.

Gloucester, the spokesman for Thomson's patriotic philosophy, articulates sentiments as idealistic as the greater-love-no-man-hath love story. *Edward and Eleonora* is more romantic in atmosphere and more exotic in incident than the author's previous plays. Edward is stabbed by a poisonous sword. The captive Arabian Princess Daraxa tells Eleonora that Edward can be saved if the wound is sucked, but the extractor will die. Eleonora drains the poison and becomes moribund. Her protracted pleas with her wounded husband to be permitted to sacrifice herself are manifestations of dialectic rather than personal emotion.

> Ah, what am I, with nameless Numbers weigh'd?
> With Myriads yet unborn? All Ranks, all Ages,
> All Arts, all Virtues, all a State comprizes?
> These have a higher Claim to thy Protection.
> Live then for them. —O make a great Effort!
> What none but Heroes can, bid the soft Passions,
> The Private stoop to Those that grasp a Public,
> Live to possess the Pleasure of a God,
> To bless a People trusted to thy Care,
> Live to fulfil thy long Career of Glory,
> But just begun. To die for Thee be mine.
>
> (II. 4)

Selim, the noble sultan, who has had no part in the attempted assassination of the English king, enters the Crusaders' camp in disguise, and saves the dying Eleonora. Selim's unselfish act preserves peace; as the distraught Edward attacks the infidels Eleonora reappears, and the opponents in "righteous mean agree." As the curtain closes Selim expresses the humanitarian solution Thomson continually offers for political imbroglios.

> Let holy Rage, let Persecution cease;
> Let the Head argue, but the Heart be Peace;
> Let all Mankind in Love of what is right,
> In Virtue and Humanity unite.
>
> (V. 4)

When pro-Frederick propaganda, that made George II almost as apoplectic as his father, ceased to be controversial, *Edward and Eleonora* was presented at Covent Garden on 18 March 1775. The play was altered by Thomas Hull, who deleted prolix passages and inserted

melodramatic action. Hull's style is typical of late century imitators
of Thomson.[8]

The year after *Edward and Eleonora* was barred from the stage,
Thomson collaborated with his friend, David Mallet, on *Alfred*. Mallet
seems to have done the first draft, then Thomson rewrote the masque.[9]
Alfred premiered at Cliveden on 1 August 1740, where the nobility,
whom the theatrical supports, witnessed the conglomeration of chau-
vinism and pastoral convention. The initial suspense is inaugurated by
Corin and Emma. These shepherds suspect that their unknown guest
is no ordinary mortal. Alfred reveals his identity in the second scene as
he discusses England's desperate condition with Devon. The shepherds
learn that their guest is royal from a hermit, who has overheard
the King's conversation. Spirits visit Alfred and console the divinely
inspired ruler who will drive out the Danish invaders.

In the second act, Alfred is reunited with Eltrude, defeats the
Danes, and captures their king. The hermit, the agent of Thomson's
political views, shows the British king his illustrious successors. The
last hero in the historical montage is George II, who will produce a
princely descendant as virtuous as Alfred. The masque closes with

---

8   Thomas Hull's insertion of an additional romance between Selim and Daraxa
shows the adapter's accommodation of Thomson's romanticism to the taste of the
next generation.

> *Selim*. The Selim!
> *Dar*. Kill me not
> With thy contempt, but rather let thy poignard
> Inflict the punishment my crime deserves,
> And let me die at least like Selim's wife!
> *Selim*. Like Selim's wife!
> And art thou she? Is't possible
> Her generous bosom could descend so low,
> Where noblest confidence—
> *Dar*. One erring moment
> Made me unworthy of the name—but cannot
> A life of sorrow and unceasing tears
> Obtain thy pardon for one fatal rashness?
> O, I will never quit these honour'd knees,
> Ne'er cease to fix these flowing eyes on thine,
> Till thou relent, and speak the voice of pardon
> To thy once-lov'd Daraxa!
> *Selim*. Oh! that look!
> It melts my best resolves!
>
>   (V. 1)

Thomas Sheridan altered *Coriolanus* (1755), and Thomas Hull published *Coriolanus: or the Roman Matron* (1797). Both authors make use of the previous
dramas by William Shakespeare and James Thomson.

9   *Cambridge History of English Literature*, 10:109.

"Rule Britannia." The merit of the famous patriotic song is in Thomas
Arne's melody rather than in James Thomson's lyrics.

When it was mounted in commercial theatre, *Alfred* appealed to the
audience because of the combination of belligerent patriotism, music,
spectacle, and romance. The success of the joint effort and a shared
interest in Socrates made Mallet and Thomson consider doing a play
on the Greek philosopher. Lyttelton mentions the project in a 1743 letter to Mallet, and when Voltaire published *Socrate* (1759), he passed
off the play as a translation of Thomson. Lyttelton denied this allega-
tion in *The Monthly Review*. The masque of 1741 was the Scots' sole
dramatic collaboration.

In *Tancred and Sigismunda* Thomson increased the romantic color,
and the hue that would entrance Europe brought him his greatest theatrical success. *Tancred* opened at Drury Lane on 18 March 1745. The
tragedy ran nine performances. It was revived by London theatres during the eighteenth and early nineteenth centuries. The drama was one
of the few plays by a Scot presented in Edinburgh which played more
than one season. *Tancred and Sigismunda, The Gentle Shepherd,* and
Douglas became repertory favorites in the North. *Tancred* was translated into French and German, an indication of the trend away from
neoclassic tragedy in favor of melodrama.

Tancred and Sigismunda is substantially changed from the Italian
original. Thomson uses a favorite motif, the conflict of public duty and
private feelings. This source of tension provides scope for inclusion of
political opinion, but, as its continued revival testifies, theatre patrons
were more interested in the tale of love and duplicity in Sicily. Tancred has been adopted by Siffredi, the Lord Chancellor. Siffredi tricks
his charge into marrying Constantia, the dead king's sister. Tancred is
in love with Sigismunda, the daughter of the chancellor who wishes to
manipulate the throne. Sigismunda, deceived into believing that the
hero has been unfaithful, agrees to wed Osmond, the Lord Constable,
who slays his bride.

> OSM. [*Entering.*] Turn, Tyrant! turn! and answer to my Honour,
>   For this thy base insufferable Outrage!
> TANC. Insolent Traitor! think not to escape
>   Thyself my Vengeance! [*They fight. Osmond falls.*]
> SIGIS. Help here! Help!—O Heavens!
>   [*Throwing herself down by him.*]
>   Alas! my Lord, what meant your headlong Rage?
>   That Faith, which I, this Day, upon the Altar
>   To You devoted, is unblemish'd, pure,

Tancred and Sigismunda (1745) by James Thomson.

As Vestal Truth; was resolutely yours,
Beyond the Power of aught on Earth to shake it.
OSM.   Perfidious woman! die!—
[*Shortening his Sword, he plunges it into her Breast.*]
And to the Grave
Attend a Husband, yet but half aveng'd!
TANC.   O Horror! Horror! execrable Villain!
OSM.   And, Tyrant! Thou!—Thou shalt not o'er my Tomb
Exult—'Tis well—'Tis great!—I die content.—[*Dies.*]

(V. 7)

The emphasis upon the sensational reduces the neoclassic coldness.
The characters are less frigid than the bachelor playwright's previous
heroes and heroines. Bonamy Dobrée adopts the explanation that the
greater emotion found in *Tancred* is related to the poet's love of Miss
Young.[10] Even in Thomson's most melodramatic play there is aloofness
which results from exalted language and thematic priorities. Thomson
valued philosophical expression above psychological motivation. The
presidence of the abstruse is particularly apparent in his last play.

   Coriolanus opened at Covent Garden on 13 January 1749, and ran
ten nights, but Thomson did not live to see this dramatic effort through
production delays. In 1748, the author wrote William Paterson of his
frustration with the Drury Lane manager: "Coriolanus has not yet
appeared on the stage, from the little dirty Jealousy of Tullus [Garrick]
towards him who alone can act Coriolanus [Quinn]. Indeed, the first
has entirely jockeyed the last off the Stage for the Season, like a Gyant
in his Wrath."[11] Thomson's Coriolanus is distant, but unlike Shakespeare's general, the eighteenth-century character is not haughty by
intent. Thomson's hero possesses justice, temperance, and courage in
sufficient abundance to deprive him of humanity. Coriolanus and other
characters speak rather than act in a series of scenes which transpire
in the Volscian camp. Galesus, Thomson's philosophical spokesman,
laments corruption, but is optimistic for the renewal of mankind by
return to simple virtues of the past, the most important of which is love
of peace. As Thomson had stated in *Liberty*, the Whig panegyric, peace
means progress. This moral-theme so preoccupies the dramatist that,
until the fifth act confrontation of Coriolanus and his mother, there is
little occurring on stage to hold an audience.

   Despite frosty figures, lengthy philosophical musings, and artificial

10 Bonamy Dobrée, *English Literature of the Early Eighteenth Century* (1700–
1740), vol. 7, *Oxford History of English Literature* (Oxford, 1959), pp. 252–53.
11 McKillop, *James Thomson Letters*, pp. 196–97.

dialogue, Thomson managed to combine classic and romantic elements into a viable amalgam. Although this pre-romantic exerted great influence upon poetry, his forte—natural description—did not lend itself to the stage. Rather than producing intrinsically significant drama, Thomson is of interest as a purveyor of Whig ideals during the storm-tossed Walpole era. He is noteworthy as an exponent of the shifting emphasis from reason to emotion taking place in British theatre. Devotion to the romantic would deprive the theatre of substance for generations. The reflection found in Thomson's dramas proved as destructive as his appropriation of the form of heroic tragedy Nicholas Rowe had evolved in an age which had little in common with the pattern. In the balance of terror and admiration with love and pity, Rowe injected an aura of sentimentality, which proved detrimental to drama. Thomson produced plays which at best exhibit "pleasing anguish"; such tragic vision is myopic.

David Mallet, a one-time Edinburgh High School janitor who became under-secretary to Frederick Maurice, was skilled in the craft of getting ahead. He was of the same political persuasion as Thomson, and worked in close association with his friend. Mallet's tragedies are similar in design and character. He worked in the Rowe tradition, but subordinated classic as well as romantic concepts of tragedy to fierce partisanship. His political propaganda in blank verse is laborious in comparison with Thomson's poetry. Also the spurious biographer of Marlborough, he capitalized on the thirst of the age for details of the famous, and continually cast political figures in tragic guise.

Mallet originally entitled his first play *Periander*, but he abandoned this more accurate designation after John Tracy's *Periander* opened the month before his own tragedy was scheduled to premiere. The dauntless Scot rechristened his play *Eurydice*, and the drama opened at Drury Lane on 22 February 1731. It was acted more than a dozen times. When it was revived, 3 March 1759, the play was a failure. Thomas Davies describes the dramatist's atrabilious behavior on this occasion: "Mallet sat in the orchestra, and bestowed his execrations plentifully upon the players to whom he attributed the cold reception of his tragedy."[12] Twenty-eight years after *Eurydice* first appeared, its full significance was undoubtedly lost upon the Drury Lane audience. In Mallet's treatment of the classic tale, Eurydice agrees to become Procles' consort to save her love, Periander. The Corinthian king has become estranged from Eurydice because of jealousy, and he is infuri-

12   Davies, *Memoirs of David Garrick*, 2:30–31.

ated at Procles' usurpation of wife and country. Periander slays the
tyrant. Meanwhile, the guilt-ridden Queen takes poison. Periander
becomes despondent at Eurydice's suicide and kills himself.

Political intrigues concern Mallet more than the unities, with which
he dispenses in favor of choppy, far-flung scenes. Characters are car-
tooned in slashes of black and patches of white. Procles, the despot of
Epidarus, who has taken possession of Corinth, is a villain without
Machiavellian subtlety. Noble Periander provides antipodal contrast.
Even in his unfounded jealousy, the hero is exculpated by his Queen's
self-recriminations. Such motivational concerns are secondary to the
political implications. *Eurydice* is a plea for the Jacobite cause. Periander (James Stuart) says to Procles (George I):

> How!—but thou darest not—Could I find thee there,
> In open day, and honourable arms!
> Opposing war to war, as monarchs should;
> That our embattled legions, front to front,
> While we betwixt them met, might judging see
> Whose sword, with keener edge, descending fell!
> Who best could earn the lawrel-wreathe of fame!—
> For that wish'd hour, I could forgive thee all;
> My throne usurp'd, these slave-like bonds, the shame
> I have endur'd—but hopes like these are vain!
> The fears that haunt my soul—
>
> (III. 5)

The author of *Remarks on the Tragedy of Eurydice in which It is
endeavoured to prove the same TRAGEDY is wrote in favour of the
"Pretender" and is a scurrilous Libel against the present Establishment*
(1731), interprets Periander's flaw of jealousy as the misunderstanding
between the Old Pretender and Princess Sobieski. This then gives
Eurydice two functions: she is James's neglected love, and as the desire
of two monarchs, she represents England. Medon (Bolingbroke), who
has served Procles in intriguing fashion, comes over to Periander who
orders the politician placed under guard. Eurydice is rescued from
Procles by her son Polydore (Prince Charles). The author of *Remarks
on the Tragedy of Eurydice* believes that this is based upon Maria
Sobieski's abduction by "two Irish Traytors, Talbot and another, both
desperate Fellows and as biggotted to Popery as the Pretender." Aris-
ton (Colonel Hay) works against Eurydice's reunion with Periander in
the fourth act. Hay did prevent a reconciliation between the Pretender
and the Princess. Periander's victory in the play is dismissed by the
pamphleteer as a mere ruse to boost sinking Jacobite morale. In addi-

tion to discarding factors which do not fit his hypothesis, the author laments that this subversion was not more transparent to playgoers. This key may not represent Mallet's precise intention, but it does illuminate a number of obscure political correspondences.

Mallet's second play, *Mustapha*, ran fourteen performances when it premiered at Drury Lane on 13 February 1739. Mallet probably was acquainted with Sir Roger Boyle's *Mustapha, The Son of Solymon the Magnificent* (1665). In both treatments of the story, Mustapha and Zanger are friends, and Solymon is convinced of his son Mustapha's innocence. The histories of the period make no mention of the friendship of the stepbrothers. Mallet's drama is not an imitation of a previous work, but a commentary on current affairs of state. In this Oriental tragedy, Mallet makes use of the anti-Walpole reaction Thomson employs in *Agamemnon*. In the tragedy produced the year before *Mustapha*, Agamemnon speaks of

> Insinuating, speckled, smooth Court-serpents,
> That make it so unsafe, chiefly for Kings,
> To walk this weedy World.
>
> (II. 4)

In *Mustapha*, Rustan the grand vizier (Walpole), is portrayed as a Court serpent, who plots with the royal family until his death in the last act at the hands of Mustapha's loyal brother, Zanger.

Mustapha is dedicated to Frederick, and there is little doubt that the Prince has the title role. Frederick was sure that Walpole concurred with, if he did not originate, George II's policy to keep him dependent financially and curtailed politically. Roxolana (Caroline) drives her son, Mustapha (Frederick), from her husband, Solymon (George II). Caroline was as notorious for her intense hatred of Frederick as she was famous for guiding her husband in affairs of state. Solymon, in the Hanoverian tradition, is plagued by suspicion and doubt; he fears any successor to his throne. Mallet gives a dangerously accurate portrait of the monarch:

> But yet, the genius of imperial rule,
> All-incommunicable, knows no equal;
> Nay knows no second. Thou hast borne thy self
> Above a subject's state: by secret arts,
> By dangerous popularity, hast dar'd
> To taint my armies, and divide their homage.
> Too well I know the native bent of man:
> From towering thoughts to traiterous designs

He climbs apace. If I at last must fear
A rival in my slave—for such thou art—
Thy virtues all are crimes. And were there none,
Not one of Othman's blood to heir his empire;
By that eternal Mind who form'd my soul!
If guilt is found upon thee—true, thy father
Will be unhappy—but thou art undone!

(II. 7)

The machinations of Roxolana and the vizier to place Mustapha in an unfavorable light, are momentarily thwarted when Mustapha, knowing of court plots, proves his worth by rescuing Solymon. Since the Turkish emperor once more trusts Mustapha, the Queen and her minister sow doubts by suggesting that his rescuer is in league with Persia. Zanger, Mustapha's brother, pleads with the hero to flee. Later Roxolana disowns Zanger for refusing to be an accessory to the murder of his brother. Emira, Mustapha's Persian wife, begs Solymon to be merciful to her husband. Solymon, furious that his son has married an enemy, refuses to believe that this match means an alliance. Persia recalls Prussia, the country with which George II arranged a matrimonial league by marrying his son Frederick to Augusta of Saxe-Gotha without consulting him. Frederick favored a German alliance.

The conventional fifth act deaths of Mustapha and Zanger bring the sovereigns to their knees. They express remorse in the last few lines of the play in a cursory nod at the requirement of poetic justice. The brevity and lack of preparation for this about face, especially on Roxolana's part, only serves to point up the strained and unnatural relations of the real royalty.

The most remarkable thing about *Mustapha* is that the Lord Chamberlain permitted its production. Its intention was patent, according to the *Scots Magazine* critic.

The pit was before five o'clock filled with gentlemen who made a very polite appearance, and were mostly of the Scots nation. . . . The whole play was acted without one hiss or mark of dislike. . . . The best description and the most moving distress passed in silence, while any casual expression which was capable of being interpreted into a meaning unintended, I believe, by the author met with the loudest applauses.[13]

The year after *Mustapha* opened, Mallet collaborated with Thomson on *Alfred*. Mallet altered the masque eleven years later for a Drury

13   *Scots Magazine* 1 (1739):88.

Lane presentation which opened on 23 February 1751; it ran eight performances. Although the production was less than polished, the play
was quite popular.[14] Mallet expanded the piece, but did not change it as
substantially as his prefatory remarks would have one believe. Since
he mentions his fatigue from his labors on Marlborough's life in this
same preface, one is prepared for the insignificant additions of which
Mallet boasts.

On the strength of the acclaim "Rule Britannia" had received, Mallet
wrote a masque entitled *Britannia,* which appeared at Drury Lane on
9 May 1755 and ran about seven performances. This patriotic piece,
which makes a plea for fighting the French, is peopled with mythologi-
cal figures as well as sailors and their girls. The nautical mortals give
the entertainment a *Pinafore*-like quality. In the seventh and final
scene, the boatswain sings a recitative which anticipates Ralph Rack-
straw's patter songs:

> See where young NAN and SUE appear,
> Away—or you are wind-bound here.
> Ah let them not, my lads, come nigh:
> Each carried witchcraft in her eye.

Nancey then sings:

> Hear me, gallant sailor, hear me!
> *While your country has a foe,*
> He is mine too—Never fear me;
> *I may weep: but you shall go.*

Eight years after Mallet saluted young love and patriotism, he wrote
Elvira. This tragedy opened at Drury Lane on 19 January 1763. *Elvira*
was performed about thirteen times. The vehicle starring Garrick was
one of the most frequently performed plays of the season. The run is a
mark of the actor-manager's drawing power, rather than a measure of
the esteem in which the Iberian melodrama was held.

The plot of *Elvira* owes something to Antione Houdard de la Motte's
best work, *Ines de Castro* (1723). Mallet's adaptation involving love
and political intrigue combines these popular facets in a politically
expedient manner. A play boasting a villainous Spanish Queen and a
declaration of war against her homeland suited the British, who had
sided with the Portuguese against the Spanish in the Seven Years War.

14   *London Stage,* Part 4, 1:238, 247–48.

The politically popular position is ensconced in sentimental story. Don Pedro and Elvira are secretly married. Alonzo IV, King of Portugal, insists that his son, Don Pedro, marry Almeyda, sister of the Spanish king. The hapless heroine is then committed to the Queen's custody. Don Pedro attempts to rescue his wife, but the King thwarts the escape, and Don Pedro is confined to quarters. Later he is condemned to death. Almeyda tries to save Don Pedro, the man she loves. The Spanish noblewoman persuades the royal father to give Elvira an audience. In a crowd-pleasing scene, Elvira announces her marriage and produces her two children. The monarch pardons his son, but comedy again turns to tragedy as Elvira dies, having been poisoned by the Queen, who is the King of Portugal's second wife. Her motive stems from heritage; she is mother to the King of Spain. Because of his step-mother's wicked deed, Don Pedro is on the verge of committing suicide, but he is stopped by his father.

On the opening night of the play, which treats of the struggles between a father for power and a son for independence, a triumvirate of Edinburgh wits, James Boswell, Andrew Erskine, and George Dempster, determined to eat at Dolly's Chop House, then take in *Elvira* to hiss it off the boards. The efforts of Boswell and company were of no avail, for Mallet's claque was larger and squelched the dissenters.[15] Edward Gibbon, who was in the playwright's faction, describes the evening in his *Journal:*

> My father and I went to the Rose, in the Passage of the Playhouse, where we found Mallet, with about thirty friends. We dined together, and went from thence into the Pitt, where we took our places in a body, ready to silence all opposition. However, we had no occasion to exert ourselves. Not withstanding the malice of a party, Mallet's nation, connections and indeed imprudence, we heard nothing but applause. I think it was deserved. The play was borrowed from de la Motte, but the details and language have great merit. A fine Vein of dramatick poetry runs thro' the piece. The Scenes between the father and son awaken almost every sensation of the human breast; and the Council would have equally moved, but for the inconvenience unavoidable upon all Theatres, that of entrusting fine Speeches to indifferent Actors. The perplexity of the Catastrophe is much, and I believe justly, criticized. But another defect made a stronger impression upon me. When a Poet ventures upon the dreadful situation of a father who condemns his son to death, there is no medium; the father must either be a monster or a Hero. His obligations of justice, of the publick good, must be

15 James Boswell, *London Journal 1762–1763*, ed. Frederick A. Pottle (New York, 1951), p. 152.

as binding, as apparent, as perhaps those of the first Brutus. The cruel necessity consecrates his actions, and leaves no room for repentance. The thought is shocking, if not carried into action. In the execution of Brutus's sons I am sensible of that fatal necessity. Without such an example, the unsettled liberty of Rome would have perished the instant after its birth. But Alonzo might have pardoned his son for a rash attempt, the cause of which was a private injury, and whose consequences could never have disturbed an established government. He might have pardoned such a crime in any other subject; and the laws could exact only an equal rigor for a son; a Vain appetite for glory, and a mad affectation of Heroism, could only influence him to exert an unequal and superior severity.[16]

The young historian was more kind to Mallet's last play than *The St. James Chronicle*. The newspaper critic who constructed "Brief Criticism on the New Tragedy of Elvira" dispensed with the drama in five lines:

Act I	Indifferent
Act II	Something Better
Act III	MIDDLING
Act IV	Execrable
Act V	Very Tolerable[17]

Boswell, Erskine and Dempster, frustrated in their cat-calls at the premiere of *Elvira,* decided to publish their imprecations, in order to annoy the Scot whom they considered had forsaken his nationality. "Mallet alias Mallock," as Johnson characterized him in his *Dictionary,* was a thorn not only in the lexicographer's side but in the flanks of a number of his countrymen who were disgusted with the name changer's opportunism. Erskine wrote a draft and his cohort collaborated upon the refinement of *Critical Strictures on the New Tragedy of Elvira Written by Mr. David Malloch* (1763). This mordent pamphlet convinced *The Monthly Review* that the criticism was written by an anti-Scots bigot.[18] Since Bute's opponents were continually fostering such prejudice, this was a natural assumption. The following citation from *Critical Strictures* indicates the tone of the sallies:

Our great Author possesses, in its utmost Perfection, the happy Act of uniting rival Ladies, and of setting, at Variance a virtuous Father and

16 D. M. Low, ed., *Gibbon's Journal* (New York, 1929), pp. 202–04. Gibbon also attended a rehearsal of *Elvira* (see pp. 185–86).
17 *St. James's Chronicle*, 20 January 1763.
18 *Monthly Review* 28 (1763):67–68.

Son. How intimate his Acquaintance with Human Nature! How deep
his Knowledge of the Passions! No less exquisite and refined in his Morality, like a true Disciple of Lord *Bolingbroke,* he unites Vice and Virtue most lovingly together; witness this memorable Line of the King's
addressed to *Elvira;*

> *Midst all your Guilt I must admire your Virtue.*

Let us invert this Line,

> 'Midst all your Virtue I must abhor your Guilt

Let us parody it:

> O Mr. *David Malloch!* 'midst all your Dullness
> I must admire your Genius.[19]

Contrary to the opinion of *Critical Strictures,* Mallet's ability was not
uniting the disparate, but in transformation to suit his purposes. His
tragedies are all based upon other plays. The political significance
which he incorporated makes his dramatic efforts different from the
originals. As a theatrical propagandist, Mallet is effective, for his portraits of prominent persons, whether condemnatory or complimentary,
are recognizable. One knows that the suspicious Solymon in *Mustapha*
is George II; he also recognizes the same monarch in the eulogistic
insertions Mallet placed in the 1751 version of *Alfred.* Mallet possessed
sufficient dramatic skill to give his dramas some nonpartisan interest.
Feathering one's political nest is a relative act. Compared with Thomson's obscure musings, Mallet's intrusions seem blatant. When considered in the light of James Baillie's work, Mallet's incursions appear
subtle.

James Baillie[20] published *The Patriot, being a Dramatic History of
the Life and death of William the First Prince of Orange, founder of
the Republic of Holland, etc.* (1736). In his preface Baillie defends the
use of prose as the natural way to express a "Treatise made up of
Conversation." He also attempts to convince the reader that the Mau-

19 James Boswell, Andrew Erskine, and George Dempster, *Critical Strictures
on the New Tragedy of Elvira Written by Mr. David Malloch,* ed. Frederick A.
Pottle. Augustan Reprint Society (Los Angeles, 1952), pp. 14–15. Frederick A.
Pottle, *James Boswell: The Earlier Years 1740–1769* (New York, 1966), pp. 102–
03.
20 *Biographia Dramatica,* 1:15, identifies the author of *The Patriot* as John
Baillie, an advocate. A notation in a copy of the play identifies the author as
James Baillie (NLS). Although *The Patriot* and *The Married Coquet* are vastly
different in feeling, there are stylistic similarities in both plays.

rice in the play is the Prince of Orange rather than the Prince of Wales. The romantic aspects of the play vitiate Baillie's halfhearted claim of historical veracity. Maurice, son of William the Silent, was a roving bachelor who sired seven bastards. The hero of *The Patriot* is the beau ideal.

Baillie, who used "Lover of Liberty" as his by-line, tells the tale of libertarian lovers, Maurice and Augusta. There is no conflict, for there are no serious romantic or political impediments. Eleonora is infatuated with Maurice, and Duke Medina professes love for Augusta, but neither principal is attracted to others. Counts Hostrate and Teligny are both charmed by Eleonora. The coquette sends Teligny off to war against Spain to prove herself an enchantress, since she has not captivated the hero. Between the desultory amorous proceedings Maurice delivers political manifestos of Whig aims:

> . . . For a Prince is guilty of all Ills, in Heaven's Eye, if he allows his Ministers to commit them. My fix'd Resolution is to have my Country independent of the Crown of *Spain,* or any other Prince, or die in the Attempt; for without Freedom, Life's a Burthen; and I swear I wou'd not part with this Glorious Thing call'd *Liberty,* for all this World can give me in Exchange. Without it, all the other Joys of Life must be insipid; Nor can the Prince himself who's absolute, be happy, because, upon the least Reflection, he must find his Subjects must abhor him; for it is impossible one can love a Person who deprives him of the greatest Good.
>
> (III. 6)

The couple announce their engagement to William, and the elated father gives them his blessing. William, who advises Maurice to "give a People a Taste of Liberty; this makes them rich by Industry," points up the deficiencies of George II by contrast. Eleonora suffers remorse, because she has sent Teligny to his death. The *femme fatale* then discusses marriage with Hostrate. Her fortune is better than Medina's, who mourns losing Augusta to the point of death. Before he expires, the Duke reveals a Roman Catholic plot against William. In the last scene of the play Gerrard, who has sworn on a crucifix to be faithful to the first Prince of Orange, shoots his liege. Despite a fatal neck wound, William sinks into an easy chair and councils his son. The gist of these pages of advice is: trust England and tolerate all religions save Popery.

Ten years after the fatuous and unintentionally humorous political drama appeared, Baillie's *The Married Coquet* was published posthumously. The author was a physician, who had an uncommon discernment in patterns of sexual behavior. The sex comedy of 1746 is ostensibly a conflict between the moral and immoral, but the author is more concerned with dialogue for the dissolute. The cameos of the deviants are finely chiseled case studies. Leonora, a procuress more interested in the money than in the assignations which take place in her house, keeps Marlowe, a rapist, who looks upon women as apples: "some fair, some brown; but at the core they are alike hollow and deceitful." This pair bait Belfield to court Melinda, the married coquette. Melinda, like Eleonora of *The Patriot*, loses interest the moment she receives adulation. Belfield, who is at odds with Cynthia, his love, is attracted to Melinda; she then indicates willingness to have an affair with Beaumont. Beaumont, a self-indulgent egoist of Buddhistic girth, believes the ladies should love him because of, not in spite of, his rotundity. Melinda later dismisses the would-be adulterer as "a miracle left for the day of judgment, when some sinful woman shall call out for the mountain to cover her."

Claremont, a pious soul from the country, tries to take his errant sister away from temptations of the city, but Melinda prefers urban titillation to rural seclusion and fidelity to her absent spouse.

Cynthia and Belfield discuss marriage. The immoralists, who feel threatened by such talk, plot to make Belfield believe Cynthia loves Sir Charles Modish, a narcissistic homosexual, whom Beaumont describes as having a "squeez'd-out voice of the epicene gender, which sounds neither masculine nor feminine, cry'd Egad the poor soul loves me; then turning to the looking-glass, he caper'd about the room like a flea in a blanket, and skip'd away." Belfield is duped by manufactured circumstantial evidence into thinking that his girl prefers Modish; the hero then takes up with Melinda. To be rid of Beaumont, Melinda has Modish impersonate her, which he delightedly does, much to the frustration of the sweating fat man.

In the fifth act the lovers are reunited, Claremont saves his sister from being attacked by Marlowe, and delivers a sermon against promiscuity to allay the consciences of readers who have enjoyed the risqué proceedings.

William Paterson served as deputy to James Thomson during his tenure as Surveyor-General of the Leeward Islands. Before this association, the two Scots had been friends. Paterson made the fair copy of *Edward and Eleonora* in 1738. Two years later he presented his own work, *Arminius*, to the Lord Chamberlain, who refused to license the tragedy then in rehearsal at Drury Lane, because it was in the same hand as the drama containing dangerous political allusions.[21]

21 *London Stage*, Part 3, 1:liii.

The caprice of the censor prevented presentation, but *Arminius* was published in 1740. Paterson's pseudoclassical play bears Thomson's impress. The rhetoric and philosophical point of view are Thomsonian, as Segestes' pacifistic plea illustrates:

> What Woes attend on War! when the dire God
> Rides forth in red Array! around him rage
> Despair and Ruin; at his iron Wheels
> Captivity is dragg'd; and in his Train
> Come rav'ning Famine and devouring Plague,
> Before him should luxuriant Nature pour
> Her richest Treasures; lo! he comes, he treads,
> And waste behind him lies the howling Desart.
> Such are the Fruits of War!
>
> (II. 3)

As the play begins, the German Prince, Segestes, is jealous of Arminius because of the younger Teuton's influence over the Germanic tribes. Segestes has promised his daughter, Artesia, to Arminius. Because of envy, Segestes joins forces with the Romans. The disloyal prince compounds his treachery by persuading his daughter to marry Quintilius Varus, the Roman general, to secure more power. This departure from Tacitus had dramatic appeal for an audience which had followed the machinations involved in Prince Frederick's marriage.

Arminius goes to the united camp of Varus and Segestes. Although he is under a promise of safe escort, Segestes holds the hero prisoner. Arminius escapes from this confinement with the help of Egebert, at the request of Sigismund.

Sigismund is the son of Segestes, who is in love with Herminia, Arminius's sister. The convenient intertwining of relationships is pat, but relatively free from the melodramatic excesses of later tragedies. The relationships involving the primary and secondary lovers can be interpreted as a means of strengthening the theme that love is mightier than war.

Arminius is extricated from the grasp of Segestes, but is captured once more by Romans. When the German leader is brought before Varus, the confrontation scene provides marked contrast to the one which took place between the hero and Segestes. The noble Roman general gives Arminius his liberty, because he does not consider the captured prince a prisoner of war. Varus also makes clear that he will not wed Artesia without her consent. Such magnanimity is in the tradition of the heroic drama.

The last act is more in the mainstream of eighteenth-century dramatic conclusions. The Romans lose a battle against the Germans.
Varus commits suicide, and Segestes is about to fall upon his sword
when he is stopped by Sigismund. The lovers, Arminius and Artesia,
Sigismund and Herminia, are united; all who sided with the Teutonic
leader are happy.

Robert Morris published *Fatal Necessity: or, Liberty Regain'd* in
1742. This version of the Appius and Virginia legend, taken from René
de Vertot's *History of the Revolutions of the Roman Republick*, is dedicated to Charles Edwin. Edwin won in the bitterly contested 1742
election as an independent parliamentary representative. The political
significance seems to be in the exposition of liberal Whig principles
rather than in the correspondence of dramatic to actual characters.[22]

In the first scene of *Fatal Necessity* Numitorius and Valerius discuss
the danger of Appius's gaining strength. In the second scene Icilius
and Virginia profess their love, thus establishing the pattern of the
play, which shifts back and forth between power politics and tender
romance. After Virginia faints at the mention of Appius's name, a fore-
shadowing of the tragic outcome, the scene shifts to Appius and
Claudius who plot sedition. The villain is a Cataline who knows that
hoodwinking the public is a *sine qua non* for despots:

> Yes, *that* is the secret Pleasure.
> To hold the Reins of Government secure
> From envious Eyes, to trace its hidden Springs,
> And know my Friend, I've always held it prudent
> And best; to gain a popular Applause,
> By outside Gentleness and Affability,
> To win Affection by obsequious Carriage,
> And Shew of Sanctity; or, if that fail,
> To bribe the leading Traytors into Silence:
> Yes, *Claudius*, 'tis this outside Tinsel Lustre
> This glittering Blaze, that awes the giddy Vulgar,
> And makes the trembling Coward wear his Chains.
>
> (I. 3)

Icilius joins forces with those who oppose the murderous decemvirs,
and swears to rid Rome of Appius. Icilius does not get the opportunity
to assassinate the first decemvir, because Appius falsely accuses the
hero of attacking Claudius, "the pretended master of Virginia." The
trial of Icilius precipitates the parricide and functions as a showcase

---

22 See *Biographia Dramatica*, 2:120–21.

for patriotism, which is presented as a hierarchy of responsibilities to state, family, and individuals. The rescue of Rome is accomplished by Virginius's sacrifice of Virginia, which prompts the Icilian party to drive out the corrupt politicians.

Morris features the love of Icilius and Virginia and minimizes the father-daughter relationship. He achieves a good balance of neoclassic and romantic, and incorporates Whig idealism with considerable skill. *Fatal Necessity* has more vitality than many of the dramas indebted to Thomson's thought and technique.

In 1739 a young Scot set out for London with play in pocket, quite like Samuel Johnson had descended upon the city with *Irene* tucked under his arm two years before. Tobias Smollett had written *The Regicide or James the First, King of Scotland* during his student days in Glasgow, and expected that his tragedy would meet with unanimous approbation. Smollett submitted the play to Lord George Lyttelton, the patron of Thomson, Mallet, and other Scots abroad. Lyttelton declined sponsorship, and with characteristic pique, Smollett "resolved to punish this barbarous indifference," by discarding his patron, as he says in the preface to his first play. Garrick rejected the tragedy. The disgruntled playwright retaliated by attacking the baron and the actor in *Peregrine Pickle.*[23] With the money he had received from the publication of *Roderick Random* (1748), Smollett had his tragedy published the following year.

Smollett used George Buchanan's account of the murder of James I as the point of departure for his tragedy. Dunbar, a noble loyal to the King, loves Eleonora, daughter of Angus, another loyal thane. Eleonora loves Stuart, the rebel who would usurp the throne. She prevails upon the smitten Dunbar to release Stuart, his imprisoned enemy. After several uninteresting advances and losses on both sides, the tragedy ends with a collection of corpses in the blood-and-thunder tradition of Elizabethan melodrama.

The dialogue is the product of a young writer. Rather than striving to fit speech to character or situation, Smollett attempts elegance. The overwritten diction, which does not vaguely resemble human utterance, abounds in epigrammatic endeavors that are circumlocutory rather than pithy. Dunbar's profession of love for Eleonora is a typical example of the abundant artificiality:

23 In *Roderick Random*, Chapters 61–63, Smollett presents a fictionalized account of the rejection of *The Regicide*. He excoriates Garrick and Lyttelton in *Peregrine Pickle* (1751), but treats both men more kindly in *The History of England* (1757–58).

DUNBAR.

O! thy words
Would fire the hoary hermit's languid soul
With ecstasies of pride! —How then shall I,
Elate with ev'ry vainer hope, that warms
Th' aspiring thought of youth, thy praise sustain
With moderation? —Cruelly benign!
Thou hast adorn'd the victim; but, alas!
Thou likewise giv'st the blow!—

Tho' Nature's hand
With so much art has blended ev'ry grace
In thy enchanting form, that ev'ry eye
With transport views thee, and conveys unseen
The soft infection to the vanquish'd soul,
Yet wilt thou not the gentle passion own,
That vindicates thy sway!—

ELEONORA.

O gilded curse!
More fair than rosy morn, when first she smiles
O'er the dew-brighten'd verdure of the spring!
But more deceitful, tyrannous, and fell
Than syrens, tempests, and devouring flame!
May I ne'er sicken, languish and despair
Within thy dire domain! —Listen, ye powers!
And yield your sanction to my purpos'd vow—

(I. 3)

Smollett submitted his tragedy "Alceste" to the Covent Garden manager in 1749, and expected it to be produced in 1750.[24] John Rich decided upon a spectacular production of this play based on Euripides. He engaged Servandony to paint the scenery and Handel to compose the music. When the production was scrapped, Handel fitted his score to a new libretto, and the music composed for "Alceste" was introduced in 1751 as "The Choice of Hercules," an appendage to *Alexander's Feast.*[25]

Smollett may have written "The Absent Man"[26] and "The Israelites, or the Pampered Nabob," but *The Reprisal: or, the Tars of Old England* is the only comedy known to have come from the pen of the irreverent novelist. The author's brief tenure as surgeon's second mate aboard the H. M. S. *Chicester* enabled him to create authentic nautical

24 *London Stage*, Part 4, 1:97, 179.
25 Abraham, *Handel: A Symposium*, pp. 149–50. Otto Erich Deutch, *Handel: A Documentary Biography* (London, 1955), pp. 679–81.
26 Allan Dugald McKillop, "Smollett's First Comedy," *Modern Language Notes* 44 (1930):396–97.

atmosphere in *The Reprisal.* The prologue refers to the two-act farce as a "sea ragout." The comic concoction, which contains ingredients Smollett used in his novels, consists of a rescue. A naive Heartly and his adroit servant, Brush, must retrieve Harriet, Heartly's fiancée who is in the clutches of Champignon, a French frigate commander who has captured the Englishman's pleasure craft. The captives are abetted by Oclabber, an Irishman, and Maclaymore, a Scot. Both Gaels are members of the tatterdemalion French crew. The proceedings provide opportunity for dialect, humor, and satirization of national pecularities. Smollett concentrates upon patriotic ridicule of the French to entertain an audience dissatisfied with the Treaty of Aix la Chapelle.

Of the humour characters who romp through incidents showing French naval incompetence, one of the more interesting is Block. He is an authentic seaman, yet eccentric. The caricature of a brutal man is analogous to naturalists' portraits, but comic violence gives the character necessary distance. This remove provides the humor those who later advocated the slice of life technique rarely achieved.

> BLOCK.
> All's fair plunder between decks—we ha' n't broke bulk, I'll assure you—stand clear—I'll soon over-haul the rest of the cargo.
> [*Pulls out a long leather queue with red ribbons.*]
> What's here? the tiller of a monkey!—s'blood the fellow has no more brains than a noddy, to leave the red ropes hanging over his stern, whereby the enemy may board him on the poop.
> [*The next thing that appears, is a very coarse canvas shirt, with very fine laced ruffles.*]
> This here is the right trim of a Frenchman—all gingerbread-work, flourish and compliment aloft, and all rags and rottenness alow.
> [*Draws out a plume of feathers.*]
> Adzooks! this is Mounseer's vane, that, like his fancy, veers with every puff to all the points of the compass—Hark'ee, Sam—the nob must needs be damnably light that's rigg'd with such a deal of feather. The French are so well fledg'd no wonder they are so ready to fly.
> [*Finds a pocket-glass, a paper of rouge and Spanish wool, with which he daubs his face.*]
> Swing the swivel-ey'd son of a whore! he fights under false colours, like a pirate—here's a lubberly dog, he dares not shew his own face to the weather.
>
> (III. 15)

There are four songs which add a sprightly touch to *The Reprisal.* In one of the exchanges between Harriet and Champignon, all of which prove that a Dorsetshire girl is wittier than a French *roué,* she

eases into her solo with admirable sophistication. Smollett's care with
introductions to the songs is unusual for eighteenth-century comic
theatre.

> HARRIET.
> Oh! you sing inchantingly; and so natural, one would imagine you had
> been a cobler all the days of your life. —Ha, ha, ha!
> CHAMPIGNON.
> Hai, hai, hai—if you not flatter me, madame, I be more happy dan
> Charlemagne—but I ave fear date you mocquez de moi—tell a me of
> grace, my princesse, vat sort of lover you shoose, I vil transform myself
> for your plaisir.
> HARRIET.
> I will not say what sort of lover I like; but I'll sing what sort of lover
> I despise.
> CHAMPIGNON.
> By gar, she love me eperduement.   (*Aside.*)
> SONG
> I.
> From the man whom I love, tho' my heart I disguise,
> I will freely describe the wretch I despise,
> And if he has sense but to balance a straw,
> He will sure take the hint from the picture I draw.
> II.
> A wit without sense, without fancy a beau,
> Like a parrot he chatters, and struts like a crow:
> A peacock in pride, in grimace a baboon,
> In courage a hind, in conceit a gascoon.
> III.
> As a vulture rapacious, in falsehood a fox,
> Inconstant as waves, and unfeeling as rocks;
> As a tyger ferocious, perverse as an hog,
> In mischief an ape, and in fawning a dog.
> IV.
> In a word, to sum up all his talents together,
> His heart is of lead, and his brain is of feather:
> Yet, if he has sense but to balance a straw,
> He will sure take the hint from the picture I draw.

(I. 3)

Smollett's former foe, David Garrick, who wished to put an end to
the bad press he was receiving in *The Critical Review*, produced *The
Reprisal* on 22 January 1757; it ran six nights. According to Richard
Cross the comedy received great applause.[27] The play was revived sev-

---

27 Cited in *London Stage*, Part 4, 2:577.

eral times in London theatres,[28] but patrons could not have been more
elated with the piece than the *Critical Review* writer. Assuredly,
the playwright hovered over the reviewer, if he did not insert the rave
notice himself in the magazine he helped establish.

> Impartial judges, and those who have real taste, allow the author of
> this piece to be not only a master of genius and invention; but happily
> just at drawing characters.
>   The blunders of the *Irishman* are none of them forced, they are such
> as cannot fail to strike and make you laugh, because there are none of
> them that have not been heard at some time or other to fall from the
> mouth of such a character.
>   There is a mixture of pride, pedantry, stiffness, and humanity in the
> Scotchman that mark him very strongly; but his dialect is not quite
> intelligible.
>   The *Frenchman* is intirely new, his gasconading, his cowardice, his
> making love, and his rage, are all of a piece, and share largely in the
> *vis comica*.
>   It is remarked of the sailors, that they have a dialect and manners
> peculiar to themselves, and that they are a species of men abstracted as
> it were from every other race of mortals. In drawing *them* our author
> has been scrupulously exact, and the following quotation will, while it
> justified our opinion, induce every judicious reader to adopt it.[29]

Northerners writing plays in London during the second quarter of
the eighteenth century concentrated upon tragedy, the genre considered the highest form of drama. They selected stories from
history and myth dealing with nobles who speak dignified blank verse,
which is rhetorical rather than emotional. Scots were preoccupied with
language. Their attention to the manner of statement may be the result
of self-consciousness arising from accented speech. Thomson's diction
exerted considerable influence upon North British writers, because his
pseudoclassic tragedies were the first to gain prominence. This poet's
language continued to affect dramatic writers into the nineteenth
century.
  The diction which Scottish writers employed is not as distinctive
as their inclination to romanticism. The incorporation of classic and
romantic components is in the same spirit of accommodation which
most of these dramatists exhibited in conceding historical accuracy to
give ancient characters contemporary political significance. They com-
promised critical tenets in modifying the use of the unities to suit the

28   Genest, *Some Account of the English Stage,* 7:517.
29   "*The Reprisal, or the Tars of Old England,*" *Critical Review* 3 (1757):159.

tastes of the audience. These concessions are concomitant with the aesthetic strictures of the Common Sense School, which holds a middle
ground experimental in method and ethical in end. Scots dramatists
were partisan and their political concerns hinged upon distinctions
such as justice and injustice, a natural stand for a minority group. The
romantic idealism manifested itself in practical rather than speculative
topics. Thomson, Mallet, and Paterson opt for peace, because it is
constructive and prosperous; war is destructive and vain.

There are allusions in the Scots' dramas which indicate the common
sense approach to the reconciliation of opposites. The king in Smollett's
Regicide exemplifies this motif when he counsels his Calpurnian queen
who has premonitions of doom:

> No, my queen,
> Let us avoid the opposite extremes
> Of negligence supine, and prostrate fear.—
> Already hath our vigilance perform'd
> What caution justifies: and for thy dream;
> As such consider it. —The vain effect
> Of an imagination long disturb'd—
> Life with substantial ills, enough is curs'd:
> Why should we then, with frantic zeal, pursue
> Unreal care; and with th' illusive form
> Which our own teeming brain produc'd, affright
> Our reason from her throne?
>
> (V. 1)

The common sense approach becomes increasingly difficult to establish as a contributory factor in Scots' plays as the trends associated with
romanticism increased in popularity. The homogenizing of the dichoto-
mous neoclassical and romantic styles, while in keeping with the tenets
of the school, occurred outside its sphere of influence. As the tendencies toward romanticism became stronger, the conciliatory attitude
diminished. When revolution was in the wind, and individualism in the
heart, Common Sense ceased to be a valid, or more correctly, a useful
framework.

1750-1775

During the third quarter of the eighteenth century, Scots favored melodrama, a natural selection for romantically inclined writers. The crescendo that would blast the British stage with sensational incidents and violent appeals to the emotions was rising. "Ye woods and wilds, whose melancholy gloom / Accords with my soul's sadness, and draws forth / The voice of sorrow from my burning heart," Lady Randolph says at the beginning of *Douglas*. Northerners, who have ever loved a good gray gloom, were delighted with the melancholy story of a national figure. English audiences also acclaimed Home's play. His idealistic portrayal of a flawless hero from the primitive past appealed to an increasingly large segment of society which was concerned with the natural goodness of man. As Ernest Bernbaum observes in his *Guide Through the Romantic Movement,* Ossian and Omai were both lionized, because they reassured the adherents to sensibility that the ideal human condition existed. The vision of a rose-tinted world lends itself to emotional rather than rational expression. The emphasis upon feelings, like melodrama itself, discourages moderation. Dramatists less capable than Home relied increasingly upon sentiment. The more limited the writer, the more he tended to exploit emotion to thrill his audience. Such distortion resulted in theatricals which reflect the confused state of many late century minds.

Andrew Henderson, a bookseller in London, wrote a pro-English *History of the Rebellion 1745–6, etc.,* and published a complimentary biography of the Duke of Cumberland, whom Scots generally regarded as the butcher of Culloden. Henderson is an exception that partially proves rules, for Scots in London were a tightly knit group. As David Daiches stresses in *The Paradox of Scottish Culture: The Eighteenth Century Experience,* North Britons were fiercely nationalistic politically, while they schizophrenically aped English models in the arts. Henderson, who dedicated his tragedy to Robert Walpole, was not in the Scottish political mainstream; his *Arsinoe; or the Incestuous Marriage* (1752), does exemplify the imitative instinct. The play is a Shakespearean pastiche. The majority of British dramatic writers of this time were indebted to Shakespeare to some degree, but Henderson's appropriation of Elizabethan material is so blatant that he could have subtitled his tragedy "Hamlet in Egypt."

King Ptolemy loves his sister, Arsinoe, and feigns affection for her children, the heirs apparent. Young Ptolemy worries that his mother and uncle are intimate:

> Accuse my Mother why accuse?
> For why tho' they each other ought to love,
> Yet carefully they ought to shun Extreams;
> Extreams in every thing prove dangerous,
> Ending in Folly and in Madness wild.
>
> (II. 1)

Shortly after the Prince speaks for moderation, he rants to members of the court against the sinful union of Ptolemy and Arsinoe. The heroine enters in the middle of her son's tirade, and questions his sanity.

In the third act, Ptolemy's machinations come to light; the ghost of Arsinoe's husband warns her of his successor's deception, and reminds her of the pledges of their marriage bed. Arsinoe does not see the apparition, but her son does. When Ptolemy's ambassador informs the widow that the King wishes to marry her, Arsinoe is shocked. She stalls, hoping to extricate herself from the dilemma, but eventually consents to wed him. Her sons are murdered. Ptolemy is defeated by the Gauls. The lustful tyrant's head is carried on stage as a symbol of "the fatal ills of ambition."

John Moncrieff shared with Andrew Henderson the penchant for imitation. Moncrieff brought out *Appius* the season after Samuel Crisp's *Virginia* opened. *Appius* premiered at Covent Garden on 6 March 1755 and ran six nights. The Roman story had been presented in the theatre since the sixteenth century, because the tale of the girl who chooses death at her father's hand rather than submission to the evil aristocrat was a crowd pleaser. The legend was popular with dramatists because the plot admits variations. Moncrieff's *Appius*, which was probably suggested by Crisp's tragedy, is a mediocre treatment of the familiar subject, but it is not a slavish imitation. In *Appius* the villain approaches Camilla, Virginia's nurse, in an effort to corrupt the heroine. Moncrieff thus stresses the deep-seated malice of Appius. The Scot also introduces Valarius and Horatius, patricians who function as foils to point up the treachery of Appius. Moncrieff shifts the emphasis from the bravery of the hapless father and daughter to the wickedness of Appius.

Moncrieff permitted Thomas Sheridan to revise *Appius*. Sheridan states that he expunged the entire fifth act.[1] It may have been his idea

---

1   *Biographia Dramatica*, 2:34. Also see Genest, 4:421–22.

to elevate the rank of Virginius to commander of a legion, since he played the centurion.

Although the staged version may have been four acts, the play was published as a five-act tragedy. Moncrieff introduced extra characters, who are relevant, but hardly necessary. Working with classic and well-known material, dramatists seem to have felt the need of change for its own sake. Moncrieff disposes of Appius by poison, which is no more effective than his portrayal of Virginius as senile. The long colloquies between father and daughter in the fifth act attempt the poise of high tragedy, but the chatty exchanges are mere prolongations to give the play the proper number of acts. Such rhetoric militates against Virginius's killing his daughter as an act of passion. Desperate actions are hard to see as drastic emotional reactions, when so much dialogue is expended before they occur.

The year after *Appius* was produced, a new play opened in Edinburgh. John Home's *Douglas* caused such a sensation when it premiered that four months to the day after the first Scottish production of the tragedy it was staged at Covent Garden on 14 March 1757.

Home had wanted to have his plays produced in London from the beginning of his dramatic career. He completed his first play, *Agis*, in 1746. The next year he took his patriotic tragedy to Garrick, who refused to produce the drama about an obscure ancient monarch. The minister expressed his bitter disappointment in a verse he wrote on Shakespeare's monument in Westminster Abbey:

> Image of Shakespeare! to this place I come
> To ease my bursting bosom at thy tomb;
> For neither Greek nor Roman poet fired
> My fancy first, thee chiefly I admired;
> And day and night revolving still my page
> I hoped, like thee, to shake the British stage;
> But cold neglect is now my only mead,
> And heavy falls it on so proud a head.
> If powers above now listen to thy lyre,
> Charm them to grant, indulgent, my desire;
> Let petrifaction stop this falling tear,
> and fix my form for marble here.[2]

After Garrick rejected *Agis*, the crestfallen divine returned home to his manse at Athelstaneford, where he constructed a play based on a national legend. "Gil Morice," the ballad which recounts the murder of

---

2   Henry Mackenzie, ed., *The Works of John Home* (Edinburgh, 1809), 1:35.

a youth by his mother's jealous husband, forms the germ of *Douglas*. Home changed the material to a great extent. He supplanted the ironic and earthy qualities of the ballad with romantic and mysterious atmosphere. In "Gil Morice" Lady Barnard's child is illegitimate. In *Douglas* the hero's birth is wrapped in secret for a nobler reason. Douglas married Matilda, despite the hereditary feud between their families. Shortly after their marriage he died, and Matilda's father had her marry Lord Randolph. Sir Malcolm hated his grandson, who carried the blood of his enemy, and had the infant abandoned. Old Norval, a shepherd, saved the child from exposure and raised him as his own.

After Lady Randolph recounts much of this background, which Richard Sheridan burlesqued in *The Critic*, young Norval (Douglas) saves Lord Randolph's life and is rewarded with an army commission. Randolph's heir presumptive, Glenalvon, hates the hero. In a fight precipitated by the villain, Douglas slays Glenalvon, and is then killed by Lord Randolph. Lady Randolph despairs over the loss of her son and commits suicide.

Shakespearean echoes sound throughout the play. The antagonism of the families recalls the Capulets and Montagues of *Romeo and Juliet*. The noble raised as a shepherd is reminiscent of Perdita's situation in *The Winter's Tale*. Villainous Glenalvon is analogous to evil Iago in *Othello*. Home modeled his blank verse on Shakespeare's, but the creative imitator's flowing cadences are Romantic rather than Renaissance. Oratorical speeches slow the action, but these poetic excursions found favor with audiences. Norval's speech became a favorite piece, which countless students of rhetoric declaimed during the eighteenth and nineteenth centuries.

> My name is Norval: on the Grampian hills,
> My father feeds his flocks; a frugal swain,
> Whose constant cares were to increase his store,
> And keep his only son, myself, at home.
> For I had heard of battles, and I longed
> To follow to the field some warlike lord:
> And heaven soon granted what my sire denied.
> This moon which rose last night, round as my shield,
> Had not yet filled her horns, when, by her light,
> A band of fierce barbarians, from the hills,
> Rushed like a torrent down upon the vale,
> Sweeping our flocks and herds. The shepherds fled
> For safety, and for succor, I alone
> With bended bow, and quiver full of arrows,
> Hovered about the enemy, and marked

> The road he took, then hasted to my friends;
> Whom, with a troop of fifty chosen men,
> I met advancing. The pursuit I led,
> Till we o'ertook the spoil-encumbered foe.
> We fought and conquered. Ere a sword was drawn,
> An arrow from my bow had pierced their chief,
> Who wore that day the arms which now I wear.
> Returning home in triumph, I disdained
> The shepherd's slothful life: and having heard
> That our good king had summoned his bold peers
> To lead their warriors to the Carron side,
> I left my father's house, and took with me
> A chosen servant to conduct my steps;—
> Yon trembling coward, who forsook his master.
> Journeying with this intent, I passed these towers,
> And, heaven-directed, came this day to do
> The happy deed that gilds my humble name.
>
> (II. 1)

Melancholy tone pervades in *Douglas*, but it is the particular speech and the specific episode rather than the entity that is memorable. This is a frequent occurrence in poetic drama, when the mode of expression preoccupies the writer. At a time when numerous convention-bound tragedies had little but performers' virtuosity to recommend them, *Douglas* is notable for its genuine idealism and sincere emotion.

Although Garrick thought *Douglas* "too simple and undrammatic" to produce, the play appealed to a wide spectrum of theatregoers. Individuals as diverse as Thomas Gray and David Hume praised the play that became a dramatic staple. Garrick determined not to let another hit slip away, and asked Home if he could produce the play he had rejected ten years before. *Agis* premiered at Drury Lane on 21 February 1758. It ran ten performances in London, and the next month, when it opened in Edinburgh, it played four nights.

Agis deals with the rivalries of Agis IV and Leonidas. There is a romantic subplot involving Lysander and Euanthe, complicated by Amphares. The tragedy of the King of Sparta, who attempted to restore the laws of Lycurgus and failed, shows that Home compounded his dramatic formula at the beginning of his career. Using the classics and Shakespeare in an original manner, he develops Amphares, who is briefly mentioned in Plutarch, into a villain of Iago-like dimensions. The author is also indebted to Elizabethan history plays, but the dominant tone is preromantic. Agis and his mother, Agesistrata, share the same fate at the hands of the opposition. The close and tragic relation-

John Home (1722–1808).

ship of mothers and sons is a recurring motif in Home's plays. Scenes
such as Agesistrata's weeping over the dead Agis are characteristic.

> Alas! alas! my son!
> . . . .
> O son of Jove, great author of our race,
> Sustain my soul! For he who was my stay,
> My comfort and my strength is now no more.
>
> (V. 1)

This pietà episode is on the same emotional plane as the farewell scene
between Lady Randolph and her offspring. It is in the reflective passages that Home exhibits the strength of emotional power. His fluent
flights of verse are more oriented to the human condition than Thomson's, and they avoid the sentimental excesses of tearjerkers.

> Let never man
> Say in the morning that the day's his own:
> Things past belong to memory alone;
> Things future are the property of hope.
> The narrow line, the isthmus of the seas,
> The instant scarce divisible, is all
> That mortals have to stand on.
>
> (II. 1)

Home puts forth ideals in *Agis* which he reiterated throughout his
dramatic works: honor offers the warrior a single alternative—victory or
death; virtue must be defended to the death; kings are born for the
good of their people. *The story of the Tragedy of Agis, With Observations on the Play, the Performance and the Reception* (1758), praises
Home's high-mindedness, which the pamphleteer recounts so moved a
lady in the audience that she fainted in her box. The line, "Dangers
when necessary ought not be shunned," inspired a Mr. Rochefort to
lead a round of applause and huzzas that interrupted the performance.

The *Theatrical Review* was less enthusiastic in its appraisal of *Agis*.
The critic exhibits the caution often found in reviews of an inferior
work that follows a major achievement: "*Agis* inspires us with admonition; *Douglas* speaks forcibly to our softer feelings. In *Douglas* he has
shown himself perfect master of nature and the human heart; in *Agis*
of contrivance in point of plot and incidents. What a masterpiece may
not we expect from such talents when united in one tragedy!"[3]

3 *Theatrical Review, 1757 and Beginning of 1758*; cited in *London Stage*, Part
4, 2:648.

The *Critical Review* complained that the story of *Agis* was obscure.[4] Home continued to employ unfamiliar backgrounds for his tragedies. *The Siege of Aquileia,* which opened at Drury Lane on 21 February 1760 and ran nine performances, deals with the struggle for an Adriatic fortress town and includes an heroic youth's early death and a mother's grief. Aquileia is besieged by Maximin, a Dalmatian chief. The town is defended by Aemilius, a Roman consul and his sons, Paulus and Titus. The brothers are captured by the Dalmatians. Maximin threatens to execute his prisoners unless their father surrenders Aquileia. Aemilius cannot capitulate honorably. A priest then proposes that the consul yield the city after four days, if no relief arrives. Cornelia, a typical Home mother, begs her husband to take this advice:

> This city is not Rome,
> Nor your small garrison the Roman host.
> A part, a little part, a very grain
> Of public interest, in your mind outweighs
> Your children, all your children. Oh! Aemilius!
> Alike the father and the mother bear
> The name of parent; but a parent's love
> Lives only in the tender mother's heart.
>
>   (III. 1)

When the troops arrive at Aquileia, Maximin feels that he has been duped, and orders a gallows erected. Titus then returns to his father and proves his bravery by not pleading for his or his brother's life:

> The cause of honour, of my father's honour,
> The cause of Rome against myself I plead,
> And in my voice the noble Paulus speaks.
> Let no man pity us; aloft we stand
> On a high theatre, objects, I think,
> Of admiration and of envy rather.
>
>   (IV. 1)

Titus returns to Maximin's camp. In the ensuing fray, he slays the Dalmatian tyrant, but is mortally wounded, and is carried back to Aquileia by Paulus, for a scene between the dying hero and his mother:

> TITUS. I stood the chance of war. Do not bewail
> A fate so far above my highest hope
> When last we parted. Men are born to die.

4   "Agis," *Critical Review* 5 (1758):237.

> Cor.   But not, like thee, in youth untimely slain.
> Titus.   This active day has been an age of life.
>
> (V. 1)

The prologue indicates that Garrick had relied on the audience's acceptance of this play, because of its memories of the recent Seven Years War, but the conflict of patriotic duty and parental love, told with a plethora of words and a dearth of action, met with a lukewarm reception.

Home's *The Fatal Discovery* was produced at Drury Lane on 23 February 1769 and ran ten nights. Again the dramatist tried an ancient Scottish theme. Ronan, Prince of Norven, and Durstan, King of the Picts, both desire Rivine. Through a false report Durstan wins the hand of the princess, although she loves Ronan, to whom she was first betrothed. Rivine's brother, Connan, tells her of Durstan's falsehood. This is a variation on the Lady Randolph love story. Rivine believes that Ronan has drowned at sea, but he is the sole survivor of a shipwreck and is living in a hermit's cave. This echoes the long lost Norval element. Rivine and Ronan meet at the cave; and on bended knee Ronan professes his idealistic love. The heroine's rhetoric foreshadows the sanguine ending:

> Even when I thought thee false, and strove to hate thee,
> Even then my tortured heart was full of thee:
> 'Tis this that sends me to an early grave;
> I could not bear to be and not be thine.—
>
> (III. 1)

The Fatal Discovery contains the same devices and the same flaws which appeared in Home's earlier plays. The familiar variation of the formula was produced anonymously because of Home's known association with the unpopular Lord Bute. When playgoers learned its author's identity, the play closed.[5]

Home's next drama, *Alonzo*, was produced at Drury Lane on 27 February 1773 and ran eleven performances. This tragedy, set in Spain during the days of the Moorish invasions, contains many of his stock themes. Ormisinda secretly marries the jealous but noble Alonzo, from whom she has been estranged eighteen years because he imagined she had been unfaithful. Ormisinda tells her confidante, Teresa, that her

---

5   Frederick S. Boas, *An Introduction to Eighteenth Century Drama 1700–1780* (Oxford, 1953), p. 276.

father, the King of Spain, ignorant of her first marriage, has arranged
to wed her to the winner of a duel between Mirmallon, a Moor, and a
Spanish champion. The stranger who duels with the Moor is Alonzo
disguised as Abdallah, a Persian prince. The victorious Alonzo accuses
Ormisinda of infidelity, and as Alberto, their son, is about to fall on his
father, Ormisinda rushes between husband and son, and stabs herself,
as she reveals Alberto's identity. Alonzo, realizing his wife's innocence,
kills himself. The complicated story of a martyr-heroine caught in an
Oedipal dilemma, a noble youth who does not know his identity, is,
as Frederick Boas observes, a Latin *Douglas*. *The Public Advertiser* for
22 March 1773 carried a bit of doggerel which indicates that Home's
charm had worn thin:

> Epigram on the New Tragedy ALONZO
>
> No wonder that each female voice
> Resounds Alonzo's praise;
> A sure foundation of Applause,
> The crafty Author lays.
>
> Against the Virtue of his wife
> A Husband, if he's wise
> According to the Gallant HOME,
> Should not believe his eyes.

Home's last play, *Alfred*, opened at Covent Garden on 21 January
1778 and closed after three performances. The earlier Thomson-Mallet
treatment of the story stresses love of country. The Home version concentrates on love. A disguised Alfred makes his way to the Danish
camp, not for political or patriotic motives, but because Ethelswida, his
betrothed, has been captured. Alfred is not the only one to mask.
In his visit to King Hinguar's camp, the Davidian hero entrances
the Dane with his music. The king asks his guest to soothe the madness
of his beloved. The Dane's love, who enters dressed in outlandish garb,
singing snatches and rambling, is Ethelswida. The complexities of the
eternal triangle are increased by Hinguar's jealous wife; and before
Alfred and Ethelswida are reunited in a happy ending, the plot tangles
an implausible skein.

To say that Home is a one-work author is not a fair appraisal. There
is merit in his post-*Douglas* plays. His blank verse is proficient, at times
commanding. His formulaic elements do provide scope for legitimate
variation. Home's tragedy is that he produced *Douglas* at the inaugura-
tion of his dramatic career.

In his last three plays, Home veered away from the neoclassical to follow an increasingly melodramatic direction. This was the way of Alexander Dow as well. Classicism restrained Home. Orientalism pushed Dow to melodramatic excess. Dow, a captain in the East India Company's Bengal infantry, was familiar with the exotic lands then influencing British art and letters. He published a translation of Mohummud Casim Ferishta's *History of Hindostan* (1768), and later in the year his first play was accepted at Drury Lane. *Zingis* opened on 17 December 1768. The elaborate spectacle ran eleven nights. In spite of Dow's experience in the East, his tale of Genghis Khan is more Brighton Pavilion than Xanadu. Dow's plot, which deals with usurpation and romance, is notable for its fast moving exposition and rising action. The seeds of the intrigue against the "all subduing" Zingis are sown, and the romantic complications unfold with intensity. Mila, Cubla's wife, begs Ovisa's assistance. Ovisa is the daughter of Aunac, the dethroned emperor whose throne Zingis occupies. Timur, the son of Zingis, is in love with Ovisa, and joins the conspiracy against his father. The tensions of Ovisa's doubts about two wrongs making a right, and Timur's anguish over what may mean parricide, neatly dovetail to arouse sympathy for the lovers' plight. Melodrama has the edge as the second act ends with Ovisa pleading on bended knee with Timur to spare his father.

In the third act Zingis enters. This ruler, whose ambitions are world-encompassing, attains the necessary mystery and stature by under-exposure. Because Zingis is on stage only at critical times, his presence is commanding when he does appear. As with most melodramas, the last acts weaken the play. Although some of the action is necessary, such as Aunca's murder, which fixes Ovisa's determination to avenge her father, the ultimate approach to the pile of corpses at the feet of Zingis is overlong, and far inferior to the fast moving beginning.

Dow's second drama, *Sethona*, which opened at Drury Lane on 19 February 1774, was performed nine times and was more beautifully mounted than his first play. Philippe Loutherbourg did the Egyptian sets which received rare reviews, but reactions to the melodrama were mixed.[6]

Sethona and *Zingis* share more than exotic settings. The motif of government usurpation, which had a peculiar fascination and significance for Scots, recurs in Dow's second play. The Egyptian tale of political intrigue laced with romance opens lavishly. Sethona is discov-

6 *Public Advertiser*, 21 February 1774.

ered in the temple of Osiris. The heroine prays she will not have to marry Amasis, who has taken the throne from her father, King Seraphis. When the unwanted wedding is announced, Sethona bursts out with romantic dialogue containing solitary longings, imagery of untamed landscape, and Gothic touches:

> O could I fly
> To some brown desart, far remov'd from man,
> And in the shade of some poor lonely tree,
> Beside a ling'ring stream, in silence sit,
> And muse from morn to eve, from eve to morn.
> Or tell my sister of the sky, that wanes
> With me apace, the story of my woe;
> There undisturb'd, I might devour my grief,
> Like some sad ghost, that nightly sits alone,
> Pale, bending o'er the slowly twinkling flame
> Of a decaying meteor.
>
> (I. 1)

Menes, the supposedly murdered heir presumptive, enters shortly after Sethona refuses Amasis' proposal. In a soliloquy Orus, a priest, reveals that Menes is the son of Sethos.

The second act opens with Menes' discovering himself to Sethona. He then recounts his escape from the sepulchre. The action continues in an upward sweep as Menes is caught by one of the usurper's men. Otanes, an officer of Amasis, frees Menes and tells him his plans to subvert the throne and return it to Seraphis, who has returned from Ethiopia in disguise. Otanes directs Sethona to wed Amasis. This marriage will aid the plans for the restoration of her father's throne. As in *Zingis,* the heroine is essential to the political plot, and reluctantly cooperates.

In the third act identities are revealed at the expense of plausibility. Abortive attempts at characterization through emotions impede the play's progress, which has gone rapidly thus far. Orus recognizes Seraphis, but Sethona does not penetrate her father's disguise as Pheron the seer. As Amasis is about to discover Pheron's true identity, Myrtaeus enters with news of the conspiracy. Orus reveals to Sethona that Seraphis was Pheron, whom they both believed dead. Sethona faints on a convenient couch; later she revives and tries to kill herself. The heroine then pleads with Menes, if he thinks she loves Amasis, to stab her. When Sethona reveals her true motivation for marrying Amasis, Menes begs forgiveness on his knees—a favored position for Dow's characters.

In the last acts, the author attempts to sustain interest by additional surprises and twists. Seraphis, like Menes, has survived the house of death. Otanes prevents Seraphis's attempt to suicide, only to have his king captured by Myrtaeus, Amasis's general. Myrtaeus recognizes Seraphis as Pheron, who saved his life in the desert. Myrtaeus sinks to his knees and grasps his captive's feet, then defects to Seraphis's camp. The reunion of Sethona and her father is marred by her tears for Menes, whose present fate is unknown. Seraphis induces her to faint once more by revealing that Menes is her brother. The rash Menes bursts upon the scene thinking that Seraphis has struck Sethona; but he is told of the kinship, and before he digests this news Amasis's men seize him. All hope for the noble characters seems lost in the fourth act which ends with a downward sweep.

In the final act Amasis promises to kill his prisoners, but feels remorse as his distracted wife, again thinking her father and lover are dead, delivers a mad speech. Seraphis and Menes are not dead, and during the course of the prolonged last act, Menes kills Amasis. Menes' true parentage is revealed, which makes him Sethona's cousin and not her brother.

One can dismiss the story of *Sethona* as Cumberland did in the prologue:

> Sethona is the lady's name—
> She lives at Memphis—of unsullied fame:
> A Tyrant woo'd her—but she lik'd another,
> And once 'twas fear'd her lover was her brother.

The contorted incidents of this melodrama illustrate the turn drama took in the latter part of the eighteenth century. *Sethona* is labeled a tragedy, yet the ending neatly doles out happiness to the good characters. Poetic justice is secured superficially by last-minute contrivances. Although the difference between serious and comic drama does not hinge on whether the ending is sad or happy, it does depend upon how seriously one takes the actions or fortunes of the characters. The concern which one feels for the characters in the melodrama is emotion increased through suspense or surprise used for its own sake. There is little regard for convincing motivation. The story is developed by action and circumstances, rather than charting of motives or personal revelation. Dow's main concern in *Zingis* and *Sethona* is in providing an exciting plot. Like most melodramatists, in his fervor for action, Dow neglects characterization. He pays little attention to human nature and dispenses with internal action. The "within" which causes tragedy is absent.

John Armstrong contributed to the corpus of dramas which caused tragedy to wane in the late century. Armstrong, an Edinburgh physician, published *The Art of Preserving Health* (1744), a popular didactic poem of home remedy and grotesque medical advice.

> Avoid the stubborn ailment, avoid
> The full repast; and let sagacious age
> Grow wiser, lesson'd by the dropping teeth.

The doctor was long in the tooth himself before his bourgeois tragedy was published. He wrote *The Forced Marriage* in 1765, and submitted the play to Garrick, who refused it. In a foreword Armstrong argues that the drama could have been staged had he "dangled after Managers" or "prostituted patronage." These remarks substantiate Thomson's observation that Armstrong's great defect was spleen.[7]

The situation of the melodrama Armstrong included in his *Miscellanies* (1770), is stock. Streni, an Italian noble, insists that his daughter, Olympia, marry Count Claudio, a man old enough to be her father, rather than Alphonso, whom she loves. Victoria, Olympia's cousin and confidante, who is given to platitudes, assures her kinswoman that Streni will relent, and that she will marry Alphonso. Victoria does not realize that Claudio is an embezzler. Complications and developments requiring action, too frequently unfold through letters. In the fifth act, Olympia, crazed by the news of her lover's death at the hands of Claudio, who has fled, dies in her father's arms. The heroine's mad scene and demise illustrate the exorbitancy of melodramatic dialogue:

> OLYMPIA.
>   As you will.
> Do with me what you please. —Ha! there again!
> Now if you do not see him you're blind.—
> Dear father
> Behold! see there! —I come, I come,
> ALPHONSO!
> Receive me Heaven—and you—
>   STRENI.
>   Ah! hold her up!
> She falls like one shot thro' the brain.

7 See Rev. George Gilfallan, ed., "Introduction," *The Poetical Works of Armstrong, Dyer, and Green* (Edinburgh, 1863).

VICTORIA.
                              Alas!
She's dead! dead! dead!
       STRENI.
                        'Tis but a fit I hope.—
Hold up her head. —Help, help! Oh all the world
To hear her speak again! —Ah me! that face
Is fix'd in death. She's cold, cold—poor
OLYMPIA!
I've liv'd too long. She's gone, my faultless child
For ever gone—and I her murderer—Oh!

                                                            (V. 2)

There are elements in this tragedy of fated lovers, such as Alphonso's banishment, which indicate that this playwright bowed to Shakespeare. Armstrong also appreciates Shakespearean drama in his essays. His *Essays* by "Launcelot Temple" (1763), contain dramatic criticism which indicates that his tragedy was probably a reaction against the heroic verse tragedy which he considers pompous and monotonous. His high regard for Shakespeare, and acknowledgment of blank verse as superior to rhymed couplets, raises the question of whether *The Forced Marriage* is intended to be poetry or prose. It is almost entirely prose. The lines which are set up to resemble verse in a number of sections are as difficult to scan as his *Art of Preserving Health,* which abounds in mysteries of accentuation. Armstrong's critical sketches belie a common-sense approach to the theatre of his day, and exhibit ability to spot flaws in contemporary dramas. His animadversions fit his own play:

> As to the Characters .... Those that appear in most of our modern plays, tragedies call them or comedies, are like bad portraits; which indeed represent the human features, but without life or meaning, or those distinguishing strokes which, in the comparable HOGARTH and in every great history painter, make you imagine you have seen such persons as appear in the picture. In short, those mechanical performances are as imperfect and unnatural representations of human life, of the manners and passions of mankind, as the *Gothic* Knights which lie along in armour in the Temple church are of the human figure.[8]

The Scots whose plays were produced or published in London during the third quarter of the eighteenth century contributed little which can be considered unique. Real innovation is rare in drama, particularly in

8 John Armstrong, "On Characterization," *Miscellanies* (London, 1770), 2:166–67.

the actor-dominated theatre of eighteenth-century London. Henderson and Moncrieff closely adhered to English models. The two most talented Scots playwrights of the era, Home and Dow, each stamped his plays with his individuality. Both men were formulaic; neither succeeded in improving his formula in later works. Also, the works of Home, Dow, and Armstrong exhibit the progress of melodrama. One may consider the incongruous line in *The Forced Marriage*, "She's dead! dead! dead!" a rattle signaling the immoderate emotionalism which gagged late Georgian drama.

1775-1800

During the last quarter of the century, dramatists favored melodramas with too many thrills, and farces with too little substance. Rather than desperate measures to resuscitate the expiring theatre, these extremes were the result of incremental use of pyrotechnics to mask dramatic deficiency. Many productions were placebos to satisfy a society in a state of revolutionary upheaval which wanted escape rather than a mirror of its disconcerting age. Northern melodramatists and farceurs continued to follow Southern fashions, and with few exceptions, manufactured works which helped create the denouement that was to grip the stage for nearly a century. Joanna Baillie made a distinctive contribution at this time. Her dramatic aesthetic of the dominant passion points a solution to the uncontrolled romanticism. The precedence of emotion over reason was debilitating British drama. Emotion is a necessary but dangerous theatrical prescription. When feelings are used for their own sake, one must continually increase the dosage of sentiment and excitement. These ingredients may stir an audience once, but they are rarely effective a second time. When productions do not merit revival, novelty becomes essential. One of the less taxing ways of assuaging the craze for newfanglement is spectacle. As the *Westminster Review* observed in dismissing John Burgoyne's 1774 hit, *The Maid of the Oaks*,[1] spectacle often supplanted dramatic worth as a criterion of success.

1 Cited in *The London Stage*, Part 4, 3:1846–47. A less spectacular version of John Burgoyne's five-act vaudeville was produced in Scotland. *The Maid of the Oaks Altered into an After-Piece of Two Acts by a Gentleman of the Theatre-Royal, Edin-*

Extravaganza and variety go hand in hand. Countless short pieces flickered briefly on the stage. James Stewart supplied this kind of *ignis fatuus*. His farce, *The Two English Gentlemen, or the Sham Funeral*, was presented at the Haymarket on 21 March 1774. Genest labels the comedy poor, and the notice in *Biographia Dramatica* states that the performers who presented the piece were as despicable as the play itself. Five years later Stewart's comedy, *The Students, or the Humours of St. Andrews*, was performed at the Haymarket on 13 October 1777. It was played as the afterpiece the night Cornelius Vanderstop's translation of *The Gentle Shepherd* opened. In his dedication to George Coleman, Stewart describes his 1779 production: "I waited for the Opinion of the Town, and found it past my Expectations favourable, notwithstanding, as 'tis often the Case with Benefits at your House, two of my Performers was wretched, although I took every Precaution, but those not used to the Stage, rehearse one way, and play another."

After *The Students* was staged, Stewart rewrote some of the speeches and added six songs to the university high jinks. The play opens with an old school custom: three students hold an archery contest, the goal of which is to shoot an arrow over the spire of St. Leonard's. Frederick is the loser and has to buy drinks for his friends Byron and Freeport. Frederick then outlines his scheme to trick McDowell, the exciseman, into believing he has come into an inheritance. The pranksters adjourn to the tavern, where they agree to include the Drover, who wishes to make McDowell a cuckold.

At this point the author introduces the romantic plot. Freeport and Harriot, abetted by Byron and Emily, foil Graspall, Harriot's guardian, who wants her to marry his son, thus keeping the girl's money in the family. After putting McDowell through humiliations he has done nothing to merit, Frederick, who now has Harriot and her fortune, decides to give McDowell a generous estate. The two threads of plot in the two acts never truly entwine. The construction and the dialogue are such that Stewart's prefactory admission that he never attended university is unnecessary.

Charles Stuart may be considered a member of James Stewart's clan, if a penchant for the ridiculous entitles one to share a tartan.

---

burgh, in *A Collection of the Most Esteemed Farces and Entertainments performed on the British Stage* (Edinburgh, 1792), pp. 263–91, keeps Burgoyne's better dialogue, and wisely deletes more spectacular numbers beyond the capabilities of a provincial playhouse. James Dibdin, *Annals of the Edinburgh Stage* (Edinburgh, 1888), p. 185, notes an Edinburgh performance of *The Maid of Oaks* on 26 April 1783.

"The Experiment," a two-act comedy which opened at Covent Garden on 16 April 1777, and *The Cobler of Castlebury*, a musical which played once at Covent Garden on 27 April 1779, are attributed to Stuart. Genest disliked the *Cobler*.[2] As the curtain opens Lapstone is getting drunk. The cobler passes out, providing Sergeant Bluff opportunity to make love to Kate Lapstone, who encourages him. Nancy Bluff gets satisfaction by provoking Lapstone's advances. The wife swapping ends with the happy reunion of Lapstone and Kate, Bluff and Nancy.

Stuart concocted "Ripe Fruit; or, The Marriage Act," which served as a morsel for "The Feast of Thalia; or A Dramatic Oglio"[3] given at the Haymarket on 22 August 1781. Seven days later the same theatre staged Stuart's "Damnation; or the Playhouse Hissing Hot" on 29 August 1781. John O'Keeffe assisted the Scots farceur in the writing of *Gretna Green*, which opened at the Haymarket on 28 August 1783. The operatic farce ran nine nights and was revived a number of times. The musical involves elopements to Gretna Green, where Rory, the blacksmith-parson, weds couples using an anvil for an altar.

The play set in the Dumfries honeymoon resort, which became synonymous with runaway marriage,[4] has an international cast. Signora Figurante, an Italian duenna, accompanies Miss Plumb who intends to marry Captain Tipperary. This Irish rogue deserts his fiancée and woos Lady Pedigree, who has come to Gretna Green to prevent her daughter, Maria, from marrying Captain Gorget. Maria and Gorget are finally wed, because the officer unmasks Tipperary, who is his thieving servant. The Irishman marries Miss Plumb in the double wedding finale.[5]

The script was published in London and Dublin in 1783. The score of borrowed music with new lyrics was sold at the theatre. The music consists of British and Continental songs burdened with Stuart's banal verses. In comic numbers he relies on nonsense such as "Hotchity, Botchity, Shakity, Quakity." In romantic lyrics he does no better:

> My fond heart sweetly basks in the bright beams of hope,
> without it these roses and lillies would droop:

2   Genest, *Some Account of the English Stage*, 6:98.
3   "Ripe Fruit" was "by way of Entremet" in "The Feast of Thalia; or, A Dramatic Olio. Bill of Fare, in which every Dish belonging to the Drama will be served up: Prelude, Tragedy, Comedy, Opera, Interlude and Burlesque." *London Stage*, Part 5, 1:446.
4   Under Scots law, couples needed only to declare their wish to marry before witnesses. This law, which was abolished in 1940, made the village of Gretna Green just across the English border a famous elopement resort.
5   Genest, *Some Account of the English Stage*, 6:286.

'Tis the Sun that illumes this parterre of true Love;
without hope I shou'd droop like the 'lorn turtle Dove.
When my Jamie brav'd danger on Gib'ralters fell rock,
hope kept off the balls, made my heart stand the shock,
and drew him return'd in all vict'rys grand charms,
after conq'ring his foes to submit to these Arms.

Stuart dedicated *The Distress'd Baronet* to George, Prince of Wales:
"But your Royal Highness, by relinquishing your splendor for the satisfaction of your creditors, voluntarily obeyed the admirable laws of a
most honourable heart." The comedy in which the protagonist is modeled after the Regent opened at Drury Lane, on 3 May 1787. It ran six
nights. The prodigal Sir George Courteous finds himself penniless upon
reaching majority. The distressed baronet wishes to woo Sophia, and
inaugurates the romance with a letter which he entrusts to his French
servant.

> LA ROCHE. For when she put it in her pocket—
> SIR GEORGE. Her pocket! Why sirrah, you said just now that she put
> it in her bosom.
> LA ROCHE. Ah, mi Lor!—(*aside*). What shall I say? —Ah, mi Lor! de
> pocket of de lover, you know, is de bosom, de breast—dat be de lover's
> pocket in France, mi Lor.
> SIR GEORGE. Psha! Sirrah don't call me my Lord! I have no title to it.
> [Exit]
> *La Roche.* Pardonnez moi! I tought all de English men de lords of de
> creation.
> (I. 4)

Sophia pretends to be twins in order to captivate Sir George. Before
the hero wins Sophia, who extricates him from financial difficulties, Sir
George becomes involved with Jewish moneylenders. One of these is
Peter Pop, the pawnbroker, who is Sophia's stepfather. (This most
interesting character is modeled after Shylock.) Pop's lament for the
loss of the money Sophia has stolen provides insights into life of the
time.

> I can't forget the insult!—The parish officers to come to me in a drunken
> fit with a bastard child to pawn! Do they think my shop a Foundling
> Hospital? —Demme, I never took in a child in my life but once—that
> was Miss Sophy—and now the jade has taken me in. O! if her mother
> had but given me a duplicate of her to heir my fortune, I would have
> advertised her in the Hue-and-cry, and put her into Newgate.

Pop threatens to disinherit Sophia and leave his fortune to public
charities,

to spunge off my sinful peccadilloes—and ere I die it shall be the business of my life to follow the example of a worthy Borough justice, by
searching all Middlesex and Surry for six black and four white sattin
virgins to support my pall, and strew my coffin with Covent Garden
nosegays.

(II. 3)

Five days after *The Distress'd Baronet* opened, Stuart's *Box-Lobby
Loungers* played at Drury Lane on 16 May 1787. This piece makes use
of Scots and Irish characters, one of the author's favorite devices. In
The Stone-Eater Stuart again featured stage Irish to get laughs. This
interlude, which opened at Drury Lane on 14 May 1788, is built on one
joke. There was, according to Genest, a geek at the time who swal-
lowed small stones, then wiggled to enable the crowds to hear the
pebbles rattling in his stomach.[6] In the play inspired by this attraction,
Holdfast believes that his daughter is destined to marry a stone eater.
The girl's two suitors, Captain O'Thunder, who was born at Stoney
Batter and has lived by the Black Rock, and Captain Leek, who was
born in Flintshire, are served a meal of marble to decide who is a freak.
   Stuart's *The Irishman in Spain* opened at the Haymarket on 13
August 1791. The farceur had submitted the play under the title of
"She Would Be a Duchess" to the Lord Chamberlain earlier in the
year but the censor, at the request of General John Gunning, refused
to license the piece. Stuart cut the two acts to one after the opening,
and changed some of the business in his satire of Gunning's daughter,
Elizabeth, and her amorous involvements with the heirs of the Dukes
of Marlborough and Argyll. The general could not keep his family
affairs under wraps, for Elizabeth Gunning rattled the private skeletons
in her novel *Memoirs of Mary* (1793).
   As *The Irishman in Spain* begins, Olivia and her servant, Viletta,
arrive at Don Guzman's house after a long residence in a monastary.
This may be a reference to Gunning's ejection of Elizabeth from his
house, after which she moved in with the Duchess of Bedford. Olivia
decides to interest her vascillating swain, Carlos, by pretending to join
the Poor Clares. Carlos is upset by this development and threatens to
become a monk. Kilmainham, the Irish footman, tries to discover
Olivia's true intention. When the servant is unsuccessful, Guzman disguises as a confessor, and has his footman impersonate a Spanish
grandee. Viletta then pretends to be an abbess. The masking brings

<hr>

6   Genest, *Some Account of the English Stage*, 6:481.

about the union of Carlos and Olivia, whom Viletta and Kilmainham decide to join in Ireland for a double wedding.

Stuart used standard comic tools such as dialect and disguise in his fast-moving contrivances; the irreverent allusions to contemporary men and mores are of greater interest. These are manifestations of the revolutionary spirit. Making light of sacred cows of the establishment is a perennial prerogative of satire. Stuart's implied questioning of the intrinsic value of the status quo is a reflection of the drastic change then taking place.

When a society is disturbed it seeks surcease from its worries, and the theatre, preoccupied with appearance versus reality, can provide illusory retreat from a shattering world. Zany farces as well as romantic tragedies permit audiences to forget cares, which intellectual comedy and tragedy frequently bring into sharper perspective. Sensibility encased in an action-packed plot or in poetic elegance tranquilizes by reassuring patrons that natural human goodness triumphs. Henry Mackenzie's dramatizations in this mode created torpor rather than a sense of well-being. As a contributor to the London stage, the man of feeling was less successful than Charles Stuart. Mackenzie had submitted tragedies to Garrick as early as 1773, but did not get a play accepted in the English capital for another decade. On 10 February 1784, *The Shipwreck: or Fatal Curiosity* opened and closed at Covent Garden.

George Coleman had done an adaptation of Lillo's tragedy in 1782, which was quite popular. Coleman improved the role of Young Wilmot and changed the catastrophe. Mackenzie's five-act treatment is inferior to the earlier versions. Lillo's three-act structure is more suited to the simple story of the couple who unknowingly kill their son for material gain. Mackenzie's incretions turn the sentimental original into a mawkish debacle. His statement of intention belies his weakness as a dramatist:

> The principal objects of the alteration are, to remedy a defect which had been observed in the original, a want of connexion and increasing interest in the scenes; to afford, from the pressing necessity of the moment, a better apology for Wilmot's commission of the crime, and to show Agnes tempted to it by slower degrees, and the seduction of opportunity: for a like purpose, her character of pride and fierceness is endeavoured to be more strongly brought out in the conversation she holds with her husband and Charlotte. The additional character of the Boy is introduced, not only to infuse somewhat more of pity into the calamities of the Wilmot family, but to give an opportunity of showing

the distresses resulting from their poverty, on which the pride and delicacy of a more advanced age do not easily allow it to dwell.

Of the new characters introduced, the most noisome is Charles, the grandson of Old Wilmot and Agnes. The lad's function is to bring tears to the eyes of the audience. In this adaptation which substitutes pity for terror, Agnes's grandson becomes the decisive figure in the drama. His pathetic situation is dominant, and it complicates the action unnecessarily. Since Charles is a factitious pretext, he may be considered Mackenzie's "fatal curiosity."

Mackenzie's final attempt to entertain London is an elongated comedy which lulls like laudanum. He modeled *False Shame, or the White Hypocrite* on *La Fausse Inconstance; ou Le Triomphe de l'Honnête* by Fanny de Beauharnais. *False Shame* was presented as "The Force of Fashion" when it played one night at Covent Garden on 5 December 1789. The author attributed the failure of the play, in part, to the improper interpretation of Mountfort, the lead. In his introduction he also states the theme and accurately appraises its execution.

> The general idea of the piece, exhibiting a young man, of the most virtuous dispositions and amiable feelings, overpowered by a false shame, and led into conduct unworthy of him, certainly admitted of a dramatic representation, susceptible both of the lighter and more serious excellencies of comedy, and capable of a very useful moral effect; but it must be owned, that this idea is imperfectly brought out.

The play opens in a drawing room. Sensibility taints the dull comic dialogue which comprises the lengthy exposition. Several characters describe Julia's father, Mountfort, who is presumed dead. The preparation of this father's return is more than adequate.

In the second act Mountfort uses the pseudonym Wilkins. He and Sedley meet. Charles Sedley has been established as a good, middle-class, Clochester School young man, but he makes a miserable impression on Wilkins, because he assumes a pseudo-sophisticated pose. He pooh-poohs Mountfort, his old tutor, then runs amok by deriding sentiment. Mr. Wilkins next encounters Julia, his daughter. Wilkins's stammering reticence exudes overly-apparent clues to the speaker's true identity:

> JUL. [*After a pause.*] This letter, sir, which you were kind enough—
> pardon me, sir, its contents have too much moved—The friend of my
> father!—his friend when dying—entrusted by him!—it is foolish, very

foolish; but when I remember!— [*She bursts into tears. When she recovers, she curtsies, and makes a sign to him to be seated.*]

WIL. Madam, I—I feel the reception one of the most interesting to me,—most favourable to you,—such as Mountfort—I mean the friend of Mr Mountfort, the friend of his daughter—

(II. 1)

In the last acts, intrigues spring up to extend the play to a full five acts. Sir Charles fancies Julia, whom Sedley loves. Miss Danby plots with Sir Charles because she is infatuated with Sedley. An old retainer identifies Wilkins as Mountfort, and testifies to Sedley's humanitarian generosity. Sedley is properly contrite for his foppish behavior; this signals his union with Julia. Mountfort has the last homily in the play:

But tell your white hypocrites, my lord, that the colour of this hypocrisy is apt to grow darker. He who is first such a hypocrite from vanity, or from fear, will be in danger of becoming, in truth, the character he personates. A fool in the attempt, he will be a villain in its accomplishment; and will suffer equally in both. Tell them, my lord, that to be really good is a much shorter way to be happy;—to procure the only reputation an honest man can value; the only happiness a reasonable man can enjoy.

(V. 1)

It is ironic that Mountfort preaches on hypocrisy, since his masquerade is as deceptive as Sedley's. Gambits such as this lead one to question Mackenzie's sincerity in purveying sanctimonious sentimentality. The sensibility that made his novels popular is unsuited to the dramatic form. Catherine Metcalfe's dramatic adaptation of Mackenzie's novel, *Julia de Roubigne*, for a 1790 production at Bath, is a study in the incompatibility of the two genres. Sensibility is better read than said, for virtuous humanitarianism demands readers' imagination rather than actors' interpretation.

In comedy, under the influence of sensibility, the pathetic overrides the incongruous. This results in unintentional incongruities of the variety that abound in *False Shame*. Lady Eglantine Maxwell Wallace wrote comedies under the influence of sentimentalism, but she drew much from Old Comedy, which provided the mirth she achieves. In 1787 Lady Wallace wrote her first play, which she patterned after a French source, as was common practice in the late eighteenth century. Dumaniant's *La guerre overte; ou la ruse contre ruse* is the basis of Lady Wallace's *Diamond Cut Diamond* and Mrs. Inchbald's *The Midnight Hour*. The latter opened at Covent Garden the same season the

Scots lady's play was published. Mrs. Inchbald's adaptation may have obstructed presentation of *Diamond Cut Diamond*.

Lady Wallace's *The Ton; or the Follies of Fashion* opened at Covent Garden on 8 April 1788. In the preface she infers that her comedy is theatre of fact. The promiscuous and materialistic preoccupations are typical of *beau monde* satire. Lord Bonton seeks a friend's mistress. Lady Bonton keeps Daffodil, a *cavalier servante* who is "for shew rather than use." Lord and Lady Raymond are involved with Ben Levy, a moneylender. The usurer provides scope for anti-Semitic remarks similar to those in *The Distress'd Baronet*. Macpharo, an Irish rogue who lives by duping the gullible, describes the fashionable way of life: "Faith it bestows every advantage that empire can. It aggrandizes the low born—sets at nought ancient titles—makes the great do *little* things without reproach, and little people do *great* ones, without praise or reward." In the fourth act, there is a scene in which an assortment of characters hide in an armoire. This Molieresque device indicates Lady Wallace's ability to incorporate physical business, but the author focuses upon dialogue at the expense of incident. Conversation loaded with French phrases is calculated to make one see that the palanquin set are as brittle as the writer is clever. The production did not achieve the desired sophistication. *The Public Advertiser* of 9 April 1788 admonished the audience not to think that "the prompter has a part in the play from his frequent audibility."

Lady Wallace was better at self-dramatization than playwriting. Her pamphlet, *The Conduct of the King of Prussia and General Dumourier* [Charles Dumouriez] (1793), is more entertaining than her comedies. According to the author, whose snobbery rivals that of the characters in *The Ton,* she was on intimate terms with Dumouriez and numerous other important figures in Revolutionary France. Her account of adventures, which stemmed from writing a letter to England warning that Austria and Prussia would not be able to rescue Louis XVI, is a better source of social custom than political information.

After her return from Paris, where she purported to have engaged in espionage, Lady Wallace published *The Whim* in 1795. The play was in rehearsal at Margate, but was refused a license. Genest attributes John Larpent's revocation of the permit to political sentiments in the play, and cites Fag's speech to Nell:

Why faith, Nell you have a great fault, as time go—you know, old women are quite the fashion—you are too young—But, egad, I shall

please myself—I shall prefer the symmetry of Venus, and the rosy
health of young Hebe, to all the fat Forties of fashion.

(II. 1)

Genest believes the key to the censorship is the phrase "fat Forties of
fashion."[7] If Larpent considered this variation of the Regent's description of the ideal wife, "fat, fair, and forty," unfit for the stage he must
not have scrutinized John O'Keeffe's *The Irish Mimic, or Blunders at
Brighton.* This farce opened at Covent Garden on 23 April 1795,
despite the line in Act II, scene 3: "Fat, fair, and forty were all the
toast of the young men." *The Irish Mimic* and *The Whim* have more
in common than a contemporary allusion. Both pieces share a leading
lady named Julia, who is united to a Captain by machinations of a
clever servant.

The Whim derives its title from Lord Crochet's capricious one-day
revival of the Saturnalia. Fag and Nell, a pair of servants, are made
master and mistress of the house. Lord Crochet assumes Fag's culinary
duties, and his daughter, Julia, becomes Nell's maid. The play progresses in the established pattern of sentimental comedy, where servants best masters, and love triumphs without much trouble. Fag, as
master, unites Julia to Captain Belgrave, who loves her. Although Crochet at first objects, he plays his Saturnalian game, and being a
sporting Briton, finally consents to the marriage.

Lady Wallace also wrote "Cortes," a tragedy which was never
published. There is a quotation from this play on the title page of
The Whim, which newspaper advertisements of the comedy identified
as a passage from "Cortes."[8]

Andrew MacDonald, a deacon in the Scottish Episcopal Church,
resigned from his Glasgow parish and went to Edinburgh to develop
his literary talents. Like so many of his predecessors, he then made the
four-hundred mile trip to London, where he published a variety of
writings, some of which appeared under the pseudonym "Matthew
Bramble." MacDonald's *Vimonda* premiered at the Haymarket on 5
September 1787.[9] At Coleman's suggestion MacDonald omitted several
speeches for publication.

7 Genest, *Some Account of the English Stage*, 10:212. Nicoll, *A History of English
Drama*, 3:19, states that *The Whim* merited condemnation on artistic grounds.
8 *Biographia Dramatica*, 2:131.
9 Nicoll, *A History of English Drama*, 3:391, states that *Vimonda* was first performed in Edinburgh. Dibdin, *Annals of the Edinburgh Stage*, p. 208, gives the date
of the Scottish premiere as 4 May 1789. Mackenzie, *Anecdotes*, p. 206, says that the
play was scheduled to be presented at the Royalty Theatre, which opened 20 June
1787. Refusal of the patent forced this playhouse to close until July 3.

Vimonda, set in the border country between England and Scotland during the Middle Ages, opens with a scene between Melville and Vimonda. The heroine gives the impression of preternatural possibilities and hints at the delicate emotional balance necessary for a heroine who loses her senses and dies of a broken heart.

> Why do I toss each night in shudd'ring dreams,
> And rave of bloody swords, and ghastly wounds?
> 'Tis the dread phantom of my murder'd father
> That haunts yon towers, that tears my heart with terror,
> That cries revenge! and frowns—and vanishes.
> His monument shall be my oratory;
> There shall my constant knees the marble wear,
> There will I cry for vengeance on the wretch
> Who brought the deed accurs'd of Heaven, and there
> I'll pray the restless spirit to repose.
>
> (I. 1)

The lovers then exit. Dundore and Barnard discuss the recent black night on which they plunged the dagger into Rothsay's heart. This conversation substantiates Vimonda's vision of her dead father, which Melville tended to pass off as the fancy of a sensitive lady in mourning. The villain, Dundore, reveals his love for the heroine, thus adding another familiar complication.

In the second act Vimonda and Alfreda, her confidante who is not the shepherdess she seems, are interrupted by a servant who reports having seen Rothsay's ghost. The feeling of other-worldly forces afoot is strengthened by the light-dark imagery of the poetry spoken by characters whose torches create physical shadows. Vimonda commissions Dundore, who killed her father, to apprehend her father's slayer. The audience has just about digested this dramatic irony, when Rothsay confronts Alfreda. Since Alfreda is the only character who thus far does not seem emotionally involved in the events which have transpired, Rothsay's revelation is most effective. Rothsay is not a ghost but a long lost Lear. Alfreda's counsel to the bitter man exhibits MacDonald's poetic capability:

> Look on this night—how mild, how calm, how lovely!
> Wouldst thou enjoy it, court the fanning breeze,
> Run o'er with raptur'd eyes the clear blue vault,
> Hail the sweet moon curtain'd in rolling clouds,
> And welcome each bright planet as it rises?
> Or wouldst thou rather sit dejected down,

> In deep suspicion of a sudden storm,
> Watching till night's cold Queen shall burst in flame
> And burn the skies, while all her glorious train
> Stop in affright, and backward wheel their orbs?
> What hast thou more? What canst thou here perceive
> To ground thy doubts upon? —A noble youth,
> From distant regions, crown'd with glory, comes;
> Rescues from death thy daughter; gains her heart;
> And, after decent space to sorrow given.
> Has gain'd her hand too, but for thy appearance
> Thus wrapt in gloom. 'Tis dotage, folly, frenzy,
> But to surmise that they could plot thy death,
> Who deeply mourn it; who delay to reap
> The fruit of ardent love, till thou shalt rest;
> Who rear sad tombs, and weary Heav'n with prayers
> For thy unquiet ghost.
>
> (II. 1)

In the third act Dundore tells Barnard of his poisoning Vimonda against her lover. Melville and Vimonda meet, and relations are strained. Alfreda tells the hero how he can win back Vimonda's esteem. Alfreda soliloquizes about her love for Melville, and the revelation tempts one to question her motives. When Alfreda tries to reason with Vimonda to overcome her hatred of Melville, one doubts the confidante's sanity, but not her sensibility. Alfreda's implausible nobility is characteristic of the flaws in motivation which mar the last two acts.

When Rothsay reveals himself to the assembled principals, he directs his scorn at Melville. Again Alfreda calls attention to the old man's senility. The fourth act ends with Barnard's confession to Rothsay that Dundore and he are the real villains.

In the final act Dundore gives Melville a cup of poison, which he says is from Vimonda. Melville takes the brew which he believes fatal and, thinking himself poisoned, kills the cowardly Dundore. Vimonda, who has not sent the potion, learns that her love has been poisoned and dies heartbroken. Barnard enters with the news that he did not put a deadly drug in the cup as Dundore had instructed. Melville then reenters and Rothsay gives Alfreda to the grieving hero. The greatest irony in *Vimonda* is that MacDonald, possessed of genuine dramatic sense in some aspects, displayed a lack of common sense in the last acts of his tragedy. The melancholy foreboding is admirably sustained in a drama that follows the romantic path through the Gothic arch.

MacDonald's other plays, *The Fair Apostate, Love and Loyalty,* and *The Princess of Tarento* were published posthumously in his *Miscella-*

neous Works (1791). *The Fair Apostate* is a tragedy which makes a
plea for peace and true Christianity. Benascar the Saracen proposes
peace terms, which Manfred the Norman refuses. Corbred plans to
turn traitor and join the Saracens for selfish reasons. Zimorna, the sister
of Valdemar, defects to the Saracens, because she is convinced that the
Christians err in aggression. Tamira, Manfred's daughter and Valdemar's love, soliloquizes about the hostilities. Her position is congruent
with that of the author, who in Act II stresses pacificism:

> War, detested monster,
> Murd'rer of joy, and mother of despair,
> Shall thy pestif'rous breath ne'er cease to taint
> Each noble disposition? Ev'ry youth,
> Form'd to inspire affection, and to feel it,
> Infected by this frenzy, flies to arms;
> And by defeat or victory alike
> Destroys what most he loves. . . .

Zimorna, who calls her brother's objections to her joining the infidels
"jargon of hood-winked prejudice," confronts Valdemar with the observation that in the Saracen kingdom there is no bigotry. The heroine in
Act III asks questions more disarming than the usual rhetorical queries
of melodrama:

> What is it to be Christian? To be cruel?
> In blood and desolation to delight?
> To spurn all laws? To hate mankind? To have
> No sigh for woe; for misery no tear?
> If so, then Corbred is the first of Christians.
> Or is it to be generous and gentle?
> Honor to cherish? Justice to protect?
> To have a heart expanded as the air,
> And warm as the bright sun?

Corbred's treachery is discovered. Tamira's capture by the Saracens
provokes the Christians. In a mature manner, both sides are shown less
than perfect. Zimorna, the fair apostate, learns that she is a cause of
the impending battle, and tries to prevent bloodshed by showing both
sides their common emblem, the cross. Her efforts are of no avail, and
when Alcansor dies in the field, the heroine expires from grief. Zimorna's love for the Saracen makes her defection more credible. The ideas
MacDonald expresses in this drama are provocative. Despite many
characters, much intrigue, and numerous romances, the play moves

slowly. The reflective passages are comparable to Home's. As with the works of the more famous Scots dramatist, these sentiments give the remote mediaeval saga an air of detachment.

MacDonald's *Love and Loyalty* is a fairy-tale opera. This fantasy, set in twelfth-century Bohemia, resembles a Christmas pantomime. King Alphonso loves Juliana; DeZegri desires Juliana and the crown as well. The villain imprisons the girl. With the initial tension established, the scene shifts from the woods to the salon, and the mood changes from the melodramatic to the comic. Matilda examines a confiscated note-book of a supposed English spy, and learns that the owner is Dr. Didymus Drybone, "body physician and poet laureat to the most valient hero Richard Coeur de Lion," who is writing a travel account. Matilda, an Anglophile, summons the doctor. Drybone, who enters in Act I with a beautifier in one hand and a love lyric in the other, introduces himself with the following song:

> In Delphi where the Mogul is,
> I batter'd at Love's portcullis,
>   Admitted to dine
>   In Haram divine,
> Where never a tabby nor trull is.
>   Wherever I was
>   I gain'd the applause
> Of loveliest ladies—'tis true Ma'am;
>   I tumbled their paws,
>   And mumbled their jaws,
> As now I could do to you Ma'am.

Matilda asks Drybone to manage an entertainment in honor of Alphonso's visit and gives him Triboulet as assistant. The aide is Doll Dumpling, Drybone's wife in disguise. Spiridof, who cannot, in con-science, further DeZegri's wicked plans, helps Juliana to escape from the dungeon, and they flee to the home of her brother, Alexis, who loves Matilda. Before the assembled principals Drybone and his com-pany present a pastoral in which Matilda, Juliana, and others partici-pate. This play within the play foreshadows the happy conclusion. DeZegri is killed by Juliana who saves the king's life, and she becomes queen. Matilda marries Alexis, Drybone and Spiridof are knighted.

The Princess of Tarento is a two-act comedy which is more involved than *A Midsummer Night's Dream*. Julia loves Stephano, Matilda's ser-vant. Hippolitus, in menial guise, professes his love to Julia. Matilda, betrothed to Prosper because he can reinstate her as Princess of Tarento, loves Hippolitus.

In the second act, King Alphonso and Manfred pretend to be Moors to test Camilla, whom Alphonso wishes to be his queen. Alphonso believes that she loves Prosper. A mock battle is staged in which Fulvio, dressed as a Muslim, captures his love, Julia, who has jilted him because of Prosper's trickery. Duplicity by Manfred, who capitulates to the Moorish camp in an attempt to seize Alphonso's throne, a pastoral, and other previously used devices, make *The Princess of Tarento* resemble self-parody. In the happy ending Matilda chooses Hippolitus, and Julia is reunited with Fulvio. The too involved business is interspersed with lyrics set to operatic melodies by Handel, Corelli, and other classical composers. Despite all of its faults and foolishness, *The Princess of Tarento* is a delicately wrought rococo bauble.

John Oswald's *Humours of John Bull* is as crude as Andrew MacDonald's opera is refined. Oswald's "Operatical Farce" is a more typical product of a Scots closet dramatist than MacDonald's fantasies. Oswald, who used the pen name, "Sylvester Otway," produced a number of publications, which are frequently eccentric and invariably favor isolationism. The play which he describes as a "fantastic ebullation of whim," Oswald included in his *Poems* (1789). In his preface, the author acknowledges that the political allusions could never have passed the censor, "even if the Author's stomach had not been too squeamish to digest the various disgusts of theatric solicitation."

In the first scene, two blades, Classic and Ingenuous, discuss their loves, Lucy and Lucinda. In the second scene Mr. Worthy and his Hindu servant arrive at Timothy Pimpleface's inn. The proprietor tries to impress his guest with malapropisms, but the humor becomes offensive with the introduction of Mrs. Pimpleface, a French woman. Lucy is told that her foreign stepmother desires the Indian menial.

The concert Pimpleface has promised Worthy takes place in front of the hotel. The entertainment, which satirizes current operatic tastes, is a study in strident nationalism. The chorus sings a song of British superiority which is typical:

> *The Frenchman vends us caprioles,*
> *The Italian sells us squall,*
> *Windy, flighty gifts, while we*
> *With roast beef pay for all.*

(I. 3)

Lucy is surrounded by admirers after the concert. These men provide a departure for Oswald to stereotype various nationals: the Frenchman capers about the stage; the Irishman displays arrogance; the Italian sings of his castration, then introduces Trillini, the former John Bull, who has been emasculated by foreign powers.

In the final scene the army and navy are represented by hostile drunks. An inebriated parson, as well as Saunders, point up discrepancies in religion. Saunders informs Pimpleface that he is a cuckold:

> And fatigued at length with holy cogitations I fell fast asleep, and I saw in a vision the Whore of Babylon sitting in the midst of her iniquities, and the muckle de'il advanced towards her:— She flew into his arms. I shrieked out, started up, and rushing between them to prevent the propagation of Antichrist, what should I see ayont the shrubbery, but your gude wife here in the arms of Tippo Saib.
>
> (II. 2)

The innkeeper sends his wife home to France and amid rejoicing over the divorce, the young couples get together. *Humours of John Bull* is as poorly put together as it is extreme in its prejudice. When pieces such as *The Princess of Tarento* contain anti-Semitic punch lines, bigotry used as a source of humor is worth consideration, for it mirrors the insecurity of the age of revolution.

Sir David Dalrymple's *The Little Freeholder* (1790), is a more polished advertisement for the British way of life. In his comedy, Dalrymple manages to convey his social message, insert patriotic sentiments on British liberty, and individuate characters. To improve his view, Lord Montorgueil orders Blast, an old soldier, to remove Tailor Snip's home to a new location. They plan to make Snip believe that the hovel was removed from his freehold by witchcraft. Robert, the footman, and Savon, the valet, are jealous that Blast converses so long with their master. Their vaudeville exchanges prevent the situation from turning pathetic.

SAVON:

> . . . .
> I never knew a man that had visited foreign parts, so ignorant of *sça-voir vivre* as Blast is—quite a bore; gives no body elbow-room, as *Swift*, Dean *Swift*, said of Mat. Prior. You love anecdotes, Robert?
> ROBERT:
> I can't tell, I never tasted them.
>
> (I)

Shortly after the servants' banter, Snip, Blast, and two maids enter drinking punch, courtesy of the noble. The smooth Savon and the harsh Blast get into an argument. Snip tries to effect a peaceful settlement by inviting the company for breakfast. As all enthusiastically discuss what they will bring to the "house warming," Blast warns Snip of witches on the road home and tells a tale of Moggy M'Kissock, a house-moving sorceress. After Snip departs, Blast reports to Montorgueil, who offers his henchman a two shillings a day post as reward for service. The crippled soldier tells of his plight as a pensioner and, as the Lord sneaks away, Blast realizes how ungrateful the noble is.

The second act opens with Snip searching for his house. His kinsman, Hacquill, who passes himself off as a solicitor, wishes to take the case to court. Snip tells Hacquill that the magic of Moggy M'Kissock caused the phenomenon. Hacquill tells him that "witchcraft was abolished by the statute of *somethingmo Georgi secundi*," but "that is a *law* of police, and does not extend to Scotland, and other parts beyond seas." Hacquill is busy taking down particulars when the house mover confesses his deed to Snip, who is hurt that a friend would mistreat him, but the two settle differences without litigation. Blast then acts as intermediary with Montorgueil for Snip. Although the freeholder wishes only to have an apology and his house moved back, one of the maids prevails upon him to live in the new and better locale and to obtain a large indemnity.

The dramatic output of Simon Gray of Dunse, Berwickshire, rivals the prolificacy of Archibald McLaren. *The Historical Catalogue of Writings, Published and Unpublished, of Simon Gray* (1840), lists twenty-nine comedies, twelve history plays, ten tragedies, and five burlesques, as well as dramatic criticisms. Most of this work Gray completed after 1800. His first play, a tragedy, *The Spaniard; or Relvindez and Elzora, the True, though Injured Lovers* (1787), was printed in London in 1839. A number of his plays deal with Scottish history. Gray used the Gowrie Conspiracy, Sir William Wallace, George Wishart, and other national events and personalities as subject matter for his plays, most of which remained in manuscript. Multitude proved a many-headed monster; the checklist apparently survived all copies of Gray's fifty-six plays.

Lady Elizabeth Lyndsay, Countess of Hardwicke made a French fable into a play for her children in the late 1790s. The youngest member of the original cast of *The Court of Oberon, or The Three Wishes* was two when the fairy tale was performed in the nursery of Wimpole. Later, the piece was done at a bazaar "for the aid of the distressed Irish" sponsored by Princess Victoria, to whom the 1831 publication is dedicated. The entertainment begins with an assembly of the fairy court. After repetitious dialogue suited to very young players, Queen Mab advises the sprites:

> Leave wayward mortals to themselves,
> They are but peevish, froward elves;
> Still anxious for some fancied blessing,
> Though, when attained, not worth possessing.
>
> (1)

Oberon gives three wishes to Hodge. The simple woodman wastes the first when he wishes his adviser, Justice, had a roasted eel. When Margery complains of his stupidity, Hodge longs for his wife to be struck dumb. Susan gives up the third wish her father has promised her, in order that her mother may speak again. Margery then permits Susan to marry her love, Harry Ploughshare, and the generous girl gets her desire.

Scott dubbed Joanna Baillie the female Shakespeare, and Byron considered her the only dramatist since Otway. The enthusiastic accolades are understandable upon examination of contemporaneous theatrical artifacts such as Lady Elizabeth's playlet. Miss Baillie's first play, "Arnold" (1790), does not survive. Her earliest extant volume, *A Series of Plays: in which it is attempted to Delineate the Stronger Passions of the Mind each Passion Being the Subject of a Tragedy and a Comedy,* was published in 1798. Its aesthetic theory of playwriting is as innovative as *Lyrical Ballads,* published the same year. In a sense, Miss Baillie shared with Wordsworth and Coleridge the desire to portray common human experience. Realizing the commonality of the passions, humours, weaknesses and prejudices, she concentrates upon interior rather than external struggles favored by action-oriented melodramatists. The function of tragedy, she believes, is to unveil situation rather than mere physical action. The purpose of tragedy then is not to reveal the hero in clashes, but "To our nearer regard, in all the distinguishing varieties which nearer inspection discovers; with the passions, the humours, the weaknesses, the prejudices of men." The second and more important function of tragedy is: "to unveil to us the human mind under the domination of those strong and fixed passions, which, seemingly unprovoked by outward circumstances, will, from small beginnings, brood within the breast, till all the better dispositions, all the fair gifts of nature, are borne down before them."

Miss Baillie focuses on the drawing of a persona who embodies a great passion. The purpose of the characterization is to inculcate moral-

Joanna Baillie (1762–1851).

ity. As with most theoreticians, the scheme of capturing love, hatred, anger, etc., leads her to inconsistencies in application of the theory. At times, the passion rather than the proposed moral takes command.

The three plays which appeared in 1798, *Basil*, a tragedy on love, *The Tryal*, a comedy on love, and *De Monfort*, a tragedy on hate, have common qualities. The simple plots stress their main themes. Concentration upon a single character's dominant emotion necessarily limits the plot. If the plot is circumscribed so are the characterizations. Protagonists are driven by an *idée fixe*. Subordination of all other characters to the central figure results in flat and inconsequential supporting roles.

In *Basil* (never produced) the hero is a victim of love at first sight. As the play opens the stage is filled with spectacle. Count Basil arrives with his victorious armies. The procession is a favorite feature in Miss Baillie's plays. Aware of the popularity of extravaganza, she incorporated splendid pageants frequently and effectively. Although only about seven of her twenty-six dramas were staged, the author was always consciously striving to make her plays acceptable for professional theatrical presentation. The story of Basil's ensnarement progresses in a direct manner. The Mantuan Duke secretly conspires with France. To ensure Basil's delay in joining forces with the emperor, who is at war with the French, the Duke uses his innocent daughter, Victoria, as a pawn. Basil falls in love with her at their first encounter. The infatuated hero stays in Mantua while the Battle of Pania rages. Disgraced because of his neglect of duty, Basil commits suicide.

The theory of the importance of the individual passion breeds artificiality. When accompanying feelings that give perspective are absent, the representation becomes monomaniacal. The success or failure of this psychological approach depends on how forceful the author can make the protagonist. Since there is little relation of character through action, and the supporting cast is virtually ineffectual, the main character must reveal himself. The protagonist has many speeches, which show the working of the passion itself, but when such a figure moves in a world of nonentities, passion, which should grow out of interaction, is dubious.

The exclusion of all other elements but the dominant feeling is more suited to tragedy than comedy, which thrives on complications. These are absent in *The Tryal*. Mariane has become engaged to Withrington's favorite nephew without the uncle's consent. Mariane and the elderly uncle achieve a reconciliation of sorts in the first act, but no mention of this facet is made until the end of the play, when Withrington pompously announces that Mariane "is already engaged to a very worthy young man, who will receive with her a fortune by no means contemptible." This comedy is over-simplified and never achieves the portrayal of the desired emotion. The couple's love resembles that of arranged marriages which abound in novels of the period.

De Monfort, Joanna Baillie's most effective play, more nearly encompasses the goals of her aesthetic than her other dramas. The nature of the passion portrayed lends itself to the concept of the all-consuming drive. *De Monfort* is a study of hatred. De Monfort's sister, who is more memorable than any of Miss Baillie's other supporting characters, provides relief from the monomania. The excursion in loathing results from a duel which the Marquis Rezenvelt has fought with De Monfort. The Marquis spared the loser, which increases his wrath. In the second act, a reception in the lavish apartments of Count Freberg provides spectacle and an excellent backdrop for the heroine's entrance. The minor players' comments about Jane De Monfort are an accurate description of Sarah Siddons,[10] who starred in the role in the initial Drury Lane production of 29 April 1800, and which ran eight nights.

> PAGE. So queenly, so commanding, and so noble,
> I shrunk at first in awe; but when she smil'd,
> For so she did to see me thus abash'd,
> Methought I could have compass'd sea and land
> To do her bidding.
> LADY. Is she young or old?
> PAGE. Neither, if right I guess; but she is fair;
> For Time hath laid his hand so gently on her,
> As he too had been aw'd.
> LADY. The foolish stripling!
> She has bewitch'd thee. Is she large in stature?
> PAGE. So stately and so graceful is her form,
> I thought at first her stature was gigantic;
> But on a near approach I found, in truth,
> She scarcely does surpass middle size.
>
> (II. 1)

In the third act Jane pacifies her brother, and when Rezenvelt and Monfort meet all seems serene. From this point on, the drama is anti-climactic. There is more suspense in *De Monfort* than in the dramatist's other plays, but one learns the outcome too quickly. As the fourth act opens, Conrad, a roguish sort, tells De Monfort that Jane is about

10   Margaret S. Carhart, *The Life and Work of Joanna Baillie* (New Haven, 1923), p. 118, notes the contemporary sources which mention that the author tailored the role to the actress.

De Monfort (1800) by Joanna Baillie.

to marry Rezenvelt. De Monfort fights with the noble, and later murders his enemy treacherously. In the last act, De Monfort is imprisoned
in a convent. Left alone with the body of his foe, De Monfort uncovers
the corpse. This precipitates his realization that he is mad.

> Come, madness! come unto me, senseless death!
> I cannot suffer this! Here, rocky wall,
> Scatter these brains, or dull them!
> [*Runs furiously, and dashing his head against
> the wall, falls upon the floor.*
>
> (V. 2)

After the recognition scene, brother and sister meet once again. De
Monfort on his death bed learns that Conrad's story is groundless, and
expires before civil authorities can call him to account.

Joanna Baillie seems to have been trying to give De Monfort heroic
stature. Rather than a tragic hero, this character is a villain whose fault
is jealousy. Early in the play he expresses demonic hatred:

> Oh! that detested Rezenvelt!
> E'en in our early sports, like two young whelps
> Of hostile breed, instinctively reverse,
> Each 'gainst the other pitch'd his ready pledge,
> And frown'd defiance. As we onward pass'd
> From youth to man's estate, his narrow art
> And envious gibing malice, poorly veil'd
> In the affected carelessness of mirth,
> Still more detestable and odious grew,
> There is no living being on this earth
> Who can conceive the malice of his soul,
> With all his gay and damned merriment,
> To those, by fortune or by merit plac'd
> Above his paltry self.
>
> . . . .
>
> But when honours came,
> And wealth and new-got titles fed his pride;
> Whilst flatt'ring knaves did trumpet forth his praise,
> And grov'ling idiots grinn'd applauses on him;
> Oh! then I could no longer suffer it!
> It drove me frantic. —What! what would I give!
> What would I give to crush the bloated toad,
> So rankly do I loathe him!
>
> (II. 2)

Ranting such as this leads one to suspect that Joanna Baillie is indebted to German drama for more than the setting of *De Monfort*.

There are lengthy passages about De Monfort's nobility, but he does not demonstrate any virtue through actions. The murder of Rezenvelt is not a crime of passion, but a deliberately planned criminal act. If a protagonist shows only a single passion which is of the splenetic variety, it is impossible to draw a hero.

Jane De Monfort, although only a foil of her brother, is better drawn. Miss Baillie is skilled at creating female characters. Jane is virtuous, but she does have a few failings which make her almost human. The focus shifts sufficiently from the personification of hate in De Monfort to the heroine; this relieves the monotony of constantly harping on hatred.

Joanna Baillie's theory is psychologically oriented; her ignorance of the workings of the psyche accounts for some of the technical weaknesses of the characterizations. The concept of restricting character portrayal aroused much emotion in her contemporaries. English, Scottish, and American critics who reviewed her plays were immoderate in praise or blame. M. Norton appraised the dramas justly and succinctly when he observed that in seeking to reveal the passion she loses sight of the man.[11] Despite her shortcomings, Miss Baillie made a conscious effort to restore the dramatic grandeur of true tragedy. Kurt Wittig in *The Scottish Tradition in Literature* speculates that the plays of Joanna Baillie "might have been a starting point for a Scottish theatre." A national theatre never developed in the sense that Scots produced a distinct dramatic corpus. Miss Baillie's method is Aristotelian rather than Caledonian.

11   Carhart, pp. 110–31, digests early nineteenth-century opinion of *Plays on the Passions*. M. Norton, "The Plays of Joanna Baillie," *Review of English Studies* 23 (1947):131–43, considers the author's dramatic theory.

Epilogue

From the sixteenth century onwards, drama was the most suspect of arts in the North. In England the development of professional theatre was interrupted for a generation during the Commonwealth. In Scotland no professional theatre developed until the eighteenth century. Since they had no dramatic tradition, Scots followed English models. The loss of national political identity in 1707, which reinforced the removal of the court in the previous century, fostered conformity to an anglicized culture.

Scots contributors to dramatic writing during the last decades of the seventeenth century share religio-political persuasions. Clerke, St. Serf, Lesly, Pitcairne, and Fleming the Younger were royalists. These Stuart partisans followed the Episcopal system which did not inhibit playwriting. In serious as well as in light works, most of these writers express their position on church and state matters.

Presbyterians were as unsympathetic to drama as they were to the establishment. Kirkmen were exasperated with Charles II, the covenanted king, who punished those who attended conventicles and enacted harsh measures to achieve conformity. James II escalated persecution. Presbyterians regarded William III, when he arrived on a good Protestant wind, as an ally. His policy of moderation failed to placate a number of those who suffered for their faith from the Caroline ejection through the Bloodless revolution.

North Britain had experienced much unrest during the 1600s, and the country continued to fester into the next century, when controversy flared over the union. The political canker came to a head with the Jacobite rebellion of 1715. After the uprising of 1745, restoration of the Scottish royal family was, as J. D. Mackie observes in his *History of Scotland*, "*Tout finit par des chansons.*" Scots playwrights paid homage to the Good Old Cause long after the return of the Stuarts ceased to be an important political issue. Mallet's *Eurydice* may be considered an early example of sentimental Jacobitism. Wilson's *Earl Douglas* and Dow's *Zingis* are expressions of the nationalist spirit rather than literal

pleas for the return of a Scottish king. Ossianic dramas invariably evoke
sentiments of longing for a regal and independent past. This strong
emotional appeal was responsible for the entry of Jacobitism into
Scottish mythology.

The Forty-five lacked the spontaneity romantics depicted in literature, but the nationalism the rebellion represents coincided with justifiable pride in a variety of accomplishments. There was strife when
George I came to the throne in 1714. Thirteen years later George II's
accession was generally accepted in the North. In Georgian Scotland
economic conditions gradually improved: agriculture advanced; industry developed. As the number of rich and influential people increased
so did the complacent acceptance of the political status quo. Prosperity
provided leisure for cultural endeavors. Scots in many fields contributed substantially to the Enlightenment. The Common Sense philosophy
of Thomas Reid, the histories of David Hume and William Robertson,
the economic theory of Adam Smith, the engines of James Watt, the
roads of John Macadam, and the architectural designs of the Adam
brothers added lustre to the golden age of Scottish productivity. Allan
Ramsay, Jr., and Henry Raeburn painted portraits of their enlightened
landsmen whose influence extended far beyond the homeland. William
Henry Playfair's New Town provided the proper setting for men of
achievement, and earned Edinburgh the appellation, "Modern Athens."

Modern Athenians were concerned with belletristic as well as utili-
tarian aspects of dramatic writing. When the chances for play production are slight, writers concentrate upon the programmatic. Scots who
wrote plays during the Restoration, as well as those who wrote in colonial America,[1] exhibit this tendency. Thomson and his circle used the

---

1   The first published drama in America, *Androboros* (1714), was written by the
Scottish peer, Robert Hunter, in collaboration with Lewis Morris. Hunter, the most
popular royal governor of New York and a staunch Whig, presumably devised the
manuscript key written in the one extant copy of the political play. (See Oscar
Wegelin, *Early American Plays 1714–1830 being a compilation of the Titles of
Plays by American Authors Published and Performed in America Previous to 1830*
[New York, 1900], p. 59. See also Arthur Hobson Quinn, *A History of the American Drama from the Beginning of the Civil War* [New York, 1923], p. 6.) Despite
the identification of prototypes and the vulgar dedication to "Don. Com. Fiz.,"
the satire remains obscure. The squib ridicules the Senate and Lieutenant Governor Nelson (Androboros, i.e., maneater), who is determined to attack the
French (the Mulomachians). The Senate votes "Negen Skillignen and Elleve
Pence" for expenses of the military expedition. The Keeper (Hunter), who is the
spokesman for sanity, asks why the resolution is passed before the fact. Aesop
answers "By all means, lest when it is over you should have less reason for this
Resolve." In addition to exposing political corruption, the play excoriates the
clergy.

The first drama produced in America was Mallet's 1751 version of *Alfred*, pre-drama as a forum for political opinion. They also adhered to neoclassical precepts and labored over the poetry which couched their ideas.

Thomson, Mallet, Paterson, and James Baillie crusaded for Frederick Maurice and the Whigs by modeling roles in tragedies to resemble current political figures. Fyffe, Riddel, and others fashioned eulogistic pieces to please the monarchy, a practice carried on in every kingdom

---

sented by students at the College of Philadelphia in 1757 (*Pennsylvania Gazette* 20 January 1757, gives an account of the production and stresses the students' choosing their vehicle. See also, *Pennsylvania Gazette* 27 January, 3 and 10 February 1757). Thomas Godfrey and Francis Hopkinson altered the masque to suit the sentiments of the American audience.

William Smith collaborated with musician Francis Hopkinson on a graduation exercise for the class of 1761 at the College of Philadelphia. Smith wrote commencement odes and a dialogue for the same school. This program was presented on 17 May 1775.

The most interesting plays written by a Scot for colonial audiences are the dramas of Hugh Henry Brackenridge. Brackenridge migrated to the New World when a child, but his early training in the Calvinist Scots-Irish settlements in Pennsylvania and his education at Princeton, a liberal Whig college then under the jurisdiction of a Scot, established ties sufficiently strong for him to produce the poem, "Tree of Liberty," and other dialect works in frank emulation of Ramsay and Burns. Brackenridge wrote his first play in collaboration with Philip Freneau. Brackenridge delivered the triologue at the Princeton graduation exercises on 25 September 1771. The neoclassic verses elaborate on love of country and the beauties of nature in the new land. An interesting feature of this work is the vision of New York as a metropolis.

Brackenridge wrote *The Battle of Bunkers-Hill* (1775) for students to present at his Maryland Academy. American and British military leaders give long speeches in dignified verse. The reluctance of the English to fight contrasts to the courage of the colonists. A Redcoat Captain's musing illustrates the English attitude toward the battle:

> Oh Bute and Dartmouth knew ye what I feel
> You sure would pity, an old drinking man,
> That has more heart-ake, than philosophy.
>
> (IV. 1)

About two years later Brackenridge wrote *The Death of General Montgomery* to give students declamatory experience while honoring American patriotism. The death scene of Montgomery at the battle of Quebec and characterizations of patriots taken from newspaper accounts and popular stories of the time are notable features.

Brackenridge's *Masque, Written at the Warm Springs in Virginia in the Year 1784*, honors George Washington's "royal" progress up the Potomac. Washington made no comment in his journal on this eulogy composed to obtain political advancement for the lawyer, journalist, and novelist.

Brackenridge had witnessed the destruction of his settlement by Indians when a youngster. He dwelled on Indian atrocities in *The Rising Glory of America* and *The Death of General Montgomery*. Scots at home portrayed Indians as noble savages. MacLaren, who had been stationed in America while in the service, and Richardson concentrated on the romantic aspects of primitives.

The adaptability for which Scots immigrants are noted manifests itself in the plays North Britons published in colonial America. They invariably treat New World concerns and themes.

that has produced plays. Mallet, Home, Smollett, and anonymous writers inserted popular political opinions in plays. In supporting factions, ridiculing opposition, seeking favor, or gaining audiences playwrights created tension between opposing forces within the monarchical frame. The revolutionary temper of the late Georgian period questioned the very idea of sovereignty. Logan made a plea for freedom in *Runnemede*. Although the censor thought the drama excessively libertarian, the play treats freedom as constituted by the Magna Carta. Scots writers of theatre and closet pieces favored working within the established confines of government. Jackson and Dalrymple cast freeholders as good men who triumph by patience and suffering, not rebellion. Scotland's ties with France were historic, but the longstanding affinity did not prevent criticism. Plays such as *Modern Politics* and *The Philistines* decry abuses of the French Revolution. Extremist squibs of Oswald and Smith exhort isolationism. When surveying plays by Scots the canny admonition *Look Before ye Loup* is a more frequent proposition than the new ideology expressed in *Elim and Maria*—that hope for freedom is to be found in America.

Political and religious concerns were inextricably bound throughout the seventeenth century. *The Assembly* and *The Monarchical Image* evince this commixture. Inhabitants of a land noted for Calvinistic earnestness used religious topics infrequently in literature during the eighteenth century. This is attributable to the concern for separating the sacred from the secular. School plays such as Coldstream's and Drummond's adaptations were presented to inculcate moral principles. Lesly's *Dialogues*, Hunter's *Wanderer*, Tait's translation of *Jeptha*, and late century dialogues and closet plays such as *Edinburgh Delivered* provided homiletic instruction. Religious sentiments are included in MacDonald's *Fair Apostate* and Grahame's *Wallace*, but the focus is upon adventure.

Of serious topics, one of the wealthier sources rich in dramatic potential is Scottish history and legend. Nesbit is the first Scot known to have cast this matter in dramatic form. Nesbit, Jackson, MacLaren, and Grahame based plays on the story of Wallace. Home, who proved national subjects could succeed, as well as Wilson, dramatized Douglas. Wood, and McArthur, based plays on Rothesay. Logan, Mickle, and Grahame wrote dramas about Mary Queen of Scots. Fyffe, Smollett, MacDonald, Norval, and Gray used their history and tradition in creating serious plays. Richardson, Mylne, Riddel, and Miss Edwards were inspired by Ossian.

Literati founded the Poker Club in Edinburgh in 1757, the season

Allan Ramsay (1686–1758).

Douglas opened in London. Their purpose was to promote nationalism. Playwrights as well as club members were captivated by this
spirit. Dramatists who employed subjects gleaned from their heritage
recounted their lore in an anglicized manner. Writers of serious drama
invariably wrote in English, which was more advantageous if a work
were to gain widest acceptance. Traditional qualities of Scots expression—personal and direct statements put forth to convey character, yet
possessing subtlety sufficient to elicit multiple hypotheses—were fore-
gone by playwrights who exerted greatest influence. Thomson concentrated upon comprehension rather than compression. Paterson, Morris,
Greenfield, Riddel, and Grahame followed Thomson's manner of
composition. Ramsay embroidered plain statements with neoclassic
embellishment. Home emulated the Bard rather than the *makers*.

Early eighteenth-century writers drew inspiration from the ancients,
but as the century progressed neoclassic gave way to romantic. Backgrounds became less antique and more exotic. Mediaeval and Renaissance Europe, Africa, and the Orient appealed to romantically inclined
dramatists. Stories set in unfamiliar locales aided plausibility of increasingly melodramatic action. Scots writers were disposed to the cult of
melancholy and idealization of the past. The antiquarian tendency gave
plays a derivative quality. Concentration upon the contemplative poetic
strain supplanted the truly dramatic, and the melodramatic substituted
for the microcosmic reflection of the world. A shift from neoclassic to
romantic occurs in all British drama of the period; the early use of
these elements by Thomson and Home forecast the direction drama
was to take.

The customs and manners of Scotland provided material for light
theatre pieces, and Ramsay's *The Gentle Shepherd* spawned numerous
imitations. The pastoral peopled with rustics was the Scottish play in
popular estimation. This confining concept was used by Shireffs, Learmont, and Burness who corresponded about their intentions to portray
true Scots manners. Finlayson drew material from local customs, as did
James Stewart and Charles Stuart. Heron, who wrote in English, consciously strove to create a genuine Scots comedy of manners that would
transcend the stereotype.

By the eighteenth century, the Scottish language had ceased to be
used for intellectual expression. It was chiefly a spoken tongue, vari-
ously transcribed. Playwrights who used Scots fashioned intentionally
quaint products. Their striving to be provincial may be the result of
disappointed nationalism. It is more likely that the humorous, mocking,
and homely dialect dramas, which evoke a superiority of rural virtues,

are manifestations of the romantic fantasy of the peasant. Craufurd was the first Scot who wrote native dialect to entertain a London audience. He delegated the burr to a pawky servant, Willie. Menials, rustics, and caricatures were assigned dialect by Smollett, Finlayson, Morison, MacLaren, Learmont, Brown, and other writers of comedies. Their delineations are progressively romantic, and result in the removal of the native figures from life in their dramas.

The employment of Scottish history, legend, custom and language points to the beginning of a national theatre. Scots tended to rely upon English fashions and conceptions in playwriting. Those who did free themselves from conventional aesthetic prepossessions of the London stage and struck out in new directions gained most recognition. Box office successes such as *Tancred and Sigismunda, The Gentle Shepherd, Douglas,* and *De Monfort* did not follow established patterns. Theatre is a commercial art; some who succeeded followed formulae, for as Johnson stated in a prologue: "The Drama's Laws the Drama's Patrons give, / For we that live to please, must please to live." Scots contributed Restoration comedies, sentimental comedies, neoclassical tragedies, melodramas, and farces during the decades when these genres were popular. Failure to subdue native tone and accent often brought adverse criticism. During the late 1700s when national consciousness surged throughout Europe, Scotland had good reason to be proud. The mores of Gaels and Sassenachs were the province of comedy and Scots had become the expression of a subculture.

A substantial number of Scots writers at home and abroad manifested proficiency in playwriting. Censure at home and ridicule as foreigners in London frequently confronted these dramatic writers. Although encumbered by these peculiar burdens, Northern authors persisted in creating for the theatre. The lure of writing for the stage where man speaks to man about man is stronger than all impediments.

List of Plays and Entertainments by Scottish Dramatists   1660-1800

The following list of plays and entertainments attempts to register all known dramatic works by native-born Scottish authors written during the Restoration and eighteenth century in Great Britain and America. Because of the fugitive nature of the material this list must be incomplete. The precarious position of the drama in North Britain is no doubt responsible for the loss of a number of theatrical pieces. Scots at home and abroad frequently wrote plays anonymously. This practice, which arose from necessity because of ecclesiastical and civil curtailment, and became customary, was followed from the birth of professional theatre in Scotland through the era of Sir Walter Scott.

Edinburgh was the center of the Scottish theatrical world, and the only town which offered regular dramatic presentations during most of the period under consideration. Theatres did open during the last years of the eighteenth century in Aberdeen, Glasgow, Arbroath, and Dundee. Other towns also witnessed occasional productions, but most new endeavors premiered in the Scottish capital. Scots playwrights almost invariably tried to have their dramas staged in London, and settled for a Scottish opening as a last resort.

This register, which is arranged according to authors, gives the title, place and date of premiere, place and date of first publication. When significant, other editions and printings of the text are noted. Select notices and reviews of the plays are listed.

The title of the play is followed by an indication of the type of play concerned. These designations are in no way final. Thus a tragedy may be more accurately described as a melodrama, a ballad opera may be an operatic farce. Where possible the designation employed by the playwright or playbills has been used. The abbreviations for types of dramas are as follows:

B. O.   Ballad Opera   Can.   Cantata

C.	Comedy	O. F.	Operatic Farce
C. O.	Comic Opera	Or.	Oratorio
D. P.	Dramatic Poem	P.	Pastoral
E.	Entertainment	Pan.	Pantomime
F.	Farce	Pol.	Political
H.	History	Pre.	Prelude
I.	Interlude	Rel.	Religious
M.	Masque	Sat.	Satire
Mus.	Musical	T.	Tragedy
O.	Opera	T. C.	Tragi-comedy

The theatre or place of premiere and the date of the opening are given in parentheses. If no such information is presented, the play did not appear on the stage, or there is no record of its having been presented. The abbreviations for the theatres are as follows:

Can.	Canongate Theatre, Edinburgh
C. G.	Covent Garden, London
D. L.	Theatre Royal in Drury Lane, London
Hay.	Little Theatre in the Haymarket, London
L. I. F.	Lincoln's Inn Fields, London
T. H.	Taylor's Hall, Edinburgh
T. R. E.	Theatre Royal, Edinburgh, i.e., the playhouse in Shakespeare Square, in Prince's Street.

Notices of plays which opened in Edinburgh were almost exclusively the province of the *Edinburgh Courant* and the *Caledonian Mercury*. These newspapers are abbreviated *E. C.* and *C. M.* respectively. Neither newspaper felt constrained to give the name of every play it advertised. Because dramatic criticism is almost nonexistent in the Scottish press of this period, only the first notice of the play is given. With regard to the anonymous plays, interludes, afterpieces and the like, the newspaper notice is, in many instances, the sole indication that the play existed. Because of the obscurity of these short entertainments, only those which seem to be of a Northern character are included. (See Terence Tobin, "A List of Anonymous Pieces Presented at the Theatre Royal, Edinburgh, *1767–1800*," *Studies in Scottish Literature* 7 [1969]:29–34.)

Notation of bibliographically useful data not generally known has been made under several entries. Select periodical and newspaper notices of plays, particularly contemporaneous reviews, are listed under the play to which they refer. Some recent scholarship is noted. Much valuable information about plays included in this list and which appeared in the British capital is provided in Emmett L. Avery, et. al., *The London Stage, 1660–1800*, 5 pts. in 11 vols. (Carbondale, Ill.: Southern Illinois University Press, 1960–1968). Several dramatists, whose works appear in the following list, continued to write plays in the nineteenth century. Readers are referred to Allardyce Nicoll, *A History of English Drama, 1660–1900*, 6 vols. (Cambridge: Cambridge University Press, 1959), for plays by Scots written after the terminus of the period under consideration.

ALLAN, ADAM. The New Gentle Shepherd, a pastoral comedy; reduced to English by Lieut. Adam Allan. C. Frederickton, New Brunswick and London: 1798. [There are alterations in the songs, and a third scene is added in Act IV.]

[ARBUTHNOT, JOHN.] Three Hours after Marriage. C. (D. L. 16 Jan., 1717), London: 1717; 8°. [Although John Gay's name appears on the title page, this play was written in collaboration with John Arbuthnot and Alexander Pope.]

ARMSTRONG, JOHN. The Forced Marriage. T. In *Miscellanies*, 2. London: 1770; 8°. The Reverend George Gilfallan, ed., "Introduction," *The Poetical Works of Armstrong, Dyer, and Green* (Edinburgh, 1863).

[BAILLIE, _____.] Patriotism! Pol. F. Edinburgh: 1763; 8°.

[BAILLIE, JOANNA.] A Series of Plays: in which it is attempted to Delineate the stronger passions of the mind. Each passion being the subject of a tragedy and a comedy. London: 1798; 8°. Contains: Count Basil, a Tragedy. T. The Tryal, a Comedy. C. De Monfort, a Tragedy. T. (D. L. 29 Apr. 1800.) *British Critic* 13 (1799):284. *Critical Review* 24 (1798):13. *Monthly Magazine* 5 (1798):66. Margaret S. Carhart, *The Life and Work of Joanna Baillie* (New Haven, 1923). M. Norton, "The Plays of Joanna Baillie," *R. E. S.* 23 (1947): 131–43. [For a list of Miss Baillie's works published after 1800, see Allardyce Nicoll, *A History of English Drama 1660–1900* (Cambridge, 1966), 4:257–58.]

[BAILLIE, JOHN OR JAMES*.] The Married Coquet. C. London: 1746; 8°.

_____. The Patriot, Being a Dramatick History of the Life and Death of William the First Prince of Orange, Founder of the Republick of Holland. By a Lover of Liberty [i.e., Baillie]. Pol. London: 1736; 4°. [*Nicoll, 3:296, follows earlier lists which give this author's name as John Baillie. A copy in the National Library of Scotland contains the notation that the author is James Baillie.]

[BEUGO, JOHN.]   The Dream of St. Cloud. D. P. In *Poetry, Miscellaneous and Dramatic, by an Artist.* Edinburgh: 1797; 8°.

BRACKENRIDGE, HUGH HENRY.   The Rising Glory of America. Pol. (Nassau Hall, Princeton, 25 Sept. 1771.) Philadelphia: 1771; 8°. [This commencement exercise was written in collaboration with Philip Freneau. Brackenridge delivered the triologue.]

————.   The Battle of Bunkers-Hill. Pol. (Brackenridge's Academy, Maryland, Autumn 1775.) Philadelphia: 1776; 8°. *Pennsylvania Evening Post* 7 Nov. 1776. *Pennsylvania Ledger* 9 Nov. 1776. *Pennsylvania Journal* 13 Nov. 1776. Claude C. Robin, *New Travels through North America*, trans. by Philip Freneau (Boston, 1784), p. 12.

————.   The Death of General Montgomery at the Seige of Quebec. A Tragedy. Pol. T. (Brackenridge's Academy, Maryland, Autumn, ca. 1777.) Philadelphia: 1777; 8°. *Pennsylvania Evening Post* 12 Apr. 1777. *Pennsylvania Journal* 23 Apr. 1777. *Pennsylvania Weekly* 23 Apr. 1777.

————.   A. Masque, written at the Warm Springs, in the year 1784. M. (Warm Springs, Va., 1784). In *Pittsburgh Gazette* 16 June 1787; reprinted in *Gazette Publications*, (Carlisle, Pa.: 1806), pp. 35–40. [This masque was written in honor of George Washington.] Claude Milton Newlin, *The Life and Writings of Hugh Henry Brackenridge* (Princeton: 1932). Virginia Hajek, "The Dramatic Writings of Hugh Henry Brackenridge" (Ph.D. diss., Loyola University, Chicago, 1971).

BROWN, JAMES.   The Frolic. F. Edinburgh: 1783; 8°. [The earliest record of presentation is a performance at T. R. E. 2 May 1787; the premiere probably occurred in 1783.] James Dibdin, *Annals of the Edinburgh Stage* (Edinburgh, 1888), p. 200.

[BROWN, WILLIAM.]   Look before ye Loup; or, a Healin' Sa' for the crackit crowns of Country Politicians . . . by Tam Thrum, an Auld Weaver [i.e., Brown]. Pol. Edinburgh: 1793; 8°. [The play was also published in Philadelphia.]

————.   Look before Ye Loup Part Second: or, Anither Box of Healin' Sa' for the crackit crowns of Country Politicians . . . by Tam Thrum, an Auld Weaver [i.e., Brown.] Pol. Edinburgh: 1794; 8°.

BURNESS, JOHN.   Charles Montgomery . . . Written in the Manner of George Barnwell. T. (Mason's Hall, Lerwick, Shetland, 18 Apr. 1798.) Stonehaven: 1799–1801?

————.   *Plays, Poems, Tales and other Pieces.* Montrose: 1819; 8°. Contains: The Hermit; or, The Dead Come to Life. C. (Berwick upon Tweed.) [An adaptation of Smith's *Trevanion.*] Rosmond and Isabella; or, The Persisting Penitent. T. (Musselburgh.) Charles Montgomery. T.

————. The Recruit. I. (Montrose, n.d.) [An altered version of Gavin Turnbull's *The Recruit.*]

BUSHE, AMYAS. Socrates. D. P. London: 1758; 4°. ["Extracts of Amyas Bushe's Excellent Dramatic Poem," *Universal Magazine* 23 (1758): 23–25, may have preceded the publication of the entire work.]

[CARSTAIRES, CHRISTIAN.] The Hubble-Shue. F. Edinburgh: ca. 1786.

CLERKE (Clark) WILLIAM. Marciano, or the Discovery. T. C. (Holyrood House 27 Dec. 1662?) Edinburgh: 1663; 4°.

COLDSTREAM, PATRICK. Joseph. Rel. (Montrose Grammar School 25 Apr. 1732.) C. M. 25 Apr. 1732. [A translation of *Josephus* by Cornelius van Schoon (Terentius Christianus).]

————. Dido. T. (Grammar School of Crail, Fyfe, August 1737.) [An adaptation based on the *Aeneid.*]

————. Judith. Rel. (Grammar School of Crail, Fyfe, 28 Aug. 1740.) [An adaptation of *Judith* by Cornelius van Schoon.]

————. Turnus and Aeneas. T. (Grammar School of Crail, Fyfe, 24 Aug. 1742.) C. M. 2 Sept. 1742. [An adaptation based on the *Aeneid.*]

CRAUFURD (CRAWFORD), DAVID. Courtship A-la-mode. C. (D. L. 9 July 1700.) London: 1700; 4°.

————. Love at First Sight. C. (L. I. F. 25 Mar. 1704.) London: 1704.

[DALRYMPLE, DAVID, LORD HAILES.] The Little Freeholder. D. E. London: 1790; 4°.

DAVIDSON, ANTHONY. Datamis. T.

————. The Fair Hybernian. T.

————. The Sailor's Return. C. O.

————. St. Kilda, or The Sons of a Gun. F.

————. The Shepherd of Snowdon. Mus. E. (Salisbury.)

————. A Voyage to Nootka. C. O. (Winborne, Dorsetshire.)

————. Maria, or the Maid of the Rock. C. O. (Lymington, 1790s.) R. W. Babcock, "Eighteenth Century Comic Opera Manuscripts," *PMLA* 53 (1937):907–08.

DOW, ALEXANDER. Zingis. T. (D. L. 17 Dec. 1768.) London: 1768; 8°.

————. Sethona. T. (D. L. 19 Feb. 1774.) London: 1774; 8°.

DRUMMOND, JOHN. *A Collection of Poems for Reading and Repetition.* Edinburgh: 1762; 8°. Contains: The Death of Hector. T. The Redemption of the Body of Hector. T. [Both school plays are extracted from Alexander Pope's translation of the *Illiad.*]

————. The Death of Teribazus and Ariana: Extracted from Mr. Glover's Leonidas. T. In *The Art of Reading and Speaking in Public; being a Collection for the use of Schools and Private Perusal.* Edinburgh: 1780; 8°.

DUNCAN, GIDEON. The Constant Lovers; or, the Sailor's Return. Edinburgh: 1798; 8°.

EDWARDS, MISS [CHRISTIAN]. Otho and Rutha, a Dramatical Tale, in *Miscellanies in Prose and Verse.* Edinburgh: 1776; 16°. [This work is about equally divided between narrative and dramatic form.]

ELPHINSTON, JAMES. *Forty Years of Correspondence between Geniusses ov boath Sexes and James Elphinston in 6 pocket volumes, foar ov oridginal letters, two ov poetry, in which all the letters ov himself and his friends appeared with the spelling altered in accordance with the new system.* London: 1791, 5. Contains: Israel on Mount Horeb. Or. 1773. The Temple of Harmony. Can. [Both works are translations from the French.]

ERSKINE, ANDREW. She's Not Him, and He's Not Her. F. (Can. 6 Feb. 1764) [Edinburgh]: 1764; 8°. *C. M.* 1 Feb. 1764. *E. C.* 4 Feb. 1764. See *The Cloaciniad.* Edinburgh: 1761.

EWING, PETER. The Soldier's Opera, or, Life Without a Mask. C. O. London: [1792]; 8°.

[FINLAYSON, JOHN.] Marches Day: A Dramatic Entertainment . . . as annually performed by the Originals, at *** [i.e., Linlithgow]. E. Edinburgh: 1771; 8°.

FLEMING, ROBERT (THE YOUNGER). The Monarchical Image: or, Nebuchadnezzar's Dream, D. P. In *The Mirrour of Divine Love Unvail'd.* London: 1691; 8°.

FORBES, WILLIAM. Xantippe, or the Scolding Wife, done from the Conjugium of Erasmus, by W. F. of D. [i.e., William Forbes of Disblair]. D. P. Edinburgh: 1724*; 4°. [*Ralston Inglis, *Dramatic Writers of Scotland* (Glasgow, 1868), p. 131, gives 1726 as the date of publication. The title page of the copy in the National Library of Scotland notes 1724 as publication date.]

[FYFFE, ALEXANDER.] The Royal Martyr, King Charles I. O. Edinburgh: 1705; 4°. [This anonymously published opera was printed as a tragedy in 1709. In 1712 the second edition of the play appeared as *The Tragedy of the Royal Martyr King Charles I.* This edition enlarged to five acts, in prose and verse, differs markedly from the 1705 drama. The Royal Martyr, or Life and Death of Charles I (T. R. E. 7 Apr. 1794) may be a revival of this play.] *E. C.* 5 Apr. 1794.

GORDON, ALEXANDER. Lupone, or the Inquisitor. C. (Hay. 15 Mar.

1731.) London: 1731; 8°. *C. M.*, 10 Feb. 1759. James Boswell, *London Journal 1762–1763*, ed. F. A. Pottle (New York, 1950), p. 5.

GRAHAME, JAMES. Wallace. T. [Edinburgh]: 1799; 8°. [Six copies were printed privately.] Mary Stewart, Queen of Scots. H. Edinburgh: 1801; 8°.

GRAY, SIMON. *Historical Catalogue of the Writings, Published and Unpublished, of Simon Gray, of Dunse, Berwickshire.* London: 1840. Lists: The Spaniard; or, Relvindez and Elzora, the True though Injured Lovers. T. 1787; altered, 1790; rewritten, 1802; happy ending added, 1832.

———. The Spaniard, or, Relvindez and Elzora . . . and The Young Country Widow . . . With Three Letters to Dr Blair; and Thoughts on the Present State of the British Drama, and what seems calculated to improve it. London: 1839; 8°.

———. New Modes of Making Love; or, Bob Bell, Ensign-to-be, a-Courting. C. 1789–1830. [Citations of first dates in the Gray *Catalogue* (used below) indicate the period from first draft through the finished play.]

———. The Young Country Widow. C. 1790. London: 1839; 8°. See *The Spaniard.*

———. Adamana; or the Rash Maiden. T. 1791. The Lady of Lanley Hall; Or, a Manner-Scape of Scotland Three Centuries Ago. A Dramatic Romance, in Blank verse. 1791; rewritten, 1800.

———. A Lesson to Maidens; or, the Ruined Sisters. Being a Sequel to The Lady of Lanley Hall. T. 1791–1800.

———. Bachelor Convinced; or, Wife Triumphant. C. 1791. [London]: 1830.

———. The Duellist. C. 1791–1831.

———. The Courtier Grown Jealous, and Abram's Courtship. C. 1791–1831.

———. The H. F. Club; or, Church of Blasphemy. C. 1795; printed? 1830.

———. The Widower. C. 1795–1831.

———. Gowrie's Conspiracy. H. T. (Boarding School, Kensington Gravel Pits 8 June 1796.)

———. The Assasins. T. 1796–1830. Bailie Greig and His Three Daughters; alias the Retail Shop: or Characters drawn from Life; or, if ye will, a Dramatico-Epic Novel of a new kind, being intended for the Entertainment of Fifty-eight Nights. 1798; completed 1829.

———. Borthwicko Castle; or, Seven Ghosts and a Half. A Burlesque Romantic Drama. A most serious machinical play, intended for a Christmas Piece, though not a Pantomime. 1798.

———. Hume Castle Lost; or, Bustle Pertness, and Singsong. Being a True Comic Opera. B. O. 1798–1800.

———. Hume Castle Won; or, Singsong Pertness, and Bustle. Being another True Comic Opera. B. O. 1798–1804.

———. Faith and I Must; or Bachelor Subdued, and Woman still Triumphant. C. 1800–1831.

———. The Step-Mother; and Omnia Vincit Amor; or, Love the Conqueror. 1800–1834. [The privately printed catalogue of Gray's works (National Library of Scotland) lists over 50 plays by this writer. He wrote 12 plays on the seasons alone after 1800.]

GREENFIELD, ANDREW. Henrique, Prince of Sicily, T. In *Poems*. London: 1790; 8°. John Nichols, *Literary Anecdotes* (London, 1812–15), 8:261–62. [This tragedy ends abruptly in Act IV unfinished.]

HAMILTON, NEWBURGH. The Doating Lovers; or, the Libertine Tam'd. C. (L. I. F. 23 June 1715.) London: 1715; 12°. *L. S.* Pt. 2, 1:360–61.

———. The Petticoat Plotter. F. (D. L. 5 June 1712.) London: 1720; 12°. *C. M.* 26 Aug. 1754. [Hamilton wrote the lyrics for Handel's oratorio *Samson*.]

HAMILTON, WILLIAM. Mithridates. T. In *Poems on Several Occasions*. Glasgow: 1784; 4°. Nelson S. Bushnell, *William Hamilton of Bangour Poet and Jacobite* (Aberdeen: University of Aberdeen Press, 1957). [The first scene of the first act of this translation of Jean Racine's *Mithridate* was published.]

HART [SAMUEL*]. Herminius and Espasia. T. (Can. 12 Feb. 1754.) [Edinburgh]: 1754; 8°. *E. C.* and *C. M.* 12 Feb. 1754. *Scots Magazine* 25 (1754):212. [*The author is sometimes incorrectly identified as Charles Hart.]

HENDERSON, ANDREW. Arsinoe, or the Incestuous Marriage. T. London: [1752]; 8°. [This play is a translation of Thomas Corneille.]

———. In Foro. [This manuscript is unfinished.]

[HERON, ROBERT.] St. Kilda in Edinburgh, or, News from Camperdown. Mus. F. (T. R. E. 21 Feb. 1798.) Edinburgh: 1798; 8°. *E. C.* 15 Feb. 1798.

———. Pizarro, a Tragedy in five Acts, differing widely from all other Pizarros in respect of Characters, sentiments, language, incidents, and catastrophes. By a North Britain [*sic*] [i.e., Heron] T. London: [1799]; 8°. James Sinton, "Robert Heron and His Writings,"

Papers of the Edinburgh Bibliographical Society 1930–1935, 15 (Edinburgh, 1935):17–21.

HOGAEUS, GULIELMUS (HOGG, WILLIAM). Comoedia Joannis Miltoni . . . paraphrastice reditta a G. Hogaeo. M. London: 1698; 4°. [This is a Latin translation of John Milton's *Comus*.]

HOME, JOHN. Douglas. T. (Can. 14 Dec. 1756.) London: 1757; 8°. E. C. and C. M. 4 Dec. 1756. A. E. Gipson, *John Home, a study of his Life and Works, etc.* (Caldwell, Idaho: 1917). *Douglas*, ed. by H. J. Tunney (Lawrence, Kansas, 1924), pp. 94–97, contains a digest of contemporary comments on the play.

————. Agis. T. (D. L. 21 Feb. 1758.) London: 1758; 8°. *Critical Review* 5 (1758):327–41. *The Story of the Tragedy of Agis. With observations on the Play, the Performance, and the Reception* (London, 1758).

————. The Siege of Aquileia. T. (D. L. 21 Feb. 1760), London: 1760; 8°.

————. The Fatal Discovery. T. (D. L. 23 Feb. 1769.) London: 1769; 8°.

————. Alonzo. T. (D. L. 27 Feb. 1773.) London: 1773; 8°.

————. Alfred. T. (C. G. 21 Jan. 1778.) London: 1778; 8°. Henry Mackenzie, "Memoir," in *Works of Home* (Edinburgh, 1822), 1: 46–48, mentions three MSS: The Surprise, or Who Would Have Thought It. C. ca. 1774. / Alina, or the Maid of Yarrow. T. ca. 1779. / A two-act fragment of an East Indian Story. T. ca. 1780.

HOUSTON, LADY ELEONORA CATHCART. The Coquettes, or the Gallant in the Closet. C. (Can. Feb. 1759). C. M. 10 Feb. 1759. F. A. Pottle, *James Boswell the Earlier Years 1740–1769* (New York, 1966), pp. 40 and 465.

[HUNTER, JOHN.] The Wanderer and Traveller. Rel. Glasgow: 1733*; 8°. [*A MS notation in Hunter's Commonplace Book (National Library of Scotland) gives the publication date as 1712.]

[HUNTER, ROBERT.] Androboros. A Bographical [*sic*] farce in three acts, viz. The senate, The consistory, and The apotheosis. Pol. Monoropolis [New York]; 17 [09–14]; 4°. [The Brown University copy contains a MS key.]

JACKSON, JOHN*. Eldred; or the British Freeholder. T. (Capel-street, Dublin, 2 Dec. 1773.) London: 1782; 8°. [This tragedy was also called "Eldred; or the British Father." E. C. 14 Feb. 1774.]

————. The British Heroine. T. (C. G. 5 May 1778.) [A slightly different version of this tragedy entitled "Geralda; or, The Siege of Harlech" was staged in Dublin 13 Jan. 1777.]

————. Sir William Wallace, or Ellerslie; or, The Siege of Dumbarton Castle. T. (T. R. E. 26 July 1780.) *E. C.* 19 July 1780.

————. Tony Lumpkin's Ramble Through Edinburgh. (T. R. E. 26 July 1780.) *E. C.* 19 July 1780.

————. Transformation; or, the Manager An Actor in Spite of Himself. (T. R. E. 29 Apr. 1789.) *E. C.* 27 Apr. 1789. [This is probably the work of Jackson. He undoubtedly wrote a number of afterpieces and brief occasional farces and adaptations during his tenure as Edinburgh theatre manager. *Donald Mackenzie, *Scotland's First National Theatre* (Edinburgh, 1963), p. 10, notes that Jackson was Scottish.]

LEARMONT, JOHN.   The Unequal Rivals. P. In *Pastorals, Satirical, Tragic, and Comic.* [Edinburgh]: 1791; 8°. Jeannette Marks, *English Pastoral Drama* (London, 1908), pp. 122–23.

LESLY (LESLEY), GEORGE.   Divine Dialogues. London: 1684*; 8°. Contains: Dives's Doom. Rel. / Sodom's Flames. Rel. / Abraham's Faith. Rel. [*This is the second edition. Internal evidence, i.e., the dating of the dedication (1675), indicates that this is the period of the first edition, which apparently is no longer extant.]

LINDSAY, LADY ELIZABETH, COUNTESS OF HARDWICK.   The Count of Oberon, or the Three Wishes (Private theatre at Wimpole Hill, near Cambridge, ca. 1800.) London: 1831; 8°.

LOGAN, JOHN.   Runnamede. T. (T. R. E. 5 May 1784.) Edinburgh: 1784; 8°. *E. C.* 1 May 1784. "The Life of Logan," in *Poems and Runnamede a Tragedy* (Edinburgh and London, 1805), p. xxx, mentions the following manuscripts: The Wedding Day. T. / The Carthaginian Heroine. T. Electra. T. / A tragedy on the death of Mary Queen of Scots. T. J. S. Marshall, "Introduction," *Letters of the Rev. John Logan* (Edinburgh, 1961).

LYON, WILLIAM.   The Wrangling Lovers; or, Like Master Like Man. (Can. April 1745.) Edinburgh: 1845; 8°. [An alteration of Sir John Vanbrugh's *The Mistake.*]

[McARTHUR, SAMUEL.]   The Duke of Rothesay. T. [Edinburgh]: 1780; 8°. [This tragedy was written in 1764.]

MacDONALD, ANDREW.   Vimonda. T. (Hay. 5 Sept. 1787), London: 1788; 8°.

————. *The Miscellaneous Works of Andrew M'Donald.* London: 1791; 8°. Contains: The Fair Apostate. T. / The Princess of Tarento. C. O. / Love and Loyalty. C. O.

MACKENZIE, HENRY.   The Prince of Tunis. T. (T. R. E. 8 Mar. 1773.) Edinburgh and London: 1773; 8°. *E. C.* and *C. M.* 6 Mar. 1773.

———. The Shipwreck: or Fatal Curiosity . . . altered from Lillo. T. (C. G. 10 Feb. 1784.) Edinburgh and London: 1784; 8°.

———. False Shame, or The White Hypocrite. C. (C. G. 5 Dec. 1789.) In *Works*, 8. Edinburgh: 1808; 8°. ["Force of Fashion" is an earlier title for *False Shame*. The comedy was performed as "Force of Fashion."]

———. The Spanish Father, T. In *Works*, 8. Edinburgh: 1808; 8°.

———. Dramatic Pieces from the German. I. The Sister; a Drama by Goethe, Author of the Sorrows of Werter. II. The Conversation of a Father with His Children by Gesner, Author of The Death of Abel. III. The Set of Horses; A Dramatic Piece by Emdorff [i.e., Ayrenhoff]. Edinburgh and London: 1792; 8°. *Transactions of the Royal Society of Edinburgh*, 2 (Edinburgh, 1792):154–92. David W. Lindsay, "Henry Mackenzie, Alexander Thomson and *Dramatic Pieces from the German*," *Studies in Scottish Literature*, 3 (1965):253–55. [These translations have been attributed to Mackenzie and Dr. Francis Okely.]

———. Virginia, or the Roman Father. T. Edinburgh: 1820. [Mackenzie wrote a draft of this tragedy when he was sixteen, in 1761. He reworked the juvenile effort and published it privately for distribution to select friends.]

MacLaren, Archibald. The Conjuror; or, The Scotsman in London. F. [Dundee]: 1781; 12°.

———. The Coup de Main, or the American Adventurers. Mus. E. (New Theatre, Dundee, 1783.) [Perth]: 1784; 8°. [An altered version was published as *The Coup-de-Main; or, Love and War in Yankeyland*. London: 1816; 12°.]

———. The Humours of Greenock Fair; or, the Taylor made a Man. Mus. I. (Greenock, 1788.) [Paisley]: 1790; 12°.

———. The Highland Drover; or, Domhnul Dubh M'Na-Beinn [i.e., Black Donald Son of the Mountain]. Mus. I. (Inverness, ca. 1790.) Greenock: 1790; 12°; Carlisle: 1790; altered version, London: [1805]; 12°.

———. The First Night's Lodgings. F. (1790–1800.) London: [1800]; 12°.

———. American Slaves; or, Love and Liberty. C. O. (Dumfries, 1792.) [This play was doubtless published under another title.]

———. The Siege of Perth; or, Sir William Wallace the Scots Champion. I. (Dumfries, 1792.) Perth: 1792. [This piece was made into a musical and appeared as *Wallace the Brave: or, The Siege of Perth*. London: 1819; 12°.]

————. The Bonny Lass[es] of Leith; or, The Humours of Dugald McBicker. Mus. I. (T. R. E. 1793.) [Edinburgh?]: 1790–1793?

————. Scottish Volunteers. Mus. F. (Greenock, ca. 1795.) [Paisley]: 1795; 8°. [This is the same play as *The Bonny Lasses of Leith.*]

————. Siege of Berwick; or, The Brothers Devoted. Mus. D. (1792–1795.) London: 1818; 8°.

————. What News from Bantry Bay; or, The Faithful Irishman. C. O. (St. Peter's Guernsey, ca. 1794.) [Dublin]: 1798; 8°. [This piece was reprinted as an entertainment, *The Humours of the Times; or, What News Now?* London: 1799; 8°.]

————. Old England Forever! or A Fig for the Invasion. C. O. [Bristol]: 1799; 12°.

————. Negro Slaves. I. (T. R. E.? ca. 1799.) [Edinburgh]: 1799; 8°. [*Negro Slaves; or the Blackman and Blackbird.* London: 1799; 12°, is an enlargement of the earlier version.]

————. Soldier's Widow; or the Happy Relief. Mus. E. London: 1800; 8°. [*A Soldier and a Sailor.* London: 1805; 12°, is an altered version of this play, as is *Credulity; or, the Force of Superstition . . . To which is added A Chip of the Old Block; or, the Pirates Repulsed.* London: 1823; 12°.]

————. The Monopolizer Outwitted. Mus. E. London: 1800; 12°. [For a list of MacLaren's plays which appeared after 1800, see Nicoll, 4:350–52.]

[MACLAURIN, COLIN.] Hampden. T. In *Fugitive Pieces. Poems on Various Subjects by a Scotch Gentleman: A Member of the Faculty of Advocates* [i.e., MacLaurin]. Edinburgh: 1799; 8°.

————. Songs in the Justiciary Opera. Composed Fifty Years Ago, by C——— M——— [i.e., Colin MacLaurin] and B——— [i.e., Sir Alexander Boswell]. Auchinleck: 1816.

MACLAURIN, JOHN, LORD DREGHORN. The Public. A Tragedy in one Scene. Sat. In *Poems on Several Occasions*, 1. Dreghorn: 1769; 8°. [This squib privately printed on the author's estate involves the struggles between John Lee and Samuel Foote for the patent for the Edinburgh Theatre.]

————. The Philosopher's Opera. C. O. Edinburgh: ca. 1757; 8°. [This squib on *Douglas* has been attributed to MacLaurin.]

————. The Deposition, or Fatal Miscarriage: a Tragedy. Sat. [Edinburgh]: [1757]; 8°. [This squib on John Home and his circle has been attributed to MacLaurin.]

MALLET (MALLOCH), DAVID. Eurydice. T. (D. L. 22 Feb. 1731.) London: 1731; 8°. *Daily Journal* 20 Feb. 1731. *Remarks on the Tragedy of Eurydice in which It is endeavoured to prove that same Tragedy is wrote in favour of the "Pretender" and is a scurrilous Libel against the present Establishment* (London, 1731). *The Works of Aaron Hill* (London, 1953), 4:47, 97–100.

————. Mustapha. T. (D. L. February 1738.) London: 1739; 8°. *Scots Magazine* 10 (1739):88.

————. Alfred. M. (Cliveden Gardens, 1 Aug. 1740.) London: 1740; 8°. [This masque was written in collaboration with James Thomson. It was billed as an opera, with music by Thomas Arne, when it opened at D. L. March 1744.]

————. Alfred, A Masque. T. (D. L. 23 Feb. 1751.) London: 1751; 8°. [Mallet labeled his alteration of the original version a tragedy.]

————. Britannia. M. (D. L. May 1755.) London: 1753; 8°.

————. Elvira. T. (D. L. January 1763.) London: 1763; 8°. James Boswell, *London Journal 1762–1763*, ed. by F. A. Pottle (New York, 1950), pp. 56–62. D. M. Low, ed., *Edward Gibbon's Journal* (New York [1929]), pp. 185–86, 202–04. James Boswell, Andrew Erskine, and George Dempster. *Critical Strictures on the New Tragedy of Elvira Written by Mr. David Malloch* (London, 1763).

MARSHALL, JANE. Sir Harry Gaylove, or Comedy in Embryo. C. Edinburgh: 1772; 8°. Terence Tobin, "A Consideration of Jane Marshall's *Sir Harry Gaylove*," *Delta Epsilon Sigma Bulletin* 13 (1968): 107–13.

MICKLE, WILLIAM. The Siege of Marseilles. T. In *Poems and a Tragedy*. London: 1794; 4°. *Scots Magazine* 51 (1789):532–34, 581–83. Sister M. Eustace Taylor, *William Julius Mickle (1734–1789): A Critical Study* (Washington, D.C., 1937).

MITCHELL, JOSEPH. The Fatal Extravagance. T. London: 1720; 8°. Paul S. Dunkin, "The Authorship of *The Fatal Extravagance*," *MLN* 51 (1945):328–30. P. P. Kies, "The Authorship of *The Fatal Extravagance*," *Research Studies of the State College of Washington* 13 (Pullman: 1945):155–58. [Aaron Hill collaborated on this play.]

————. The Highland Fair, or Union of the Clans. B. O. (D. L. March 1730.) London: 1731; 8°.

MONCRIEF, JOHN. Appius. T. (C. G. 6 Mar. 1755.) London: 1755; 8°. [Thomas Sheridan revised the play for performance.]

MORISON, DAVID. Jack and Sue; or, the Fortunate Sailor. C. O. In *Poems. Chiefly in the Scottish Dialect*. Montrose: 1790; 8°. *Biographia Dramatica*, 2:246.

[MORRIS, ROBERT.] Fatal Necessity: or, Liberty Regain'd. A Tragedy:

As it was Once acted in Rome For the Sake of Freedom and Virtue. Pol. London: 1742; 8°.

MURDOCH, JOHN. The Double Disguise. C.(?) In *Pictures of the Heart and the Double Disguise*, 2. London: 1783; 12°. [This play was written for a private performance.]

MYLNE, JAMES. *Poems consisting of Miscellaneous Pieces and Two Tragedies*. Edinburgh: 1790; 8°. Contains: The British Kings. T. / Darthula. T. [Mylne wrote a comedy which was never published.]

NESBIT, GABRIEL. Caledon's Tears, or Wallace, a Tragedy Containing the Calamities of Scotland, from the Death of King Alexander III. to the betraying and butchering of that faithful Father of his Country, Sir William Wallace, of Ellerslie. Collected from the Chronological Records, by G. Nesbit. T. Edinburgh: 1733; 8°.

NIMMO, MATTHEW. The Fatal Secret; or, Truth Disguised. T. Dundee: 1792; 8°.

NORVAL, JAMES. The Generous Chief. T. (Montrose, ca. 1792.) Montrose: 1792; 8°.

[OSWALD, JOHN] "SYLVESTER OTWAY." The Humours of John Bull. O. F. In *Poems*. London: 1789; 8°.

PATERSON, WILLIAM. Arminius. T. London: 1740; 8°.

[PATON, _____.] William and Lucy. B. O. Edinburgh: 1780; 8°.

[PENNECUICK, M. D., ALEXANDER.] The Interlocutor. C. Edinburgh: 1803; 8°. [This play was written in the early eighteenth century.] William Brown, "Writings of Alexander Pennecuick, M. D., and Alexander Pennecuick, Merchant," *Publications of the Edinburgh Bibliographical Society 1901–04*, 6 (1906):117–31, doubts that Pennecuick wrote this comedy.

[PENNECUICK (MERCHANT), ALEXANDER.] Corydon and Cochrania, a Pastoral on the Nuptials of the High and Potent Prince, His Grace James, Duke of Hamilton, Chatelherault and Brandon, &c. Solemniz'd February 14, 1723. By A. P. Gent. P. Edinburgh: 1723; 4°. [See RAMSAY, *The Nuptials*.]

PITCAIRNE, ARCHIBALD. The Assembly. C. London: 1722; 8°. [This comedy was written in 1692, was revised by anonymous hand(s) and appeared as *The Assembly, or Scotch Reformation*. London: 1766; 8°. The second edition contains an interesting preface, which provides a key. Pitcairne's name appears on the title page of the third edition, Edinburgh: 1817. See *Tollerators and Contollerators*.]

RAMSAY, ALLAN. The Nuptials: A Masque on the Marriage of His Grace James Duke of Hamilton, and Lady Anne Cochran. M. (Edinburgh 14 Feb. 1723.) Edinburgh: 1723. [See PENNECUICK, (MER-CHANT).]

———. The Gentle Shepherd. A Scots Pastoral Comedy. P. (T. H. 22 Jan. 1729.) Edinburgh: 1725; 12°. *The Eccho; or, Edinburgh Weekly Journal* 4 (29 Jan. 1729). Burns Martin, *Allan Ramsay, a Study of His Life and Works* (Cambridge, 1931).

———. The Caledonian Villagers, a Scotch Pastoral Interlude . . . by Natives of Scotland who are to speak the Dialect of that Country. P. I. (H. 21 Jan. 1782.) [This interlude is probably an adaptation of *The Gentle Shepherd.*]

[RICHARDSON, WILLIAM.] The Indians. T. (Richmond Theatre, near London and Caledonian Theatre, Glasgow, ca. 1790.) London: 1790; 8°.

———. The Maid of Lochlin, taken from Fingal attributed to Ossian. D. P. (Glasgow College, late 1790s.) London: 1801; 8°.

RIDDEL, JOHN. George's Natal Day. M. (T. R. E. and Argyle Street Theatre, Glasgow, ca. 1780.) In *Original Poems by a Young Gentleman.* Edinburgh: 1780; 8°.

———. Malvina. T. Glasgow: 1786; 8°.

SCOTT, THOMAS. Edwin and Catherine; or The Distressed Lovers. T. In *Poems.* Paisley: 1793; 8°.

SCOTT, SIR WALTER. Goetz of Berlichingen, With the Iron Hand: A Tragedy Translated by William° Scot, Esq., Advocate, Edinburgh. T. London: 1799; 8°. [°A few copies were printed before the error was discovered. Henry A. White, *Sir Walter Scott's Novels on the Stage* (New Haven, 1927). For a list of Scott's dramatic contributions after 1800, see Nicoll, 4:397.]

SHIRREFS, ANDREW. Jamie and Bess, or The Laird in Disguise, a Scots Pastoral Comedy in imitation of The Gentle Shepherd. P. (Aberdeen, °Elgin, Inverness.) Aberdeen: 1787; 8°. [°The earliest recorded performance is Aberdeen on 12 Jan. 1788. The play premiered before this season.]

———. The Sons of Brittania. I. (Amateur production, Edinburgh, 1796.) Edinburgh: 1796.

SMITH, [EAGLESFIELD.] Sir John Butt. Pol. F. Edinburgh: 1798; 8°.

SMITH, WILLIAM. An Exercise consisting of a Dialogue and Ode Sacred to the Memory of His Late Gracious Majesty George II (College of Philadelphia 23 May 1761.) New York: [1761]. [Smith wrote the dialogue for this commencement exercise; Francis Hopkinson wrote the *Ode.*]

———. An Exercise, containing dialogue and two odes set to

music for the public Commencement in the College of Philadelphia
(College of Philadelphia 17 May 1775.) Philadelphia: 1775.

SMOLLETT, TOBIAS.   The Regicide, or King James the First King of
Scotland. T. London: 1749; 8°.

————.   Alceste. O. ca. 1749.

————.   The Reprisal, or the Tars of old England. C. (D. L. 22 Jan.
1757.) London: 1758; 8°. *Critical Review* 3 (1757):159.

STEELE, ARCHIBALD.   The Shepherds' Wedding. P. [Edinburgh]: 1789;
8°.

STEWART, JAMES.   The Two English Gentlemen, or the Sham Funeral.
C. (Hay. 21 Mar. 1774.) London: 1774; 8°.

————.   The Students, or the Humours of St. Andrews. F. (Hay.
13 Oct. 1777.) London: 1779; 8°.

————.   The Exciseman Trick'd. F. (Hay. 18 Mar. 1782.) [An
adaptation of *The Students*.]

STEWART, THOMAS.   Valentia, or the Fatal Birth-Day. T. London:
1772; 8°. [This play is based upon Nicholas Rowe's *The Fair Penitent*.]

STUART, CHARLES.   The Experiment. C. (C. G. 16 Apr. 1777.) [This
piece is attributed to Stuart.]

————.   The Cobler of Castlebury. Mus. E. (C. G. 27 Apr. 1779.)
London: 1779; 8°.

————.   Damnation, or the Playhouse Hissing Hot. I. (Hay. 29
Aug. 1781.)

————.   Ripe Fruit, or the Marriage Act. I. (Hay. 22 Aug. 1781.)
[This piece was a segment of *The Feast of Thalia*.]

————.   Gretna Green. Mus. F. (Hay. 28 Aug. 1783.) *Songs, Airs,
. . . In Gretna Green*. London: 1783; 8°. [Only the songs were
printed. This piece was advertised as "Gretna Green; or, A Trip to
Marriage" in *E. C.* 19 July 1786.]

————.   The Distressed Baronet. F. (D. L. 3 May 1787.) London:
1787; 8°.

————.   The Box-Lobby Loungers. Pre. (D. L. 16 May 1787.)

————.   The Stone Eater. I. (D. L. 14 May 1788.) London: 1788;
8°.

————.   The Irishman in Spain. F. (Hay. 13 Aug. 1791.) London:
1791; 8°. [This farce is an adaptation of "She Would Be a Duchess,"
which was banned by the Lord Chamberlain on 13 Aug. 1791.]

ST. SERFE (SYDSERF), THOMAS.   Tarugo's Wiles, or the Coffee House.
C. (L. I. F. 5 Oct. 1667.) London: 1668; 4°. *The Journals of John*

Lauder Lord Fountainhall, pp. 174–75. John Downes, *Roscius Angli-canus,* ed. by Montague Summers (London, 1928), p. 31.

TAIT, WILLIAM. Jeptha. T. Edinburgh: 1751. [This is a translation of George Buchanan's *Jepthes.*]

[THOMSON, ADAM.] The Disappointed Gallant; or, Buckram in Armour. . . . Written by a Young Scots Gentleman [i.e., Thomson]. B. O. (T. H. 1736–37[?]) Edinburgh: 1738; 8°.

THOMSON, [ALEXANDER.] *The German Miscellany; consisting of Dramas, Dialogues, Tales and Novels.* Translated from that Language. Perth: 1796; 12°. Contains: Bianca Capello A Dramatic Narrative From the same Work [i.e., Alfred Meissner's *Sketches*]. The Indians in England, a comedy, from Kotzebue. C. [This translation appeared as The East Indian . . . Translated from the German of Augustus von Kotzebue. Dublin; 1800; 8°.] The Lottery Ticket . . . translated from C. F. Bellert. C. [n.d.] [See MACKENZIE.]

THOMSON, JAMES. The Tragedy of Sophonisba. T. (D. L. 28 Feb. 1730.) London: 1730; 8°. *A Criticism of the New Sophonisba* (London, 1730).

————. Agamemnon. T. (D. L. 6 Apr. 1738.) London: 1738; 8°.

————. Edward and Eleonora. T. London: 1738; 8°. [This tragedy slightly altered by Thomas Hull opened C. G. 18 Mar. 1775.]

————. Alfred, A Masque. M. 1740. [This masque was written in collaboration with David Mallet. See MALLET.]

————. Tancred and Sigismunda. T. (D. L. 18 Mar. 1745.) London: 1745; 8°. C. M. 2 Feb. 1748; 30 Mar. 1749; 11 Mar. 1754; 10 Feb. 1755; 31 Jan. 1756; 31 Mar. 1757. *Glasgow Journal* 14 and 21 May 1753. E. C. 31 Jan. 1756; 31 Mar. 1757.

————. Coriolanus. T. (C. G. 13 Jan. 1749.) London: 1749; 8°.

TURNBULL, GAVIN. The Recruit. I. (Dumfries 1792.) Dumfries: 1794; 8°.

TYTLER, A[LEXANDER] F[RASER], LORD WOODHOUSELEE. The Robbers . . . Translated from the German of Frederick Schiller. T. Edinburgh: 1792; 8°. Archibald Alison, *Memoir of the Life and Writings of the Honourable Alexander Fraser Tytler Lord Woodhouselee. Transactions of the Royal Society of Edinburgh* 38 (Edinburgh, 1818).

WALLACE, LADY EGLANTINE MAXWELL. Diamond Cut Diamond. C. London: 1787; 8°.

————. The Ton; or, Follies of Fashion. C. (C. G. 8 Apr. 1788.) London: 1788; 8°. *The Daily Advertiser* 9 Apr. 1788.

————. The Whim . . . With an address to the public, upon the arbitrary and unjust aspersion of the licenser against its political sentiments. Offered to be acted for the benefit of the hospital and poor

of the Isle of Thanet, but refused the royal license. . . . C. Margate
and London: 1795; 8°.

———. Cortes. T. *Biographia Dramatica,* 2:131.

WHYTE, ———. The Confession. C. (T. R. E. 25 Mar. 1799.) E. C.
21 Mar. 1798.

WILSON, JOHN. Earl Douglas; or Generosity Betray'd. T. Glasgow:
1764; 8°. [This tragedy is a revision of *Earl Douglas. A Dramatic
Essay.* Edinburgh: 1760; 8°.]

WOOD, JOHN. The Duke of Rothsay. T. Edinburgh: 1780; 8°.

WOOD, WILLIAM. A Translation of Allan Ramsay's The Gentle Shepherd into English. P. [Edinburgh]: [1785]; 8°.

———. The Billet-Master; or, The Forgery: An Opera. C. O. Edinburgh: 1787; 8°. [The author may be William Woods, the actor.]

PLAYS BY UNKNOWN AUTHORS
OR OF DOUBTFUL ATTRIBUTION

I am indebted to Norma Armstrong, "The Edinburgh Stage 1715–1820:
A Bibliography," Library Association of Great Britain, an unpublished
F. R. A. thesis (1968), for a number of the anonymous entries.

Acis and Galatea, a Masque. M. (St. Mary's Hall, Edinburgh, 1 Aug.
1750.) E. C. 30 July 1750.

Adventures in Edinburgh; or, The Taylor Distress'd. (T. R. E. 22 Apr.
1782.) E. C. 17 Apr. 1782.

The Appendix, a farce, or the Spirit of the Spirit of Liberty. Extracted
from the Works of "Junius jun.," author of the *Spiritual Magazine.*
To which is added a receipt for making an Appendix to any book
after it is published and exposed to sale. By a Real Friend of Liberty.
F. Newcastle: 1770. [Ralston Inglis, *Dramatic Writers of Scotland*
(Glasgow, 1868), p. 89, attributes the authorship to James Murray.]

Away to Leith Links; or, Golfing We Will Go. F. (T. R. E. 2 May
1787.) E. C. 28 Apr. 1787.

Brissot's Ghost! or, Intelligence from the Other World; communicated
to a meeting of those who call themselves friends of the people. Pol.
Edinburgh: 1794; 8°.

The Buck's Ramble Through Edinburgh; or, A Trip to Comely Garden
(T. R. E. 21 Apr. 1779.) E. C. 17 Apr. 1779.

Burnam Wood; or, The Highland Chief (T. R. E. 16 Mar. 1793.)

The Devil to Pay, or the Play House Metamorphs'd . . . As it was acted
at the Canongate Theatre, 24 Jan. 1768. F. Edinburgh: 1767.

[This playlet commemorates the licensing of the Theatre Royal, Edinburgh.]

The Duke of Rochford. T. Edinburgh: 1799. ["Said to be from the post-humous papers of a Lady of Quality." See Ralston Inglis, *Dramatic Writers of Scotland* (Glasgow, 1868), p. 145.]

Edinburgh Delivered; or, the World in Danger. D. P. Edinburgh: 1782; 8°.

Elim and Maria. A Pastoral Tragedy. P. Glasgow: 1792; 8°. [This pastoral has been attributed tenuously to Thomas Muir. See *N. & Q.*, 1st ser., 10 (1853):263–64, and (1854):414.]

The Enraged Musician. F. (Can. 2 Feb. 1753.) E. C. and C. M. 30 Jan. 1753.

Epilogue to the Winter Session. I. Edinburgh: ca. 1780.

The Fortune Hunter, or A Trip to the Lighters. F. (T. R. E. 1780.)

The Genius of Glasgow. M. (Caledonian Theatre, Glasgow, 1792.)

Glasgow Green, or a Trip to Loch Lomond. I. (Caledonian Theatre, Glasgow, 1798.)

The Good Woman Without a Head; or, Diarmugh M'Finnan's Voyage to America. F. (T. R. E. 19 Apr. 1784.) E. C. 14 Apr. 1784.

The Greenock Landlady; or, The Sailors in Port Glasgow. F. (T. R. E. 20 July 1772.) E. C. 8 July 1772.

Haddington Grammar School Play [Name unknown] (March 1724). Haddington Council Records 28 Mar. 1724.

Hallow Fair. F. I. (T. R. E. 17 Apr. 1784.) [This may have been written by William Woods.]

Harlquin Highlander; or, a Trip to Roslin Castle (T. R. E. 15 Apr. 1773.) E. C. 7 Apr. 1773. [This may be a version of "Roslin Castle" (Hay. 22 Mar. 1776) attributed to James Oswald.]

Highland Competition Prize; or, Shelty's Trip to Auld Reekie (T. R. E. 21 Apr. 1790.) E. C. 19 Apr. 1790.

Highland Festival (T. R. E. 21 Apr. 1779.) E. C. 26 Apr. 1779.

A Hint to the Sailors; or, The Wapping Landlady (T. H. 7 July 1756.) E. C. 3 July 1756.

Hooly and Fairly; or, The Highland Lad and the Lowland Lass T. R. E. 30 Apr. 1789.) E. C. 27 Apr. 1789. [Hooly and Fairly in character by M'Donald was advertised as a singing entertainment (Hay. 17 Jan. 1780).]

The Humours of the Town. I. (T. R. E. 1776.)

The Leith Landlady. F. (T. R. E. 30 Mar. 1778.) E. C. 25 Mar. 1778.

The Mad Cap, a Comedy for the Digestion, in three acts, from the

German of Kotzebue, by R＿＿＿ H＿＿＿. C. Edinburgh: 1800.
[R. H. may be Robert Hunter.]

The Manager's Last Stake; or, the Resurrection of Digges, Ross and
Lancashire C. (T. R. E. 5 Mar. 1796.) [This is probably a dramatic
squib.]

Modern Politics, or the Cat Let out of the Pack. Pol. Edinburgh: 1793;
8°.

The New Maid of the Oaks, a tragedy as lately acted near Saratoga, by
a company of tragedians, under the direction of "The Maid of the
Oaks," by Ahab Salem. Pol. [Edinburgh]: 1788; 8°. [Ralston Inglis,
Dramatic Writers of Scotland (Glasgow, 1868), p. 90, attributes this
piece to James Murray.]

The Parting Lovers; or The Highland Recruits. (T. R. E. 20 Mar.
1776). E. C. 17 Mar. 1776.

Pastoral in Latin and English [title unknown]. P. (Dundee Grammar
School 1751.) [This was probably written by the master.]

Pastoral [title unknown] P. (Hamilton Grammar School 1722.) [Mr.
Findlater was headmaster at Hamilton at this time, and may have
written the Latin pastoral. See Ralston Inglis, *Dramatic Writers of
Scotland* (Glasgow, 1868), p. 142.]

Penance for Having Two Wives at a Time . . . after Thelyphthora by
Rev. [Martin] Madan. I. (T. R. E. 6 June 1792.) E. C. 2 June 1792.

The Philistines, or the Scottish Tocsin Sounders. Pol. Edinburgh: 1793;
8°.

The Planters of the Vineyard; or a Kirk Session Confounded. by Mr.
Lothian*. As it was performed At Forthtown by the Persons of the
Drama. C. Edinburgh: 1771; 8°. [*Lothian is almost certainly a pseu-
donym.]

Religious satire [title unknown] Rel. (Lundy 1668.) [Jack McKenzie,
"A Study of Eighteenth Century Drama in Scotland (1660–1760),"
(Ph.D. diss., University of St. Andrews, 1955), 1:276, attributes
the authorship to Mr. Bouok, a schoolmaster.]

The Royal Council of Advice; or, the Regular Education of Boys, the
Foundation of all other national improvements (Kirkcaldy Grammar
School 29 Aug. 1734.) E. C. 27 Aug. 1734. C. M. 29 Aug. 1734.

Safe Moored; or, The Sailors Return to Leith (T. R. E. 31 May 1788.)
E. C. 29 May 1788.

The Sons of Auld Reekie; or, All in Good Humour (T. R. E. 24 Sept.
1796). E. C. 19 Sept. 1796.

The Stationer's Shop. F. (Amateur production, Aberdeen, March
1772.)

The System of Lavater; or, The Knights of the Past (T. R. E. 31 July 1797.) *E. C.* 27 July 1797.

Thomson's Birthday, or the Triumph of Reason, a Serio Comic Pantomime. Pan. (T. R. E. 3 May 1794,) *E. C.* 1 May 1794.

Tollerators and Con-Tollerators. Pol. In Archibald Pitcairne. *Babell; A satirical Poem on the Proceedings of the General Assembly in the Year M. DC. CXII.* ed. George H. Kinloch. Edinburgh: 1830. [Pitcairne is probably the author of this squib composed ca. 1703.]

Tragi-comedy [no title] T. C. in *The True Loyalist, or, Chevalier's Favourite.* Edinburgh: 1799; 8°. [This play, which deals with the history of Lady Wemyss, has been attributed to Charles Salmon.]

Trick upon Trick; or, the Vintner in the Suds. I. (T. R. E. 10 Sept. 1796.) *E. C.* 8 Sept. 1796. [This may be an adaptation of John Philip Kemble, *Trick Upon Trick.* I. (D. L. 22 Dec. 1789.)]

A Trip to Leith. I. (T. R. E. 26 Apr. 1787.) *E. C.* 23 Apr. 1787.

The Virtuous Chambermaid of Auld Reekie. I. (T. R. E. 30 Apr. 1787.) *E. C.* 26 Apr. 1787.

Index